M

€67.

THE EMPIRE IN THESE DAYS

THE EMPIRE
IN
THESE DAYS

AN INTERPRETATION

BY

R. COUPLAND
C.I.E., M.A.

FELLOW OF ALL SOULS COLLEGE
BEIT PROFESSOR OF COLONIAL HISTORY
IN THE UNIVERSITY OF OXFORD

LONDON
MACMILLAN & CO. LTD
1935

COPYRIGHT

PRINTED IN GREAT BRITAIN
BY R. & R. CLARK, LIMITED, EDINBURGH

PREFACE

OF the lectures included in this volume, Nos. II and III were read from the text as printed. Nos. VI, VII, and IX were delivered from notes only, and the text now published was written afterwards from memory with some expansion and further illustration of the argument, but no change in its substance.

The author is indebted for permission to reprint No. II to the Clarendon Press, No. III to the Oxford University Press (Indian Branch), No. IX to the Editorial Board of *The University of Toronto Quarterly*, and Nos. X, XII, XIII, and XIV to the Editors of *The Times, The Christian Science Monitor, The Round Table,* and *The Hibbert Journal.*

R. C.

WOOTTON HILL,
February 1935

CONTENTS

PAGE

I. INTRODUCTION 1

II. THE STUDY OF THE BRITISH COMMONWEALTH . 6

III. FREEDOM AND UNITY 32

IV. THE GROWTH OF DOMINION SELF-GOVERNMENT 50

V. REFLECTIONS ON A VISIT TO DUBLIN . . 57

VI. THE MEANING OF THE EMPIRE . . . 79
   1. The Commonwealth of Nations

VII. THE MEANING OF THE EMPIRE . . . 104
   2. India

VIII. INDIA AND DOMINION STATUS . . . 138

IX. THE MEANING OF THE EMPIRE . . . 159
   3. British Tropical Africa

X. AFRICAN SNAP-SHOTS 181

XI. IMPRESSIONS OF NIGERIA 213

XII. THE EXPLOITATION OF AFRICA . . . 239

XIII. THE FUTURE OF COLONIAL TRUSTEESHIP . 247

XIV. THE MEMORY OF WILBERFORCE . . . 262

POSTSCRIPT. The Meaning of Dominion Status . 275

vii

I

INTRODUCTION

THE lectures and essays collected in this book are
attempts to describe and discuss the British Empire as it
is in these post-War days. They deal with each of its three
main sections—the Commonwealth of Nations, India, and
the Tropical Dependencies exemplified by the mid-African
territories—and, though any such collection must suffer
from the lack of a continuous thread of argument and of a
proper proportion between subject and subject, it is to be
hoped that, taken all together, it provides a fairly compre-
hensive and connected interpretation of the character and
purpose of the great society to which we belong.

That the Empire is a subject which no student of the
modern world can ignore is self-evident. It is not merely
the size of it, nor its unique character and organization.
Perhaps the most striking aspect of it has been its stability
in the most tumultuous times our civilization has so far
had to go through. Five Empires were involved in the
War: only the British survived it. And in the ensuing
years of disillusionment and discontent, while other great
countries have plunged into revolution and, tearing up the
very foundations of their pre-War civic life, have acquired
a new order at the price of freedom, the British Empire has
also changed, has also adapted itself to the post-War age,
but by the quiet process of discussion and agreement and
law-making, not by violence; by enlarging, not destroying
its old freedoms; by evolution, not by revolution.

The moral would seem to be, first, that this world-wide
society of ours, whatever its deficiencies and anomalies,

does somehow meet the human needs it exists to serve. Nowhere, it appears, except perhaps in the peculiar case of Ireland, has the pressure of its framework been intolerably heavy or constricting. The Unity it gave allowed for sufficient Freedom. It is noteworthy, for example, that during the greater part of the War there were only some 70,000 British troops, largely raw recruits, and some 4000 British officials in India, whose population then numbered well over 300 million. It appears, secondly, that in the period of post-War adjustment not only the political leadership of the Empire, with one or two exceptions, but also the general body of public opinion has displayed a great gift of practical, constructive common sense. We sometimes think that this sort of political realism is a peculiar product of the English soil. But in the delicate process of establishing 'Dominion Status' the statesmen of the Dominions played at least as great a part as those of the United Kingdom; and in the still more intricate and difficult task of framing the new constitution for India the co-operation of the more far-sighted Indian statesmen has been admittedly invaluable.

The process of adjustment is, of course, still far from its end. It may be that the hardest stage of it has been covered in the last twenty years, that the most decisive steps have been taken in the last ten. But there are difficulties still to be overcome and dangers to be avoided. As far as public opinion in this country is concerned, the policy of common sense will presumably continue to be attacked on either flank. Extremists on the Right, no doubt, will go on saying that to recognize our fellow-citizens in the Dominions as our equals is to disintegrate the Empire; that no terms should be made with Indian Nationalism except at the muzzles of machine-guns; that our duty to the Africans is to 'keep them in their place' as serfs of Europe. But ideas that seem so archaic in these days can scarcely prevail in the days ahead, unless indeed an unprecedented convulsion were to thrust this country into such depths of reaction that it would no longer be recognizable for what it had been: and in that event, of course, the Empire would be, and ought to be, disrupted. No doubt, too, Extremists on the Left—that body of opinion which so dislikes the Empire as it was (or more strictly, perhaps, as some 'Imperialists' used to portray it) that it cannot or will not see the Empire as it is—will go on saying that our government, say in Tropical Africa or Malaya, is merely the instrument of 'economic imperialism', and all our professions of 'trusteeship' sheer hypocrisy; and that 'sinister interests' are the only obstacle to the prompt concession of the absolute independence which full-blooded Indian Nationalism demands. But surely there can be little more serious danger in such views than in their opposites. They are so devoid of our habitual realism. It is so obvious, when the facts are known and faced, that British administration in the Tropics is not concerned only with the economic aspect of native welfare or that the immediate withdrawal of all British aid in safeguarding the peace of India would expose its peoples to the fate of China. No; in the Empire as at home, Extremism has never been and is never likely to be a formidable danger.

The risk, such as it is, would seem to lie rather in indifference or misunderstanding among men of good-will as to the meaning of the Empire and the value of maintaining it. For many such the cause that fills their hearts in this post-War era is the cause of international friendship and co-operation; and they feel that 'imperialism', however transmuted, is somehow out of tune with 'internationalism'. The fact that the nations of the British Commonwealth, though separate members of the League, preserve an inner fellowship among themselves seems vaguely to conflict with the equalitarian principles of Geneva. Why should Canada have any other loyalties than Denmark? The fact, again, that, apart from what remains of British rule in India, we occupy so large a section of the backward areas of the world seems bound to excite the jealousy of other less 'fortunate' nations. May they not think we only care for peace because there is nothing more we want to get by war? Should we not go to Geneva with cleaner hands and purer hearts if we had no colonies?

Those are not altogether idle questions, and it is not quite enough to reply that we must take the world as we find it. This little book will serve its purpose if it helps its readers to find a better answer in an understanding of what the Empire in these days really is and means. It will be argued in the following pages that the Empire serves not only the interests of its own members, themselves nearly a quarter of mankind, but also the interests of the world as a whole: that civilization has not yet finally made its choice between corporate life and suicide, that it is not yet realized that no international order can achieve its purpose without a fuller and more candid sacrifice of national self-determination than the present 'collective system' dares to ask, and that in the meantime it would be a paradoxical blunder to dissolve the international unity of our lesser league within the League. It will be argued, further, that her membership of the Empire offers India the partnership and protection she needs for the final stage of her growth to full national stature, and that, similarly, though at a wide remove, the peoples of British Tropical Africa are gradually advancing towards that footing of equality which is the only tolerable ultimate relationship between man and man.

The course of events since most of the book was written

seems to strengthen the case it tries to make. The state of the world is worse than most of us hoped it would be only a few years back. Nationalism looks, at least on the surface, to be stronger and more menacing to the peace and prosperity of us all than it has ever been. Even another war seems less inconceivable than it did. Nor is it only the material danger that has been intensified. The competition in armaments is backed by a conflict of ideas. National Socialism has ranked itself with Fascism and Sovietism against all we mean by Freedom.

Surely this is a time when such a world-society as ours, dedicated to Freedom, yet knowing it can only be preserved or rightly used in Unity, should stand firm for the defence of civilization as we understand it.

II

THE STUDY OF THE BRITISH COMMONWEALTH[1]

THOSE of you who have read Professor Basil Williams' admirable biography will remember that Cecil Rhodes once began an address to a great business meeting in London by saying that 'he supposed the most unhappy thing in the world was for a public man to make a speech'. I venture to contest that claim. Public men, it is notorious, enjoy nothing so much as making speeches; but has any Professor ever enjoyed delivering an Inaugural Lecture? And can there be a more unhappy thing in the world than the delivery of an Inaugural Lecture before a University so critical as this and by a Professor so conscious as your present victim of his lack of almost all that is generally conceived to constitute the professorial stock-in-trade— the profound knowledge which only many years of toil can give, the authorship of several learned volumes, the venerable bearing—and so dependent, therefore, on your generosity when he asks that he be judged not by what he has done but by what he means to do?

And my diffidence is intensified when I reflect whose mantle it is that I am told to wear. When, fifteen years ago, Alfred Beit created this Chair with such far-sighted generosity and in such happy consonance with the foundation of the Rhodes Scholarships by his lifelong friend, there may have been some who thought that Colonial History was a 'fancy' subject, a side-track from the old,

[1] University of Oxford: Inaugural Lecture, November 19, 1921.

6

well-trodden highway of historical teaching, attractive, indeed—if only because side-tracks are always, alas! attractive—but bordered by no such rich fields of research as is the main road, nor equipped with such famous storehouses of political experience, and leading dangerously near those forbidden haunts where the blare of trumpets and the blaze of flags reveal that the partisans and propagandists are making merry. But any such fears were quickly laid to rest by the first appointment to the Chair. Professor Egerton, beyond dispute, possesses a more thorough knowledge of Colonial History than any living man; and the wide learning, the lucid exposition, the scholarly judgement of his lectures and his writings soon proved—if proof indeed were needed—that the American Revolution, for example, was at least as fit and profitable a field for scientific study as the Revolution of 1688, and that political lessons could be learned from the development of self-government in the Dominions as well as in the Mother-country. And may I here declare, on behalf of many students known to me and not least of myself, the debt of gratitude we owe Professor Egerton for the instant sympathy and patient guidance he has given in such full measure to all who shared his own deep interest in the subject? It is a great gain not only to his successor, who means to go on drawing, if he may, on that never-failing store of knowledge and of friendship, but for the study of History throughout the University that his resignation has not meant his departure from Oxford.

The dread of this unhappy hour might well, indeed, have been my reason for postponing it for a year from the date of my appointment. But there have been other reasons. It seemed to me that the holder of a recently founded chair might be expected to devote his first Public Lecture not so much to the exposition of some particular branch of his subject as to a brief discussion of the part which it should take in the work of the University: and to this end a little time was needed by one who had had small experience of the scope and method of the School of Modern History. A year ago, moreover, the School of Philosophy, Politics, and Economics, which is also concerned with the study of Colonial History, was still in process of creation. Above all, the Oxford of 1920 was not the Oxford I had known in 1914. We have been forced to look at the world in a new perspective, to take an interest in matters to which we were once more or less indifferent, to reconsider our scheme of values in education as in other things. And if, on the whole, we come to the conclusion that no radical change is needed in the great tradition of Oxford studies, we are ready to admit that the conditions of this post-War age demand, in some subjects at any rate, a widening of the field of work or at least a shifting of emphasis from one part of it to another.

I

Of the study of History this seems to me particularly true. The development of the War presented to us, as it were, a continuous examination paper on History. And the results of it were devastating. Many of us, I fear, were 'ploughed' by the first question on Austria and the Balkans; and others went down before the second—'Describe exactly the origin and terms of the treaty guaranteeing the neutrality of Belgium'. But the questions which betrayed most severely, perhaps, the limitations of our knowledge came later in the paper. When the people of the United States of America entered the War, when the magnitude of the contribution they made to the cause of the Allies in the short period allowed them revealed how vast was their potential strength, when, above all, it became manifest that the fortunes of the world in this new age depended first and foremost on a real understanding between this mighty Commonwealth and our own, we began to ask ourselves what we knew of its history, of its great men and great achievements, of its unique economic development, of the forces which have shaped its political ideals. And what sort of marks, I wonder, did we get for our answers? Happily an opportunity has been quickly given us to lighten our darkness: and I can speak for all Oxford in cordially welcoming the appointment of the first Harmsworth Professor of American History.[1]

The War, in fact, has taught us, as nothing else could have done, how the sundering spaces of the world have shrunk before the swift advance of science. The lives of all its peoples have been brought intimately close together. A new idea is born, and in a moment it has run the circuit of the earth. A fine ideal, a perilous illusion, a resonant phrase may be enunciated one day in London, Paris, Washington, Moscow: and on the morrow, oddly transmuted sometimes on the way, it is caught up and acclaimed and does its work for good or ill in India, Bokhara, Persia, Anatolia, Morocco, Mexico, South Africa—where you will. And, binding continent to continent and nation to nation, runs the delicate, intricate web of their economic and financial interdependence. Human society, indeed, has become so close-knit, so complex an organism, that we may be tempted sometimes to wonder whether its brain is big enough to control its body. No one can doubt, at any rate, that much hard thinking must be done if the intellectual equipment of mankind is to keep abreast of its growing moral and material needs. And this applies no less to the political than to the economic organization of the

[1] Samuel Eliot Morison.

B

world. It has become not only foolish now but dangerous to cling to the old contemptible doctrine that foresight and knowledge are not essential for the handling of great political issues because, when it comes to the point, we can always 'muddle through'. There will often enough be surprises in the world to test those gifts of improvisation and adaptability on which we pride ourselves. But politics is a science as much as an art; and we cannot with impunity omit to look afield and ahead, to detect the crucial problem, if we can, before the crisis is upon us, and to prepare ourselves betimes to solve it by scientific study.

History might well have taught this lesson before 1914. The greatest disaster in British annals was not primarily due to moral or social or economic or personal causes. We lost the thirteen American colonies primarily because we never closely studied the old Colonial System, never clearly analysed the political problem it contained, never made a real constructive effort to solve it. *Per contra*, the union of the thirteen American States in one commonwealth — one of the greatest achievements in history — could never have been effected without the preliminary study so thoughtfully and thoroughly pursued, and its results so admirably expounded, by Alexander Hamilton and his collaborators. The union of South Africa, again, which was also a very big achievement, was carried into being, it is true, on a wave of enthusiasm for a great idea; but the momentum would have been checked, the ardour chilled, the unique opportunity frittered away, if the cardinal difficulties had not been thought out beforehand so that the constitutional framework of union could be swiftly and smoothly fashioned before the forces of disruption had time to rouse themselves and wreck it. And, to take a second failure for our fourth example, is it not reasonably certain that if the Irish problem had been treated as a problem of historical and political science, and studied in the light of the experience of multi-national federal states, it could have been solved, once for all, forty years ago?

2

But before a University audience it is hardly necessary to state a case for the scientific study of politics. The purpose of this lecture is to suggest the special opportunities for such study which are offered to us as citizens of the British Commonwealth, and to plead that these opportunities should not be neglected at Oxford, especially with regard to the two paramount political problems of our time.

The first of these problems is the problem of nationality —the problem which arises from the fact that a nation (whatever it is) is not, as current usage of the term might seem to imply, the same thing as a state. A whole course of lectures might well be devoted to this fascinating theme. But I must content myself to-day with emphasizing the vastly important part nationality is playing in the modern world. Though it only came to the forefront of European politics in the nineteenth century, its reactions were felt all over Europe and beyond before the century closed. The causes of the War were rooted in it. And to-day nationality, in one shape or another, is the most powerful and the most troublesome element in the whole complex of world-politics. The demon of an overweening and perverted nationalism has not been wholly exorcized by the War, although all Europe is suffering from its fruits and the nation which most indulged it is paying the penalty in defeat and humiliation and poverty. Another nation in recovering its body has apparently lost its head. A group of contiguous nations are learning that the necessity of disrupting an ill-organized multi-national state does not in itself prove the validity of the shallow nineteenth-century doctrine that ideally all states should be uninational. And, finally, this doctrine, under its new title of national self-determination, declaring that every nation has a positive right to be a state, has given a new impetus to nationalist movements not in Europe only but all over the world. It is manifest, indeed, that there can be little peace or prosperity on earth until certain truths concerning nationality are understood—that, for example, nations, like men, should strive to cherish and enrich their individuality not for themselves alone, but in order to make their contribution to the common treasure of humanity; that, in Mazzini's noble phrase, 'a nation is a living task, her life is not her own'; that somehow, in the end, the ideal of national freedom must be harmonized with the ideal of international unity.

For the study of questions such as these there exists no other political community comparable with the British Commonwealth in the quantity or diversity of the material it contains. It is a great miscellany of nations, big and little, old and young. In some the spirit of nationality is satisfied and at peace. In others it is restless, rebellious, disruptive. At this moment the Commonwealth is alive with nationalist movements of varying character and intensity—right at its centre in Ireland, further afield in India and South Africa, and throughout that Near-Eastern border-country, just within or just without its orbit, in Egypt, Palestine, Mesopotamia. On the happy issue of these movements how much depends! For the Commonwealth, in one of its two most vital aspects, is nothing else than an attempt, on a wider scale than anything that has preceded it, to solve that insistent problem of nationality; an endeavour to keep a motley company of nations living contentedly together both in freedom and in unity; a unique experiment in international relations. If it continues to succeed, as on the whole it has so far succeeded, it may do much to save mankind by its experience and example. If it fails, if the bond of a common tradition and a common purpose is snapped by the weight of narrower interests or less generous ideals, if it splits into a chaos of alien sovereignties, the hope of the world will be dimmed. If the British League of Nations dies, what other League can live?

Because of its general importance, then, in the life of the world to-day, and because of the particular part it has played, and has yet to play, in the destiny of the British Commonwealth, the study of nationality, and especially of our own British dealings with it, should form, I contend, an essential part in the work of every British student of history and politics. And nowhere, surely, could this study be more appropriately pursued than here at Oxford, itself an academic miniature of the Commonwealth, where the youth of its component nations meet in the brotherhood of learning. A thorough understanding of nationality, I suggest, should be the hall-mark of every twentieth-century Oxford historian. And while he should not by any means neglect its history in the world at large, he should make his special contribution to the general knowledge of the subject by studying and expounding the experience of the British Commonwealth. He should be familiar, first of all, with the history of nationality in the British Isles—the growth of a national consciousness in the four nations they contain, the inevitable development of the problem of adjusting their mutual relations, the international conflict, its happy issue in Wales and Scotland, its tragic issue in Ireland. He should be acquainted, secondly, with the history of the same problem in Canada—where the juxta-

position of a conquered Celtic Roman Catholic population
in the valley of the St. Lawrence and an immigrant Anglo-
Saxon Protestant population in its *hinterland* created a
situation so closely analogous at the outset to that of
Ireland, but so fortunately and so instructively different in
its development—and in South Africa, where the national
schism, opened so needlessly by the Great Trek (one of
the unwritten epics of nationality, by the way),[1] was only
closed again when the second and third generation had
endured its heritage of strife and waste and death. Thirdly,
he should have carefully studied the growth of what may
be called Dominion nationality—how the four groups of
contiguous colonies in Canada, Australia, New Zealand,
and South Africa, divided at first either by nationality like
England and Scotland, or by a jealous 'particularism' like
the thirteen American States, gradually yielded to the
forces, economic and political, which made for unity; how
sooner, as in the case of New Zealand, or later, as in that
of South Africa, the barriers were broken down and each
group was welded together in a single constitutional frame,
more loosely or more tightly as the case might be; how this
political unification stimulated and quickened the process
which, despite differences and disputes, had been silently
going on all the time—the development of an inward
unity, of which political unity was but the outward expression; a sense of common devotion to the land they had
made their home; a consciousness of the common customs
and common interests which they shared as dwellers in
one country, of something which made all who lived in
Canada Canadians, whether they were of French or British
blood, and all who lived in South Africa South Africans,

[1] An excellent account of the Great Trek has recently been published (Longmans, 1934) by Professor E. A. Walker of Oxford and
Cape Town.

whether they spoke Dutch or English; and, finally, as time went on, the gathering of common memories and the growth of a common purpose, culminating in the knowledge which all alike brought back with them from the common ordeal of war that, to quote from Renan's famous definition of a nation, they had done great things together and desired to do more of them.

The historian who has mastered this material will be able to throw some light on those difficult questions: What is a nation? and What is nationality? He will be able, too, to make the meaning of our Commonwealth of Nations a little clearer to those of his fellow-citizens who are puzzled by the emphasis which overseas statesmen have recently been laying on the 'national status' of the Dominions. He may even temper the not unnatural bewilderment with which foreign observers contemplate so queer a spectacle, for instance, as a brisk dispute between Dominion and United Kingdom delegates in the Assembly of the League of Nations. But that is not all. Nationalism is a new thing in the Dominions. It has yet to run its course. We cannot certainly foretell, however strong our belief may be, what spirit will inform it when it reaches its full power—the spirit of Mazzini or another's. But this at least is certain. If this great society of nations is to continue—its younger partners, remember, growing in those wide spaces so much faster than the motherland, that in this generation or the next their population will outstrip our own—there is nothing we can do at Oxford to promote that end more effectively than to foster a better knowledge of the history of the Dominions in this country, and thereby a better understanding of their character, their circumstances, and their ideals. . . .

3

There is nothing revolutionary in the claim that the problem of nationality in the Dominions should not be overlooked by students of history and politics at Oxford. It is merely an extension of a field already occupied. But I would go further. I would plead that no student of history and politics ought to leave this University without some knowledge of the record and the function of the British Commonwealth in Asia and in other parts of Africa than the Dominion in the South. For the second of the two transcendent political problems of our time is the Colour Problem. Behind the question of international relations looms the more difficult and no less insistent question of interracial relations. The world is one. Asia shared with Europe in the War: and Europe cannot live apart from her in peace. India, China, Japan are members, indeed, of the League of Nations; but are we not apt to regard the work of the League as primarily an effort to establish harmony between the white peoples of the world? And what if, while we labour at this task, the old familiar evils of ignorance and prejudice, of ruthless greed and arrogant ascendancy, are gathering strength beyond our limited horizon till, some far-off day, we wake to find ourselves confronted with another seemingly 'inevitable' conflict, but this time a conflict of colour, more terribly primitive in its impulses, more inexorable, more destructive than any of its predecessors, the authentic Armageddon, stamping out in blood and ruin the last hope of civilization? I am not trying to make anyone's flesh creep—there is nothing, indeed, so hateful as thoughtless scaremongering on this theme—but unthinkable as such a conflict may seem, it is idle to suppose it could not happen. It might well happen if the peoples of the West allowed themselves to be con-

vinced by dogmatic biologists that the ultimate relations
between the white and coloured races can only be a fight
to the death for the survival of the fittest, or by cynics and
materialists that a strong or civilized people can have no
other genuine object in its dealings with a weak or backward people than to exploit it solely for its selfish gain.
And it might well happen if the wisdom of Japan were
beguiled by militarist dreams which have lost (let us hope)
their charm in Europe, and were perverted by those evil
counsellors who tell her, in language now so bitterly
familiar in the West, that 'to possess the Empire of the
Pacific is to be master of the world'. And again it might
well happen if Mr. Gandhi or his disciples could persuade
the untutored multitudes of India that the East cannot
profit by contact with the West, and that all Britain has
done for their motherland has been Satan's doing. It is
safe, I hope, to prophesy that none of these hypotheses
will be fulfilled; but even without them is it not conceivable that the world may drift into a race-schism through
mere indifference and neglect? Nature and circumstance
have made the races different in more than in colour—
different in religion, in philosophy, in experience and
tradition and ideals: and these differences cannot be
harmonized simply by wishing it so. They must be studied,
they must, as far as possible, be understood.

We need not look far afield for the materials of study.
The British Commonwealth, it has been well said, is a micro-
cosm of the world. It cuts across the strata of humanity.
It includes a part of every continent and a section of all
the great families of mankind. As in the question of
nationality, therefore, so in the question of colour, but on
an even wider and more impressive scale, it presents the
essential problems in actual operation: and in this field, as
in the other, its long experience has carried it some way,

at any rate, towards their solution. Roughly, perhaps, and tentatively as yet, it bridges the gulf between Europe and Asia. Within its bounds more than three hundred million Asiatics are living side by side with Europeans. It may not be the happiest of happy families. Discontents, justifiable or otherwise, may be at work beneath the surface whose outcome cannot be foreseen. But the fact is there. These Asiatics and Europeans are at this hour living side by side, fellow-members of one political society, owning allegiance to a single Crown. And if this fact endures, if, as the years go by, the bridge across the gulf consolidates, if the political association becomes in time a genuine comradeship, yoking Europe and Asia in free service for their common weal, surely the longest and hardest stage will have been accomplished in the long, hard march towards the brotherhood of man. Is it anything less, then, than the duty of the rising generation to inform themselves by what process of history and under what conditions this fact has come about? And ought not a British University to help them to fulfil it?

I am sure, at any rate, that my friend, the Reader in Indian History [1]—who will pardon, I know, this momentary intrusion of mine into the field in which he labours with such infectious zeal—will agree with me in wishing that the history of British rule in India were more generally and more fully studied here, and not only or mainly the military and, in its outward form alone, the constitutional history, but rather the development of the ideas which have inspired the British Raj, and especially the growth of a sense of responsibility towards the Indian people, and its effect on public opinion in Britain and on British administration in India.

The origin of this sense of responsibility may be found,

[1] Sir Verney Lovett, K.C.S.I.

I suppose, in that sudden renascence of idealism with which the British people, on the morrow of the most damaging and humiliating disaster in their history, awoke from the long lethargy of the eighteenth century. Defeat may be a better moral tonic than victory; and in that interesting decade between the wars of the American and French Revolutions men like Burke and Wilberforce brought into politics the same new spirit which Wesley and Whitefield had brought into religion. Modern students of Warren Hastings' career may fairly point to exaggeration and injustice in Burke's advocacy of Indian grievances: but let it be remembered that he was rousing his countrymen, by necessarily violent means perhaps, to their first faint perception of the moral issues at stake in the government of India. Reread his speeches of 1783 and 1785, and you will increase—if that is possible at Oxford—your reverence for that great political teacher. Note how clearly he recognizes the magnitude of our task in India, the immensity of its population, and the difficulty and delicacy of the situation that arises from the intrusion of Europe into that ancient civilization with its 'venerable priesthood', its 'nobility of great antiquity and renown', its merchants and bankers, its manufacturers and mechanics, and its 'millions of diligent tillers of the earth', the whole body 'infinitely diversified by manners, by religion, by hereditary employment, through all their possible combinations'. Note, too, how wisely he emphasizes the danger of entrusting to the same men the functions of government and the interests of trade: and how clearly he affirms the cardinal principle that the powers and privileges granted to his countrymen in India ought all to be exercised for the ultimate benefit of the Indian people and are 'all in the strictest sense a *trust*'—the first public enunciation, I take it, of the modern doctrine of trusteeship. And note, finally, his stern reproof of the ignorance and apathy of Parliament. 'Let us do what we please to put India from our thoughts, we can do nothing to separate it from our public interest and our national reputation.'

It would be no less educative, surely, than interesting to watch the influence of this idea of trusteeship, once Burke had forced it on the British conscience, on the subsequent development of public opinion and official conduct—on Parliament's attempts to reform the administration of the East India Company, on the expansion of British rule, on the interpretation and the handling of the crisis of 1857 and the question of transferring political control entirely to the Crown, on the policy of a Cobden on the one hand and a Disraeli on the other, and on the methods and the purpose of the greatest bureaucracy, to judge it not merely by the multitude of human beings in its charge, that the world has ever known.

Should our student of the Commonwealth stop there, for fear of coming too close abreast of contemporary politics and treading controversial ground? Or should he press on to the inauguration of the new *régime* in India? I think he will answer that question for himself. I think, if he studies the steady permeation of British rule in India, from Burke's day onwards, by the ideal Burke proclaimed, he will be caught up by the glamour of the story and will not rest until, be it in work-time or in leisure, he has read its latest chapter and watched, with the anxious interest only his previous study could give him, the initiation of the policy of extending to the people of India the forms of political freedom or, as I would rather put it, of political responsibility, which the people of Britain have fashioned, not without dust and heat, from the lessons of a long experience. He may judge it either way. He may think it an untimely abandonment of our trust or the inception of its last, its hardest, its crowning stage. But anyhow he will be able to contribute some measure of knowledge and thought—academic, it may be, and uninformed by personal experience of India, but better, surely, than blank ignorance and indifference—to the formation of the public opinion of his time on what may prove to be the most decisive issue of this century for the good or ill of mankind as a whole.

4

The Colour Problem is most urgent and most critical in Asia. It is most difficult and morally most dangerous in Africa; and for present purposes I mean by Africa that great equatorial belt between the Sahara and the Zambesi —that vast primeval country, the birthplace, seemingly, of our race, yet to the great majority of men a dark mysterious land; a land of fabulous wealth from the days when Europe whispered of Ophir and Monomatapa to the days when Europe finds itself dependent on its palm-oil and its rubber and the countless other products of its teeming soil; a land which has always tempted the explorer since, four centuries before our era, Hanno set sail from Carthage, and, passing the Pillars of Hercules and Cape Verde, came at last to the Gulf of Guinea and there beheld those hairy, savage men and women whom his interpreters told him were 'gorillas'; the chosen land of glorious incredible romance, the home of the blameless Ethiopians who feasted with the gods, of those battles in the dawn between the pygmies and the cranes, of Presbyter John, of King Solomon's Mines; a land of tropical extremes where Nature nourishes and kills so easily, where white men rise so high and fall so low, where the vileness in *Heart of Darkness* and the nobility in *Multitude and Solitude* can both be true to life; the homeland, first and last, of that swarming fecund Negro

race, the most backward among the great races of mankind, but stirring now under the impact of new ideas,
starting perhaps on a new life of progress and achievement.

Now it happens that a wider area of this land and a
greater number of its peoples are included in the British
Commonwealth than in any other political community. It
falls to us, therefore, its European members, by what we
do or leave undone, to take the predominant, indeed the
decisive, part in settling, one way or another, the African
question. For there is an African question. The world (I
repeat the truism) is one. None of its peoples can live in
isolation. And somehow or other, at the risk of disaster to
all mankind, no less ruinous because it might be primarily
a moral disaster, the life of Africa, like that of Asia, must
be harmonized with the life of the other continents. Here
too, moreover, the course taken in the early years of this
new age will probably determine the issue for centuries to
come. Is it importunate to ask, then, that the rising generation should find among their busy hours a space in which
to study what we have done in Africa and so to fit themselves to decide—for it will rest with them—what we shall
do in Africa?

That some such study should be pursued, and prefer-
ably in the sober, impartial atmosphere of a University,
seems to me imperative if only to counteract the increasing vogue of certain dangerous half-truths. There is a type
of doctrinaire who, when confronted with that question,
What have we done in Africa? is ready with a short reply.
'Nothing but harm', he will tell you; and if asked to enlarge on this assertion he narrates the story of British
intercourse with Africa in two grim chapters. Chapter I is
called 'The Slave Trade'. It is a ghastly picture of seven-
teenth- and eighteenth-century brutality—the ruthless
man-hunt on the Guinea coast—the horrors of the 'Middle

Passage'—the sale of the human cargo in 'parcels' at the West Indian or North American ports, 'choice men' fetching £20 and upwards a head, the sick or feeble or 'much abused' lumped with little children and superfluous women and sold off cheap as 'refuse'—and at home in comfortable England British merchants battening on the trade and complacently protesting that for this negroid order of creation, so little higher than the animals, enslavement by a civilized race is positively a moral and a physical gain. And Chapter II is scarcely less appalling. Its title is 'Economic Imperialism'; and it displays the greed of Europe operating almost as injuriously in the nineteenth as in the eighteenth century on the welfare of Africa. Now and again its cruelty is naked and unashamed: and if as a rule it is outwardly less brutal and wears the disguise of a peaceful and mutually advantageous trade, its effects on the body and soul of the Negro are no less destructive than the slave traffic itself. Lawless adventurers are soon nose down along the path to wealth which the now forbidden slave-traders had trodden. Instead of the chain and the whip, the white man brings the black man now, in exchange for his little store of rubber or ivory or gold, a gun and powder with which to kill his fellows and poisonous 'Trade Spirits' with which to madden and to rot himself. And, presently, as the century draws on, the governments of Europe are seen feverishly competing to include as much as they can of this rich field within their own exclusive control, till at last all Central Africa is 'partitioned' among them, the largest share falling, as in the slave trade, to ourselves.

It is an ugly story, and, *as far as it goes*, it is true. But I would like our hypothetical student not to take it as he finds it in propagandist literature, but to build it up for himself from the materials available. And of these there are plenty, even though the *arcana imperii* of recent years are locked up in the Colonial Office—the earlier official documents in the Record Office, Parliamentary Papers and Debates, Reports of Public Commissions and Private Committees, records of missionary societies, autobiographies, letters, newspapers, and so forth. From these let him peruse that half-true story, not skimming too lightly over any of the black spots on its pages. But let him also put together the other half of the truth. Let him study in Africa as in India the growth of the doctrine of trusteeship.

The starting-point will be the same: for, at the same time as Burke was declaring the new purpose of British rule in India, William Wilberforce, that rare example of the saint in politics, was bringing the question of the abolition of the slave trade, which had been agitated for some time past in humanitarian circles and especially in the Society of Friends, to the forefront of the political stage, forcing it by his eloquence, his industry, his almost irresistible sincerity, on the uneasy conscience of the House of Commons, and rallying to its support not only the warm heart of Fox but also the cool head of his intimate friend, the young Prime Minister himself. It was a little more than seven years since Burke had spoken in Parliament of Britain's 'trust' in India when Pitt asserted the same claim for Africa in a speech which such expert critics as Fox and Grey and Windham declared to be 'one of the most extraordinary displays of eloquence they had ever heard'. You remember the historic scene? The debate had been long drawn out and dawn was already breaking when Pitt began his closing speech. As he reached his peroration the bright sunlight of an April morning shone through the windows of the House. It gave the orator a noble metaphor with which to point his ending. If they listened to the voice of reason and duty, he told the Commons, if, by a prompt and total abolition of the slave trade, they made atonement for their long and cruel injustice towards Africa, if they allowed her the opportunity and the hope of attaining to the same blessings which they themselves, under Providence, enjoyed, then they might live to see the dawn of civilization breaking over Africa, one day to illumine and invigorate that immense continent from end to end.

> *Nos . . . primus equis Oriens afflavit anhelis;*
> *illic sera rubens accendit lumina Vesper.*

The sun was to rise many times over Westminster before this call was answered. The French Revolution and the European War thrust the question of Abolition into the background of men's minds, and of Pitt's among them. But from May 1, 1807, as far as British subjects throughout the world were concerned, the slave trade was 'utterly abolished, prohibited, and declared to be unlawful' by Act of Parliament. Twenty-six years later, as you know, slavery itself was suppressed in all the British colonies.[1]

Our student will discover, then, that the first chapter of the British record in Africa closes, and the second chapter opens, with a moral revolution. British public opinion has acknowledged that it lies not in man's prerogative to pronounce the curse of Canaan. The doctrine that the black race was created to be the 'living implements' of labour for the white is dead. The doctrine that the white race has a duty towards the black has been born. And a tradition has been created of which not only a handful of humanitarians but the rank and file of the British people are proud. Just as the cutlers of Sheffield had declared for

---

[1] Except Ceylon and St. Helena, which in 1807 were administered by the East India Company and not classed as colonies.

C

Abolition in 1789, although, as they admitted, it might injure their industry, so the cotton spinners of Lancashire in the 'sixties cheerfully endured the interruption of the cotton supply and the unemployment and hardship it involved, because it served the cause of freedom for the slaves of North America. But Africa is far from England. Deeds can be done in the dark there, unseen by Englishmen at home. And our student will find, as I have said, that half-true story to be half the truth. He will find the fortune-hunter busily at work in the slave-hunter's shoes. But he will find, too, the principles, for which Englishmen at home were willing to sacrifice so much, being upheld by two groups, especially, of their countrymen in Africa, partly through an instinctive sense of justice and humanity, partly, and in growing measure as time goes on, through a deliberate acceptance of the doctrine of trusteeship.

These two groups are the missionaries and the officials. The fortune-hunters might often be first in the field, but close on their heels and sometimes in advance of them went the preachers of the Gospel, no less enterprising, no less persevering, facing as coolly the dangers of disease and violent death, though it was only the souls of the negroes they were after and not their gold and ivory. There were missionaries, it may be, who through ignorance or bigotry or tactlessness or worse did more harm than good: but on the whole, whether in Darkest Africa or among the defenceless islanders of the Pacific, their work was of immeasurable value not only for the welfare of the people they served but also for the good name of the Commonwealth. It would be an unhistorical account of British dealings with the Pacific which made no mention of Patteson and Selwyn. It would be a travesty of our record in Africa which did not set in the forefront the name of David Livingstone. Nor were missionaries fighting a lonely battle for the natives. They had friends as well as critics in Parliament, in the Colonial Office, in the Cabinet. Their influence, indeed, on government policy in the second quarter of the nineteenth century was actually too powerful because it was too one-sided. It was not in the best interests of South Africa, black as well as white, that Glenelg, for instance, should have been persuaded that no white man could do right and no black man wrong. And a similar charge might be brought against the influence of the missionaries in alienating government opinion from the early schemes of colonization in Australia and New Zealand. But it was better to err on the side of the angels, to emphasize even to unwise extremes the duty of trusteeship, than to abandon the tradition altogether and drift back into the criminal indifference of earlier days.

And if ministers in England were generally true to the tradition, so were their officials in Africa. For officials in the end were needed, in Central Africa as well as in the South. During the greater part of the nineteenth century the British Government abstained as far as possible from adding fresh territories to an Empire which already seemed too vast. But in the 'eighties the policy of annexation or, more strictly, of the institution of protectorates was suddenly and vigorously taken up. Into the causes of this our student should look closely. He will find once more that there is a measure of truth in the assertion that the motive was selfish: that not Britain only, but all the leading States of Europe, had realized the bearing on their economic future of the fact that Tropical Africa was capable of producing an indefinite quantity of certain raw materials which modern civilization could scarcely do without; and that in the ensuing 'scramble' there was more haste and rivalry than might be expected of a wholly disinterested pursuit. But, as he digs a little deeper, he will come upon other facts. He will learn, first, that annexation to the British Commonwealth was not seldom asked for, spontaneously and genuinely, by the rulers of the peoples concerned. He will read, for example, the historic reply of the shrewd Basuto chief to Governor Wodehouse when he was told that his request for annexation had been granted. 'I have become old: therefore I am glad that my people should have been allowed to rest and to lie under the large folds of the flag of England before I am no more.' He will learn, secondly, that a policy of annexation was almost always supported, nay, sometimes passionately demanded, by the missionaries. And why? Because only by annexation, only by the assumption of direct responsibility for the maintenance of law and order by a humane European Government could the native be protected from the private European fortune-hunter. And thirdly, he will learn how obstinately reluctant British Governments were to yield to these appeals; how early and easily, had they wished, they could have planted 'the flag of England' across Africa from sea to sea; but how at last, when other Powers, with France and Germany in the van, began to peg out their claims, they could no longer stand aloof.

And so the student will come again to the threshold of our own age: and on the African as on the Asiatic question he will find new ideas awakened by the War, or rather, old ideas reanimated, crystallized, expanded. He will hear men saying that we stand in Africa as we stood in India generations back; that a similar task, though more difficult perhaps and more protracted, awaits us there; that the time is coming when all British Central Africa will be consolidated like the Indian Empire in one great political system, with an African Civil Service ranking in position and prestige and opportunity with the Indian Civil Service and attracting to its ranks that British genius for adminis-

trative tutelage which India, as we hope, will cease progressively to need. And may I express a wish, in passing,
that Oxford, which takes or has taken a notable part in the
preliminary training of cadets for the Indian, Egyptian,
and Sudanese Civil Services, might also be associated, in
some degree, with the Colonial Civil Service?[1] But more
important than the formulation of these schemes of political organization is the acceptance by the Great Powers of
the world of a new principle by which the government
of backward peoples is henceforth to be controlled—the
principle of the Mandate. A new principle, did I say? A
principle, surely, as old as the days of Burke and Wilberforce. For the principle of the Mandate is simply the
doctrine of trusteeship—the doctrine that implies (1) that
a native territory must not be regarded as the private
estate of its European rulers; that the economic development of it is undertaken for the benefit of the world at
large; and therefore that the subjects of other States shall
be as free to share in its development and trade as the
subjects of the ruling State—*i.e.* the principle of the Open
Door:[2] (2) that the natives, on their part, must not be
regarded as so much labour-power for their rulers' plantations, nor as so much 'cannon-fodder' for their armies, nor
as so many clients for their liquor trade; but in spirit, if
not yet in political capacities and duties, as their fellow-
citizens, as free as they themselves to traffic in their
property or labour: and (3) that not only should their
moral and material interests be upheld against all other
interests that conflict with them, but positive efforts should
be made to raise them by wise education and in other

[1] Courses of instruction for Civil Service 'probationers', appointed
to the Tropical African colonies, were established at Oxford and
Cambridge in 1926.

[2] See p. 252 below.

ways to a higher and wider life. And since on all these heads, with one or two grave exceptions, British ministers and British officials have observed the doctrine, Britain can claim to have been a Mandatory State for many years past.

But if the doctrine of trusteeship is no new thing in the British Commonwealth, its solemn affirmation in the Treaty of Versailles and its detailed exposition in the Covenant of the League of Nations and the texts of the Mandates is a new and a great thing—on paper. How much it will mean in practice depends primarily on us. We first upheld the doctrine; we must lead the way in its application, more consciously and resolutely now, at this great turning-point in history, than ever before. That is why, I repeat, it seems to me essential that the rising generation should not entirely neglect to study its development and so to grasp its importance and its difficulty. It *is* difficult, so difficult indeed, that Mr. Worldly Wiseman may be tempted to warn us that it is really not a practical proposition among imperfect men in this workaday world, and that nothing will prevent the strong from pushing the weak against the wall. Well, we have our answer to that. It was no unpractical dreamer, inexperienced in realities, who said that 'the essential points of a sound Imperial policy admit of being embodied in this one statement, that . . . our relations with the various races who are subjects of the King of England should be founded on the granite rock of the Christian code.' Those words were written by Lord Cromer.

I have gone far afield and brought some strange figures on to our academic stage—*habitants* from the St. Lawrence, Boers from the veld, practitioners of dyarchy from India, Negroes from the Tropics. And if I ask that Oxford should make itself more familiar with these and others like them and with the problems they represent, it is because they are fellow-members with us in one Commonwealth and because, if for lack of scientific preparation we fail to solve those problems, this Commonwealth will fail to fulfil the great purpose for which it exists. A policy of excluding its outer peoples from our field of education would seem to me to be analogous to the policy, often advocated but never, happily, with success, of withdrawing our political activities within the limits of these islands, of bidding our kinsmen overseas to break away and live alone, of leaving Asia and Africa to their fate. And I would dismiss the thought of such a policy in the spirit in which Burke dismissed the thought of abandoning India in 1783. 'There we are: there we are placed by the Sovereign Disposer; and we must do the best we can in our situation. The situation of man is the preceptor of his duty.'

III

FREEDOM AND UNITY [1]

I

CHARLES RUSSELL, to honour whose memory we are gathered here to-day, was an idealist. He was a hard worker; he threw himself with tireless enthusiasm at one task after another; but this love of work was not with him, as it is with some more sombre-minded people, only a kind of anodyne, only a means of escape from the harsh realities of life. Ideals were to him the ultimate realities. The progress or the regress of mankind were determined, he believed, not by immutable fate, but by the moulding of human character and the shaping of human will. If enough of the students in any college, if enough of the citizens in any state, if enough of the peoples who constitute mankind, would *will* it hard enough, the progress of college, state, mankind was certain. According to his faith humanity is like a pilgrim, deliberately choosing his path, resolutely making his way along it, towards the sacred city,

---

[1] The first 'Russell Lecture', Patna College, February 5, 1924. 'Established in memory of Captain Charles Russell, attached 3/3 Gurkha Rifles, Senior Professor and Principal of Patna College from 1906 to 1914, who was killed in action at Nebi Samuil in Palestine on November 22, 1917, the Charles Russell Memorial provides that, from time to time, as funds permit, some eminent person should be invited to deliver in Patna a lecture on some great achievement of the human mind in Literature, Art, Philosophy, or Science, and that these lectures should be published under the general title of the Russell Lectures.'

NOTE.—Though speaking to a mainly Indian audience, the lecturer was precluded by the official position he held at the time from dealing directly with Indian questions.

never doubting that, some day or other, he will reach it. In a letter Russell wrote a few days before he was killed, 'I don't think I have ever enjoyed life more', he said; and the letter was aptly headed, 'Within distant view of a walled city on a hill which we believe to be Jerusalem'.

I am quite sure that none of you here who knew Russell will ever forget him. But the true memory of such a man is something much more than the memory merely of his outward mortal being, of his looks and bearing, of his manner of speech and the ring of his laughter. That picture, those echoes, will blur and fade: they will pass away with the passing of this generation. If he is to be remembered as he himself, surely, would have wished to be remembered, you must think of the immortal spirit of the man, of the principles that inspired his teaching, of all that he stood for in the life of your country, of those ideals for which he lived and died. And since, as one looks about the world to-day, one is sometimes tempted to think that the causes for which so many of the best amongst us gave their lives are already almost forgotten, it may be appropriate if I fix on that last theme for this, the first Russell Lecture, and try to say something about the causes —or one of the causes—those men went out to fight for, eight or nine years ago.

2

You will agree, I think, that in one aspect the War was rightly regarded as a war for national freedom. In the heat of the actual conflict each disputant was inevitably inclined to exaggerate the merits of his own case; but the austere scientific historian, recording his cold judgements in far-off years to come, will set it down—so at least I firmly believe—that the fight against the old Empires of

Central Europe was a fight against an organized system of
national aggrandizement and tyranny. The opening moves
of the War — Austria's attitude to Serbia, Germany's
attitude to Belgium — there was nothing new, nothing
extraordinary or anomalous in these things: they were
but the application of an established doctrine of national
ascendancy, which had already betrayed itself in the treatment by the Hohenzollern and Hapsburg Governments of
those weak minorities of alien nationality that lay beneath
their rule, and which, as the War went on, was to betray
itself yet more crudely in wild and ever wilder dreams
of a Pan-German Europe—nay, a Pan-German world.
'National freedom', then, was a legitimate battle-cry. It was
right to fight for the independence of Belgium, for the
reconstitution of a free Poland, for the restoration of
Alsace-Lorraine, for the deliverance of the Danube peoples
from Austro-Magyar tyranny. But battle-cries are dangerous things. They must be brief, epigrammatic—you cannot cheer your soldiers on with the recital of a complete
political programme—you must often be satisfied with
half the truth: and half-truths are sometimes worse than
lies.

It is lamentable to have to confess it, but something like
this perversion of the true issue has apparently—so far—
resulted from the War. A few months ago, a well-informed
observer of current affairs gave the following opinion of
the present condition of Europe:

Nationalism has been exalted to the dignity of a universal
religion, and in its defence the armies of Europe can boast, on
a peace footing, of one and a half million more men than in
1913. The spirit of nationalism is insatiable: no sooner has it
made political boundaries coterminous with those of race than
it is driven by a restless fever to absorb alien peoples. It infects
present minorities with a yearning not so much to be free as

to become themselves the oppressors. Peaceful co-operation between men of different races within the same state—perhaps the highest achievement of humanity in its political life—is not even sought as an ideal, but is rejected as an absurdity.[1]

That is a grey, sordid picture. It was not for that our best men died. And the cause of it is plain enough. The half-truth has done its evil work. Men and nations have been obsessed by the ideal of national freedom: they have not paused to think what it entails or how to adjust it to other equally high ideals in human life. Dazzled by the radiance of their own freedom, they are blind to the responsibilities towards others which it involves. Freedom, they tell themselves, or (to use post-War language) Self-Determination, is their absolute, unconditional right. Why should they yield a grain of it in order to co-operate with others for the common good? Let the structure of civilization shiver and crack about them. What does it matter as long as *they* are free?

I could devote this lecture to examining what might be called the academic difficulties inherent in such a philosophy. I could enquire into the meaning of 'nationality' or 'nation'. I could ask what limits can logically be set to the application of the doctrine. But I will take broader ground. I will accept it at its own valuation, and try to show you its falsity.

In the first place, I admit no *absolute* right to freedom. An individual's right to freedom is conditioned from the outset by the fact that he cannot live alone. To live alone, as Aristotle tried to teach mankind more than two thousand years ago, he must be either a beast or a god—something less or more than a man. And since he cannot use, he cannot enjoy, his freedom except among his fellow-men, except as a member of society, his individual right to

[1] *Round Table*, No. 53, December 1923.

freedom must clearly be conditioned by the rights of others. And I would go further. I would maintain the familiar principle that rights are only the converse of duties. Why should a man be free? To be able to develop to the full the faculties he is born with. And why that? In order to use those faculties for the welfare of his fellow-men. The right proceeds from the duty. Freedom implies service. 'Service is perfect freedom.'

Now the moral law is the same for nations as for men. Life sets them the same question. For nations as for men, isolation in this close-interlocked modern world of ours is quite impossible. *Sinn fein amhain*, 'ourselves alone', is worse than most of those delusive battle-cries. It is not merely immoral—it is impracticable. Far better was the motto which the greatest prophet of national freedom set in the forefront of all his teaching. 'A nation', said Mazzini, 'is a living task: her life is not her own.' National freedom, in fact, was only half Mazzini's goal: the other half was international unity—a communion of free nations, each dedicating its life to the common welfare of all. And with men like Russell, similarly, national freedom was not all they fought for. They trusted that the very revelation of what Prussianism meant must sicken mankind against the doctrine of national egoism—that its overthrow must open the way to a new age of international fellowship and peace.

Dare we say that they were wrong? The pessimists say so. They are saying it all over the world to-day. They are rejecting the bare idea of international co-operation as an 'absurdity'. It is against nature, they say. Nations always have been selfish, always will be selfish. They cannot live in lasting concord. They *must* try to get the better of one another. The problem of conflicting nationalities is insoluble. Very plausible sentiments—and curiously familiar! Are they not the very sentiments we thought so disagreeable when they were expressed, not very long ago, in German? 'It is a law of life', said Prince Von Bülow, when he was Chancellor of the old German Empire, 'that when two national civilizations meet, they fight for ascendancy. . . . There is no third course. In the struggle between nationalities, one nation is the hammer and the other is the anvil.' The pessimism of to-day is only the Prussianism of yesterday. And this is no quibble. Once reject the ideal of international concord and you will be driven back—if only to save civilization from an infinity of international conflict —to the Prussian dream of maintaining peace and order throughout the world by forcing all its nations into virtual servitude beneath one dominant Power—*Deutschland*, or any other land, *über alles*. Is that the best mankind can do?

But there is another answer to those who deride this twofold ideal of freedom and unity—the answer of history. The ideal *has* been realized; and will it be said that what men have done already they can never do again?

3

The ideal *has* been realized, the problem of nationality *has* been solved, by more than one political society; but what should interest us most—and teach us most—is that it has been solved, in more various ways and on the largest scale, by the political society to which we ourselves belong, by what we have learned to call the British Commonwealth.

I need not remind you that there are four distinct nations in the British Isles; but we are sometimes inclined to forget that the problem of nationality as between those four nations has been in the past just as difficult and dangerous in these islands as it is on the continent of Europe to-day.

It fell, so to speak, into three compartments—the relations of England with Wales, Scotland, and Ireland. Of their record in the last of these the nations concerned have little to be proud of. It may be—is there anyone who does not hope?—that, after centuries of failure, the problem in Ireland is at last moving to its solution. But in the two other fields, in Wales and in Scotland, the nations concerned have been successful, wonderfully successful.

Now the peaceful union of England with Wales and Scotland was only attained after centuries of bitter conflict. From the time of the Norman Conquest and before it, the hardy Welsh mountaineers carried on the tradition of their ancient British stock. Right on into the sixteenth century, with the ghost of King Arthur to inspire them, they fought their endless battle with the Saxon. It was bad for England, this interminable strife. As Burke said, long after, 'Wales rid this kingdom like an incubus'. But it was still worse for Wales. A nation cannot live on hate. The Welsh might hold their mountain strongholds; but within them they were distracted and degraded by intestine feuds. At times, great princes like the Llewellyns could unify and control their country; but in the long run law and order steadily declined, till, in the end, it became unsafe for a traveller to pass along the high road. Wales, in fact, was being barbarized. And in such an atmosphere the best, the really precious, elements in Welsh nationality could not live. The springs of Welsh poetry and music dried up. Even the ancient language was fast declining into a corrupt *patois*. But at last the tragic story ended. At last, by one of the greatest strokes of Tudor statesmanship, the old breach was healed. Wales and England were joined together on a basis of local freedom and international unity; and from that moment, to quote Burke again, 'as by a charm, the tumults subsided'.

The conflict with Scotland was even longer. For centuries the English and the Scots fought each other: now the English king invaded Scotland, now the Scottish king invaded England: there was incessant strife along that blood-stained Border. Generation after generation, fathers handed on to sons the terrible bequest of hatred and revenge. Even when, by an accident of intermarriage, the Scottish king, James VI, succeeded to the English throne as James I, the trouble was not over. The two nations were still separate, still enemies: and at length, in the reign of Queen Anne, they were on the brink of war again. But then, about two hundred years ago, the wisest men in both countries, recognizing the imperative need for unity, recognizing too that it was not incompatible with freedom, came together and framed the Act of Union.

Now I hold that the union of England, Wales, and Scotland in one state—they were politically fused, so to speak, into one body—was a very great achievement. So admirably has it worked that we have long ago forgotten about our historic quarrels, or, if we remember them, it is without the faintest animosity. And yet those quarrels were very protracted and very bitter. They lasted for centuries, and the conflicting nations were utterly estranged —at least as much estranged as France and Germany are now. And the fighting was very fierce. Things were done at least as horrible as any of the 'atrocities' in modern warfare. It would be difficult, indeed, to exaggerate the tradition of enmity, the gulf of blood and tears, which once lay between those three nations. And yet—now—it has all, long ago, like an unsubstantial pageant, faded. It has passed away into the romance of history. It has died quite out of the realities of life.

Moreover—and this is the essence of the matter—these three nations have achieved a solid, indestructible unity without losing their national freedom, without impairing their power freely to develop the best and richest elements in their several nationalities. They have, indeed, gained something in addition. By living and working side by side in peace and fighting side by side in war, they have attained a sense of a new fellowship, a new *British* nationality. But that does not mean, for one moment, that they have lost the old. I have many Scotsmen and Welshmen among my friends; but I should sharply strain their friendship if I had the temerity to suggest that they had ceased to be Scotsmen and Welshmen, that they had lost their sense of nationality. No. Their sense of Welsh and Scottish nationality, their devotion to their old national heritage of custom and language and literature, their loyalty to their high historic traditions, their love for the mountains and the lochs of their homelands—these things are very much alive, very proudly and properly alive. We have got Unity, but we have got Freedom and Variety too.

4

Now let me take you to newer soil—to Canada and South Africa. It was only some hundred and fifty years ago that Britain took possession of Canada. It was then a French colony, with a wholly French population; so that when, as the result of the Seven Years War, in which Britain defeated France, this French colony was annexed, the British Government was at once confronted with the problem of nationality. How were these Frenchmen to be made into loyal members of the British Commonwealth? There were some Englishmen who, forgetful of the lessons of their own islands, insisted that the only way was to turn them from Frenchmen into Englishmen. How? By force, of course. By the old, crude method. By the hammer on the anvil. The three main distinctive elements of the nationality of these French Canadians — the Roman Catholic religion, the French language, and their peculiar system of law—should be suppressed. Happily British statesmen did not adopt that impossible policy: they adopted, on the contrary, a policy of thoroughgoing conciliation and toleration. So far from combating those three elements of French-Canadian nationality, they left them wholly undisturbed. The Roman Catholic Church was not merely tolerated: it was secured by Act of Parliament in practically all its old privileges. The French language was put on an equal footing, in public affairs, in government, in the courts, with English. And the French civil law was definitely re-established—again by Act of Parliament—as the law of the land. This policy came as a great surprise to the French Canadians. They had expected to be treated as conquered people were usually treated in those days. They had expected, as they afterwards frankly confessed, the iron heel of oppression and coercion on all the cherished heritage of their national life. And they had got instead the most complete sympathy and toleration. The result was what the policy deserved. In a very short time, the people as a whole, this conquered people, these foreigners—who had fought so bitterly against the British, who had been defeated, who had been torn away by force from their mother-country—these people settled down as contented members of the British Commonwealth.

But the problem was not quite done with. It presently reappeared in a more difficult form. British immigrants began to stream into Canada—not so much into that St. Lawrence valley which was the old home of the French Canadians as into the unexplored wilds and forests and prairies in the West—till, in the course of years, there were more Britons in Canada than Frenchmen. Formerly

British statesmen in England had been dealing with a mainly French population far away. Now the two peoples, the two nationalities, were face to face on the spot. Well, there was an awkward period. Both sides made mistakes. Among the British Canadians there was a party—a sort of Orange party—thinking only of unity, that wanted to reverse the policy of toleration and force all Canada into one uniform British mould. And among the French Canadians there was a party, thinking only of freedom, that tried to exploit the race instincts of their people, tempted them with the phantom of a little independent French-Canadian Republic, and even in the end beguiled a handful of them into a feeble and futile rebellion. But happily no irreparable breach was opened; and, after twenty or thirty years of uncertainty and difficulty, the good sense of the Canadians, both British and French, achieved the final solution of the problem by the Federation of 1867.

Federation, as you know, is a constitutional device for combining Unity and Freedom. To put it in a nutshell, the adoption of a federal system meant that, in all their provincial, domestic affairs—the matters which most closely touched their nationality—the principle of *local autonomy* was applied: *i.e.* in the new, mainly British, provinces—Ontario and the rest—the government would run on British lines, while in the old, mainly French, province of Quebec the government would run on French lines. And, around and about this system of local governments, French and British would take their share in the Federal or Central Government of the Dominion of Canada as a whole. Hence they could be, at the same time, faithful adherents in politics both of their separate nationalities and also of all Canada.

Of course, the mere adoption of this federal device has

not yet done away with all the trouble. There is still occasional friction, still a flicker now and then of race antagonism. But the unity of Canada is an established, unalterable fact. Time can only strengthen it. And within that unity remains and will remain, no less defying time, the freedom of the French Canadians. And what a rich, what a picturesque element they contribute to the life of the Dominion! If you were to go to that noble St. Lawrence valley, to Quebec and the long white line of villages that cluster along the river, you would find yourself in France—not modern France, but the France of long ago. The whole atmosphere is French—the houses, the shops, the Roman Catholic churches, the convents, the priests, the people, the language—but with an air of the Old World about it all. Except in the city of Montreal, there is none of the bustle of modern days, especially of modern days in America. For the mass of the French-Canadian people remain, as they have always been, a peasant people: and if you would understand (without going there) the old-fashioned simplicity of their life, their passionate devotion to the soil, their steady industry, their wonderful endurance of the hardships of the long, rigorous Canadian winter, their frugality, their homely family virtues, their faith and resignation, you should read a novel called *Marie Chapdelaine* by Louis Hémon. It is, I think, a beautiful story in itself: but its outstanding merit is its singularly realistic reproduction of the atmosphere of life in the backwoods of Quebec. You will understand a good deal of what French-Canadian nationality is—far more than a dozen lectures could tell you—if you read that remarkable book.

And I think, if you read it, you will not, like some critics of the *habitants* (as they are called), be overmuch distressed at their relative lack of education, at their limited outlook, at their failure to keep pace with the rush of economic development in America. There is plenty of time for economic development. And meanwhile the virtues of a peasant people are virtues still. Surely it is a good thing that the unity of Canada has not meant the smothering of freedom in a barren uniformity. Surely Canada is the richer for possessing French as well as British citizens, just as Britain is the richer for its mixture of English and Welsh and Scots.

5

And now let us pass to the problem of nationality in South Africa. It began in South Africa, as in Canada, through the British annexation of a foreign colony—the Dutch colony at the Cape—a little more than a century ago. And, as in Canada, there was a marked national difference between the old Dutch colonists and the new British immigrants who began to settle in the country. Like the French Canadians, the Dutch farmers or Boers belonged to the Old World and desired to remain in it. Like the French Canadians, they were a simple, homely, hospitable country folk; and they were thinly scattered over the wide country-side. The average size of a Boer's farm was 6000 acres. The Boer, indeed, was never really happy unless all the land he could see as he sat smoking on his *stoep* was *his* land. And owing to this solitary mode of life and owing to their being a pioneer people, on the fringe of civilization, often in strife and danger with the savage native races, the Boers had learned to be a law to themselves; and they did not take kindly to any other law. They had given trouble to their own Dutch Government in the old days; and as for the new British Government, and especially its new-fangled humanitarianism, its re-pudiation of slavery, and its one-sided, doctrinaire, inconsistent policy towards the Kaffirs on the borders of the colony, they could not—and did not—abide it. Some twenty years after the annexation, all the restless spirits among them took ox and waggon and 'trekked' off, right away from the old colony, into the vast unknown spaces of the veld beyond the Orange River. And the result of the Great Trek (as it is called) was that, in course of time, there were four separate political communities in South Africa—the British colonies of the Cape and Natal and the Boer republics of the Transvaal and the Orange Free State. In other words, the problem of the two nations living together had been (so to speak) given up. They were going to live apart.

But the problem, as British statesmen should have foreseen, could not be *solutum ambulando*. South Africa was too small—as the whole world to-day is too small—for nations to escape from all contact with each other. So the almost inevitable upshot of the Great Trek was a long, miserable story of friction and quarrelling and bloodshed. There was a little Anglo-Boer war in 1848; there was another little war in 1881, the war of Majuba; and there was a third and greater war from 1899 to 1902. Most of us can remember that last struggle and the controversies it aroused. I am not going to revive them. It may be that people will never agree as to the true rights and wrongs of it. My business is not so much with that tragedy as with the extraordinary sequel to it. I said just now that I thought the union of England and Scotland a wonderful thing. Do not suspect me of indulging in enthusiastic exaggeration if I say that I think the union of South Africa still more wonderful. Let me just put the bare facts before you; they will speak for themselves.

It was one of the conditions, when peace was made, that the Transvaal and the Orange Free State should soon be given self-government; and when, in a few years' time, they were given it, the old quadruple division of political power was once more established. The Boer republics were now, it is true, British colonies, like the Cape and Natal; but in all their internal affairs they were separate and self-governing. Was it not to be expected that they would cherish their distinct existence, maintain their old tradition of aloofness, go their own way? Was it not to be expected that generations would have to pass before the breach could be healed? . . . Well, it did not need generations: it needed precisely eight years. No sooner had the old divisions been re-established than a campaign for Union was begun. It was admirably led on both sides: but it was not merely the leaders, it was the rank and file of Dutch and British in South Africa that rose to the appeal. And mark this; it was primarily a moral appeal. The economic and political advantages of Union—the promise it held out of material prosperity, of administrative efficiency and economy, of a wise and consistent treatment of the native question—those things had their due weight. But the first thing men thought of was moral unity—the burying of the hatchet, the setting aside of three generations of strife and bloodshed and wasted effort, the submergence of the old narrow tradition of Anglo-Dutch rivalry and antagonism in the new ideal of service to a single South Africa—neither a Dutch nor a British South Africa, but the one common country of both peoples. It was on a tide of real enthusiasm for this high ideal that the Union was carried—voluntarily carried by the votes of all four colonies: it could not have been forced on them—and carried in a drastic shape. The old four colonies retained their frontiers as provinces in the new body: but it was not a federal system: they were not so divided as the provinces of Canada: the separate powers of the South

African provinces were not very much more than those of counties in England: the whole of South Africa, in fact, was fused under a single unitary government, almost as closely as England, Wales, and Scotland are fused in Great Britain. And this measure was carried in 1909 and came into force in 1910—only eight years after the close of that long and stubborn war, while the bitter memories, which war always leaves behind it, were still fresh in men's and women's hearts. Surely that was a very remarkable achievement.

But, you may ask, is it lasting? I believe so: and I will give you better authority for that belief than my own. I shall never forget a long talk I had at Pretoria in 1913 with the late General Botha, then Prime Minister—the first Prime Minister—of united South Africa. He spoke with real anxiety of the future of his country. He feared that the ashes of the old national feud were still glowing: that there were even some people in the land who, in their hearts, desired to go back to the old, discordant, fighting days of quadruple division. But he spoke with hope too; with a sort of quiet trust that Providence would never allow his country, after so much suffering, to step back again into the unhappy past. His anxiety was soon justified. In the early months of the War, as you know, a recalcitrant section of the Boers broke out in rebellion. But the hope was justified too. The rebellion was crushed—and easily crushed—not mainly by the British in South Africa, but mainly by Botha and the Boers. And now that the War is over, every year that goes by, it seems to me, will mean less anxiety and more hope. There is still a strong separatist party. There is still unfriendly feeling, in places, between Boer and Briton. But the Time-Spirit is against the feud. It will steadily become more and more of an anachronism. Before our generation passes, I believe it will be dead.

6

That is history's answer to the pessimists. In Britain, in Canada, in South Africa—not to mention countries like Switzerland and Belgium—separate nations have found it possible, however deeply divided and estranged they may have been at times, to join together at last in unity. More than that. The new composite nations that have grown, or are growing, out of their unity—Great Britain, Canada, South Africa—are living, together with the other self-governing Dominions, in intimate co-operation under one Crown; commingled, yet distinct; united, yet free. It is a wonderful thing, this great society of ours, embracing a quarter of the world, including a quarter of mankind in all its infinite variety of race and creed and tongue: and we, its members, may surely be allowed to take a thoughtful, serious pride in it; to regard it as (to quote the terms of the foundation of the Russell Lectureship) 'a great achievement of the human mind in political science'.

I said a thoughtful, serious pride: for membership of the British Commonwealth, like every other human status, involves responsibilities. It is but a young and tender growth among the world's antiquities. We are only beginning to realize the possibilities of mutual intercourse and mutual understanding and mutual help it offers to its members. Nor must we forget, unless indeed we would become a sort of super-nationalists, no less blind and selfish in our loyalties than those desperate nationalists in Europe, the duty of the Commonwealth towards the world as a whole. And in both fields, in our relations between ourselves and with other peoples, the key to success, in the future as in the past, lies in that twofold ideal. 'We are the immemorial champions of Freedom', said Lord Balfour once in the course of the War. Yes; but we have been, we must always be, champions of Unity too. Where we have Unity already, in whatever shape or degree, we must think long and earnestly before we break it up—knowing that, once lost, it may never be recovered. And where we have no Unity, we must strive after it, work for it, no less zealously than we do for Freedom—knowing that it is no less fine a thing. If we shape our course by those twin stars, we may find perhaps, in time, that a new age of peace and fellowship among mankind is not, after all, an impossible dream. Perhaps the city Russell sighted before he died, far off among the hills, was really, after all, the City of God.

IV

THE GROWTH OF DOMINION
SELF-GOVERNMENT[1]

'ALL are on an equality', said Lord Balfour when he explained to the House of Lords the status of Great Britain and the Dominions as defined in the Declaration of 1926. 'That is the very essence, as I understand it, of the British Empire.' Historians would agree. The concession of political equality is the main reason why the Second British Empire still stands, just as its refusal was the main reason why the First British Empire fell. Thus the constitutional history of the Second Empire is concerned with a process of equalization or, as its initiators in the days of Fox and Pitt termed it, 'assimilation'. Beginning as it began in England with representative institutions, self-government in the colonies expanded, stage by stage, in its scope and in its quality, until at last in 'Dominion Status' it attained complete equality with self-government in Britain.

To those who are unfamiliar with the process, a brief outline of it may be useful. It must take Canada for its chief example, since the colonies which grew into the present Dominion were, with the exception of Newfoundland, the only colonies of 'white' settlement which survived the American Revolution. The process, therefore, began in Canada, and thereafter she set the pace, so to speak, for its development in the other groups of colonies founded or acquired in Australia, New Zealand, and South Africa. What was conceded to Canada was sooner or

[1] October 1934.

50

later almost automatically conceded to her 'younger sisters'.

Representative government (*i.e.* the institution of an assembly or house of commons by which the representatives of the electorate controlled legislation) began in Nova Scotia in 1758, in Prince Edward Island in 1773, in New Brunswick in 1784, and in Upper and Lower Canada (united in 1840) in 1791. As a result of the Durham Report, responsible government was introduced in all these provinces in 1846–9. It was understood that the scope of this responsible government would be limited, by usage, not by law, to the domestic affairs of each province. In particular Durham had enumerated four fields of government which should be 'reserved' (to use the term familiar in India since 1919) to the control of the British Government—the disposal of public lands, the alteration of the constitution, the regulation of external trade, and foreign affairs (including defence).

The disposal of public lands, though its connexion with emigration made it a matter of general imperial interest, was soon recognized to be primarily a domestic concern, and it was conceded to Canada by statute in 1840.

The power to amend the constitution remained 'reserved' for a far longer time.[1] The British North America Act of the British Parliament (1867) which united the provinces in a 'national' federation styled 'the Dominion of Canada', contained no such provision enabling the Dominion legislature to amend the constitution as was made in the later Acts uniting Australia (1900) and South Africa (1909). Without such provision the constitution could only be amended by the legislature which enacted

[1] An Act of 1854 empowered the legislature of the united Provinces of Canada to alter the constitution of the Legislative Council.

it, the British Parliament; and, owing to anxieties as to the safeguarding of provincial rights, especially in Quebec, even the Statute of Westminster of 1931, which empowers the Canadian Parliament to amend any other British statute affecting Canada, specifically reserves the British North America Act and the subsequent amending Acts; so that the Canadians are still unable to effect a change in their own constitution except by asking the British Parliament, as they have already asked it on several occasions, to do it for them.

The next 'reserved' field, the regulation of external trade, though of great material importance and manifestly affecting the interests of Britain and the rest of the Empire, was 'transferred' (to use the Indian term again) to local control at a remarkably early stage. While the British Government, after the abandonment of protection, desired to maintain free trade throughout the Empire, Canada wanted a tariff, in the first instance to raise additional revenue and then to protect her nascent industries against American and British competition. When the Canadian Government raised its revenue tariff to a protective level in 1858 and heightened it further in 1859, the British Government, after a useless protest, acquiesced. Canadian 'fiscal autonomy' may be dated, therefore, from 1859.

In 1867, the Provinces were federated, as mentioned above; but of course, the adoption of the title 'Dominion' for the federation had none of the implications of the modern term 'Dominion Status'.[1] Federation only meant the territorial extension of the responsible government already possessed from a provincial to a national scale.

---

[1] 'Dominion' is, of course, a generic term covering the Dominion of Canada, the Commonwealth of Australia, the Union of South Africa, and the Dominion of New Zealand. The Irish Free State possesses Dominion Status, but rejects the title of 'Dominion' as being applicable only to 'young' nations created by colonization. Newfoundland, though it did not exercise all the privileges of Dominion Status,

The next field to be dealt with was defence. British regular troops had been stationed in all the colonies from the outset not only to meet the possible danger of external attack arising from an outbreak of war with a foreign Power but also to assist the colonial police or militia in the maintenance of 'internal security'. They were constantly employed, for example, in fighting the Bantu natives on the borders of Cape Colony and Natal between 1813 and 1880 and in the Maori Wars in New Zealand between 1845 and 1866. But in the 'sixties it was agreed that the colonies possessing responsible government were competent to maintain their own local defence and security; and after a short 'transitional period', in which the local military forces were strengthened, the British regulars were withdrawn from Australia and New Zealand in 1870, and, after their employment in the suppression of the Red River Rebellion, from Canada likewise in 1871, except for garrisons retained in two naval stations till 1906. Owing mainly to the large native population British troops remained in South Africa even after the Union: they helped in suppressing the industrial disorders at Johannesburg in 1913, but, except for some artillery and other units retained for the defence of the Cape Peninsula till 1921, they were withdrawn on the outbreak of the War in 1914. By that date Australia, New Zealand, and South Africa had created national defence forces on a basis of general military service, while Canada had maintained a small regular force and strengthened her militia. As regards naval defence, the Australian, New Zealand, and South African colonies contributed for many years to the cost of the British navy, but after 1908 Australia and New

---

was counted as a Dominion till the suspension of its constitution in 1933. Southern Rhodesia, where responsible government is not yet quite complete, is not a Dominion.

Zealand established naval squadrons of their own. Meanwhile it had been understood, of course, that in time of war all the colonies or Dominions could count at need on the assistance of the British army and navy.

The last field to be 'transferred' was that of foreign affairs. By 1914 Dominion Governments had been empowered to deal directly with foreign Governments in such commercial questions as tariff agreements. They had also appointed High Commissioners in London to act as their own agents in such matters, and they sent their own delegates to the international conferences on Radio-Telegraphy and Safety of Life at Sea in 1913 and 1914. But on the political side of foreign affairs they had taken no action separately on their own account. Foreign policy was left to the management of the British Foreign Office. The diplomatic and consular services throughout the world were wholly British. In the negotiation of political treaties directly affecting their interests, such as the Alaska Boundary Treaty, representatives of the Dominions took part, but always in conjunction with British representatives, and appointed by the King always on the advice of British ministers. It is important to realize that the Dominions, while they asked that they should be consulted on questions affecting their local interests, willingly accepted this subordinate standing in the main field of foreign affairs up to the War. Remote from the chief arena of foreign policy, knowing little of its complexities, intent on the immediate task of developing their own new countries, they were content to entrust the great issues of peace and war to the closer knowledge and longer experience of the mother-country. It was not till 1917 that their entry into this last field was demonstrated by the inclusion of their prime ministers on equal terms with British ministers in the Imperial War Cabinet, charged with the

supreme control of war policy. This new standing was
formally recognised when separate plenipotentiaries of
the Dominions, appointed by the King on the request
of Dominion ministers, separately signed the Treaty of
Versailles in which, among other things, the Dominions
were recognized as original members of the League of
Nations, each in its own right and distinct from the rest
of the British Empire. Subsequent developments, such as
the appointment of Dominion ministers at foreign capitals
or the recognition of a Dominion's right to deal by itself,
though not without informing the other members of the
British Commonwealth, with political as well as commercial treaties of local concern, confirmed the new
position; so that by 1930 the long process of extending a
Dominion's self-government into every field of its political
and economic life was at last complete.

The extent or scope of Dominion self-government being
thus equalized with that of Britain, it only remained to
remove such surviving inequalities as, in law or in fact,
rendered that self-government in any way inferior in its
quality.

In the executive field this involved a change in the
status and functions of the Governor-General. Up to 1926
he was appointed by the King on the advice of British
ministers, and he acted not only as the King's representative but also as the agent of the British Government,
under whose instructions he dealt with matters of interest
to Britain or the Empire as a whole. In 1930 it was
finally agreed that his appointment was to be advised by
Dominion ministers, that he was to act only as the King's
representative and no longer as agent of the British Government (who have since appointed separate agents called
'High Commissioners' in Canada and South Africa), and
that in the exercise of his function he should follow 'the

constitutional practice that His Majesty acts on the advice of responsible ministers'. While the position of the Governor-General in a Dominion was thus assimilated to that of the King in Britain, it was also agreed that it was 'the right of the Government of each Dominion to advise the Crown in all matters relating to its own affairs' and that it would be unconstitutional for British ministers to tender contrary advice on such matters.

In the legislative field, the powers of the Crown to 'disallow' Dominion Acts on the advice of British ministers and of the Governor - General to 'reserve' Dominion Bills on their instructions, were admitted in 1930 to have been annulled by the effect of the above agreements. The remaining elements of inequality—the operation in the Dominions of laws made by the British Parliament and its unlimited power to make such laws, and the inability of Dominion Parliaments to legislate with effect outside their own territories—were eliminated by the Statute of Westminster, 1931, which, in its main provisions, repealed the Colonial Laws Validity Act, 1865, in so far as it applied to the Dominions; empowered Dominion Parliaments to repeal or amend Acts of the British Parliament in so far as they are part of Dominion law, and to make laws having extra-territorial operation; and declared that no future Act of the British Parliament should extend to a Dominion as part of its law unless at the Dominion's request and with its consent.

Thus, in its quality as in its scope, Dominion self-government became full self-government, both legislative and executive, and 'Dominion Status' became an equal status with that of Britain.[1]

[1] For a further note on the meaning of Dominion Status, see p. 275 below.

V

REFLECTIONS ON A VISIT TO DUBLIN[1]

I

THE sins of the fathers unto the third and fourth generation. . . . Excuses can be found, of course. The Irish are
'difficult' folk. They have obstinately retentive memories.
The fault was not all ours. We had to keep the peace in
Ireland because they could not keep it themselves. Much
of what we did was in retaliation for what had been done
to us. England's safety depended on Ireland's subjection.
We must not judge the past too sternly by the moral
standards of to-day. At any rate we have tried to make
amends. The Famine was not our doing, and after the
Famine we undid, piece by piece, the old ascendancy—
religious, commercial, agrarian, political. In the later years
of the Union, Irishmen were on an equal footing with
Scotsmen and Welshmen — and Englishmen. They got
security from it and more prosperity than they could have
got alone. It was a German critic who said, not long before
the War, that 'the Irish tenants have had conditions assured
to them more favourable than any other tenantry in the
world enjoy'.

But the stubborn facts remain. Cromwell, to go no
farther back, *did* leave his mark on Ireland. The Penal
Laws *were* passed, and for a time at least enforced. The
economic life of Ireland *was* strangled in the eighteenth
century in the selfish interests of British business. And,

[1] June 23-30, 1933.

though the Irish would certainly have suffered more from Russian or Prussian rule, it is perhaps not quite so surprising as we sometimes think that the past, even the ancient past, is still remembered. We, no doubt, have had things to forgive and forget, but forgiving and forgetting are easier for the victors. And it seems only natural to suppose that, wherever else the blame may lie, the wrongs we have done to Ireland in the past are the main reason why the Irish problem is still unsolved.

2

Many Englishmen still vividly remember the sense of relief they felt when the Anglo-Irish Treaty of 1921 was concluded. Its value was by no means unilateral. Mr. de Valera and his friends have constantly asserted that there was an element of force in it. Of course there was. Force is at the back of every treaty that concludes a war; but in this case it was not all on one side. We had, no doubt, the physical power to go on steadily wearing down the resistance of the militant Sinn Feiners, who were never, it seems, very numerous: but how long could we have continued to use that power? The moral compulsion had swung against us. The continuance of fighting and bloodshed, so soon after the end of the World War, was becoming intolerable to most Englishmen; and the more that was known about the 'irregular' methods we had adopted or tolerated by way of reprisal or terrorism, the less excusable they seemed on any other plea than that which had been used, a few years earlier, to excuse Prussian methods in Belgium. Was such a mood, as some thought, an early symptom of post-War 'defeatism'? Or was it, rather, characteristic of British realism, of a people that can be pugnacious and yet cool-headed, that can ask itself even in hot blood if the end is worth the means?

Anyhow, there was a deep and widespread desire in England to get some sort of peace in Ireland; and, as usual on such occasions, the hope was general and sanguine that the particular peace achieved would endure. The adoption of 'Dominion Status', so much greater a concession to Irish nationalism than any previous 'Home Rule' offer, seemed an act of generosity and trust that was bound to awaken a response. The Irish Problem was solved at last, some said, or—when reminded that 'Ulster' was not yet included in the Free State—that any rate it was now on the right road to solution.

For ten years the optimists seemed justified. The Sinn Fein 'moderates' were scrupulously loyal to the bargain we had made with them. Having obtained the confirmation of the Treaty at the polls, they rigorously repressed the 'extremist' revolt against it, but at the tragic cost of adding a new domestic blood-feud to Irish history. For ten years they carried on an efficient, orderly, soundly financed internal administration. If in external affairs they pressed at Imperial Conferences for the complete and formal recognition of 'equal nationhood' for the Dominions, it was a natural move in the light of Irish politics, and it was closely backed not only by South Africa but by Canada; nor could there be any doubt whatever, after the Declaration of 1926 and the Statute of Westminster, that Mr. Cosgrave and his party genuinely desired and intended to remain within the Commonwealth. Another decade of such firm and sensible government, and might not the old antipathies and misgivings of the North begin to weaken?

3

The causes of the downfall of Mr. Cosgrave were complex. There was first the 'swing of the pendulum': the

Cumann na nGaedheal Government had been in power
for a longer continuous period than any other democratic
Government in the world since the War. Second, there
was the 'slump', the effects of which on the feelings of
uninstructed electors were not softened by Mr. Blythe's
conservative finance and high taxation. But those reasons,
potent as they were and strengthened by the personal
bitterness arising from the conflict with the anti-Treaty
'extremists' and by the traditional unpopularity of any
Irish Government that resorts to 'coercion', would not
by themselves have accounted for the completeness of
Mr. de Valera's final victory and for the strength of his
present position. To criticism of his opponents and
promises of a new economic *régime* he added the appeal
which still so easily and deeply stirs the emotions of so
many Irishmen—the old antagonism to England, the old
passion for Irish freedom.

Most of us on this side of the Irish Channel are probably
unaware of the enmity, one might almost say the hatred,
with which not the individual Englishman, of course,
but England is still regarded by many Irishmen. It is
something of a shock—even if at times the note of melo-
drama compels an unregenerate grin—for an Englishman
who has visited Quebec or Pretoria to come to Dublin
and see his country publicly attacked. He cannot help
being startled, for example, by the numerous old inscrip-
tions painted on the walls of houses and bridges and the
embankment of the Liffey. 'Remember the foul murders
and join Sinn Fein.' 'Damn your concessions, England.'
'On to a Republic.' Doubtless they were the handiwork
of the less responsible element in Dublin society; but it
seems odd that, in all the years since the Treaty, nobody
has felt it desirable or merely decent to delete them. There
are also printed posters headed 'Boycott British Goods'

and recounting Irish grievances with special stress on the suppression of the Easter Rebellion. Even in the municipal election which occurred in Dublin during my stay, this anti-British cry was significantly, if quite irrationally, raised. 'Slogans' were painted across some of the main streets, such as 'Don't give in to England, don't let your hand shake', or 'England has Cumann na nGaedheal, Ireland has Fianna Fail'. Nor did the former party scruple to appeal to the same anti-British memories on behalf of their own candidates. One of them was commended on an election poster as 'one of five brothers who fought beside De Valera at Easter, 1916. Who of the Fianna Fail candidates can say the same? Where were they then?'

Naturally Irish candidates must be Irish 'patriots' first and last, but it is disappointing to discover that ten years of Dominion Status have so little affected the popular belief that the touchstone of Irish patriotism is enmity to England. Indeed the old hate is kept alive all over the country. In the one week of my visit the newspapers recorded a meeting of a Wolfe Tone Club, recently revived, at Limerick, attended by a brother of Sean Wall, 'who lost his life in the fight for Irish freedom'; a gathering of three thousand people in County Clare to commemorate two patriots who fell, one in the 'Anglo-Irish war', the other in the post-Treaty conflict; the opening of a 'Pearse Memorial College' in County Galway, attended by Miss M. Pearse; a meeting of the Tomas Ashe Sinn Fein Club at Galway at which Miss Mary MacSwiney foretold a world war in the near future when England would be ordered 'to clear out bag and baggage'; and a meeting in support of the Irish language at Dublin at which the chief speaker declared he would not be satisfied 'until English is entirely rooted out of the country'. The voice, no doubt, is the voice of a somewhat rancorous extremist faction:

but the sentiments are akin to those of the present Free State Government.

Antagonism to England is linked, of course, with antagonism to the dominant class in Northern Ireland. The bitterest Fianna Fail politicians are Catholics from the North. The Lord Mayor of Dublin was violently censured during my stay for attending a non-party, non-sectarian function across the border; and the Dublin newspapers of both the big parties make the most of the economic depression in Belfast and its reported 'disillusionment' at the results of Ottawa. Naturally, too, 'Ulster's' reaction to Mr. de Valera's victory and the stiffening of its veto on the unity of Ireland under present conditions intensify the old grievance of 'partition'. To one who knows the average Englishman's attitude, it is surprising to find how widespread is the belief that the partition was entirely England's fault, if not actually England's wish, and that England could wipe it out in a moment if she chose. It even seems to be thought possible that we should *force* the Northern Protestants into the Free State. It certainly seems unfortunate that our gift of a new and massive Parliament House to Northern Ireland should have somehow been squeezed into the general settlement. It is constantly cited as a proof of a deliberate English policy of permanent partition. Few Irishmen seem aware that in fact most Englishmen, if they thought or were questioned about it, would echo the impartial wish expressed in the closing words of the speech with which the King opened the new parliament at Belfast in 1921—that that ceremony might be 'the prelude of a day in which the Irish people North or South, under one parliament or two as those parliaments may themselves decide, shall work together in common love for Ireland upon the sure foundation of mutual justice and respect'.

It has been an easy task, therefore, for Mr. de Valera to fan the old fire. The treaty settlement, of course, never seemed to Irish nationalists as generous as it seemed to us. Subject peoples may recognize the wisdom of their rulers' liberalism: its trustfulness may sometimes be reciprocated: but any freedom it gives is inevitably regarded, in India, in South Africa, above all in Ireland, as a tardy concession to plain justice. Mr. de Valera, moreover, has never admitted that the Treaty made the Free State really free, has never accepted Dominion Status as really meaning 'equal nationhood' with Britain. It is not unnatural, perhaps, for Irishmen to distrust the Dominion analogy. Ireland is not a grown-up colony: it is an ancient mother-country, like Britain: and it may be difficult for Irishmen, as it was till recently for Americans, to realize that Canada is now in real fact 'in no way subordinate' to the great country that once conquered and colonized it. It is easier, no doubt for an Afrikaner to be convinced of the real freedom of South Africa from the remote control of 'Downing Street' than for an Irishman separated by only thirty to sixty miles of water from the might of Britain. At any rate, Mr. de Valera seems assured that he is speaking the truth when he denounces the treaty settlement as the perpetuation of British tyranny, and Mr. Cosgrave as Mr. Thomas' tool: and most of the electors, who have no notion what Dominion Status means, are only too ready to believe him.

So the old idea of a fight for Irish freedom—the idea which one hoped would presently be killed by realities in Ireland as the analogous idea is being killed in South Africa—has been given a new life. Irish patriots are bidden gird themselves for the last victorious battle in the centuries long campaign. The Treaty was a trick. Dominion Status is not freedom. Only a republic can be free. Close the ranks, then, and endure for a little, and the blood of the martyrs will not have been spilt in vain. 'On to a Republic' . . . . Any Irish Catholic must be a cool-headed realist not to feel at least some quiver of response to an appeal which goes so deep into Irish memories. And even to those who recognize the present fact of Irish freedom, who know that a Republic would be no more free than a Dominion, the idea has a strong sentimental attraction. Irishmen, especially perhaps young Irishmen, want to prove to the world the high qualities of Irish nationhood, to show that Ireland can stand on her own feet and make her own individual contribution to the welfare of mankind; and, in a vague sort of way, it seems easier to do this if every link with Britain and the Empire is severed. It needs cool thinking and some knowledge of post-War international relations to realize that Ireland, like any other nation, can do nothing for mankind in isolation and that she can make a better contribution to the peace and welfare of the world by fully using her opportunities of free co-operation within the British Commonwealth than by an impulsive and irrational secession from it. What is, perhaps, more obvious is that an Irish Republic cannot be a Republic of all Ireland. The Republican drift at Dublin has already deepened the gulf that separates it from Belfast. Republicanism perpetuates 'partition'. And yet to most, probably to all Republicans, certainly to Mr. de Valera, the emotional appeal of Irish unity is quite as powerful as that of the Republic itself.

It is, indeed, this question of national unity that makes one most doubtful of Mr. de Valera's immediate intentions. No one questions, he himself proclaims, that his goal is a Republic. There is a general, almost fatalistic, belief in anti-Republican circles that he can and will attain it in the near future. He can 'republicanize' the con-

stitution by amendments, overriding or at need abolishing
the Senate. If he asks the electorate to give him a mandate
for a formal declaration of a Republic, he will get it. And
the 'extremists' are constantly pressing him in that direction. Their newspaper, *An Phoblacht*, denounced his statement in the course of the Dublin election that 'every
Republican ought to support the Republican Government
that is in existence' as an attempt 'to confuse and mislead
the people'. And in the background lurks the 'Irish Republican Army'. While nobody seems to know how strong
this pressure may become, it is agreed that, if Mr. de
Valera cannot hold his ground in face of it, he will move
to the 'Left' rather than the 'Right'. But if, as seems on the
whole to be probable, he can hold his ground and make
his own choice, will he be content with a Republic without
the Six Counties? He can amend the Free State Constitution, but not that of Northern Ireland, and formally
to declare a Republic of All-Ireland would seem to be a
more than usually unsatisfying equivocation. Moreover,
it is, perhaps, characteristic of Mr. de Valera's pyschology
that, while he cannot or will not understand the British
case and refuses to concede a single point to it, he seems
genuinely to want to be on friendly terms with Britain,
and genuinely to believe that the establishment of his
Republic—and here, as so often, the hard fact of 'partition'
is curiously ignored—so far from intensifying the quarrel
is the only way to end it.

4

Nationalism often distracts a people from the task of
grappling with its more material needs; but Mr. de
Valera's Republicanism does not seem to have blinded him
to the fact that the gravest problem in Ireland is not

political but economic. Unemployment has been aggra-
vated not only by the 'slump' but by the slackening tide
of emigration. It is reckoned that, while during the last
ten years over 200,000 Irishmen have left the country, at
least as many more have had to stay in Ireland who would
in earlier years have also gone; and some observers hold
that the mass of those 200,000 are supporters, like the
rest of the unemployed, of Fianna Fail. Mostly the younger
sons of small farmers, they despair of getting anything
from Cumann na nGaedhael, which, though it can scarcely
be called a Tory party, is at any rate the party of the
'Right', of the 'haves' rather than the 'have-nots'. They
think their only hope is in the economic and social
revolution which Mr. de Valera preaches. Economic
nationalism is to create a vast new field of industrial employment. Social reform is to enforce a far wider area of
tillage, breaking up, if need be, the bigger farms. Their
fathers may suffer from the dislocation such policies involve, especially the loss of the British market; but they
themselves have nothing to lose. A further worsening of
the general economic situation seems more likely to drive
them farther to the Left than back to the Right.

There is no reason to doubt that Mr. de Valera's desire
to help the Irish poor is as genuine as his passion for a
Republic. He dreams of 'holy Ireland', freed from the
corrupting influences of British capital, a country of simple
living, wherein 'no man is rich and none hungry'. But he
seems to combine this idealism with a mastery of political
device. Fianna Fail's intensive economic propaganda has
been very skilful in its methods and quite unscrupulous in
its promises. At the election in February 1932, a list was
printed, under the heading 'Here's what a Fianna Fail
Government *will* do for YOU', of 'the number of additional workers to be employed manufacturing at home the

quantities of goods now imported', giving a precise figure for each trade, *e.g.* 5801 for boots and shoes, 6395 for hosiery, 154 for soap and candles, 4653 for paper and stationery, and so forth up to a precise total of 84,605. And the appeal to the hunger of the unemployed is boldly coloured with religion. The Fianna Fail 'platform' in the Dublin election, which made much of the claim that Fianna Fail had already given in one year as much in relief grants as Cumann na nGaedhael in ten years, headed a programme of free milk, free fuel, old-age pensions, and the like with the title, 'Practical Christian Government'. But ideals can be misused and yet be genuine: and, while the bishops are apparently moving to the Right, the young priests are said to be 'Christian Socialists' and supporters of Mr. de Valera.

But, whatever means may be used to 'put it across', it cannot be denied that Fianna Fail's economic policy is a bold and, on its own assumptions, a logical policy, and that it is being executed by a leader who is also bold and, if anything, too logical. The majority of the electorate are facing the 'slump' with the happy conviction that they possess the two great instruments of salvation to which some other countries have pinned their faith—a Man and a Plan.

Ambitious schemes of economic and social reform are not unneeded in Ireland; and, though Economic Nationalism in its extreme form is more than usually at variance there with physical realities, there are elements in Mr. de Valera's programme which might be regarded as little more than a speeding-up of Mr. Cosgrave's more cautious policy. There would be no need, perhaps, to take too serious a view of the future if the Free State were like most other democratic countries. Economic policy would be shaped by trial and error. The Plan would be given its chance. Its mistakes would be revealed in the working. Its failure would throw the majority of the electors into the opposite camp. Progress in fact would be achieved as elsewhere, rather slowly and clumsily perhaps, along a middle path. But that seems unlikely to happen in the Free State. The miserable entanglement with Britain queers the pitch. Criticism of economic and social blunders can be confused and disarmed by raising the old political cry. Mr. de Valera's policy can be represented as the only patriotic policy. Its errors in practice may not be seen as errors, for they can be attributed somehow or other to British interference. Economic nationalism can be pushed to unreasonable lengths as a defiance of Britain and a means of escape from British influence or control. Patriots can be asked to bear the hardships it involves as the price of Ireland's freedom.

It seems plain, then, that both in politics and in economics and whether he is pursuing a Republic or a social revolution, the most powerful and lasting weapon in Mr. de Valera's armoury is the quarrel with England. He has only to take it out and sharpen it and brandish it, and at once the real issues are conjured out of sight. Few of his followers are likely to bother about dull economic doctrine or the fine points of Dominion Status when they are asked to fight for Ireland.

5

Fight for Ireland? But there is nobody to fight against. Make Ireland free? She is free already. It seems, indeed, deplorable that the whole Irish situation should be befogged and bedevilled by a fiction. And of course it *is* a fiction. It is a queer experience for an Englishman, fresh from England, to be confronted with these war-cries, these appeals to Irishmen not to be afraid. There are, of course, some Englishmen or Irishmen domiciled in England who do feel at enmity with the Free State, or at least its present leaders. That is natural enough to the friends of Englishmen murdered in Ireland or of Anglo-Irish 'loyalists' who have suffered and been 'betrayed'. But these and their like are not very numerous; and it is more than doubtful whether among the great majority of Englishmen there is any feeling of hostility whatever towards any part of Ireland or any section of its people. Their attitude, rightly or wrongly, is one of indifference. To the younger generation, in particular, the Irish Question which so warmly stirred their fathers and grandfathers is simply boring. And as for Englishmen wanting to retain—or more strictly to recover, for there is nothing left—any shred of authority in the Free State, the truth is that, in so far as they have thought about it at all since the Treaty, they have congratulated themselves on being free at last from the coils of Irish politics. The 'tyranny' cry is as unreal as the call to battle. Mr. de Valera's patriots are engaged in shadow-boxing.

The annuities dispute is no disproof of this. In our view it was not primarily a governmental business. Our Government acted as agents for the transfer of money owed by one set of private persons to another set to whom they owed it: and, when the Free State Government, performing a corresponding agency-function in Ireland, retained the money, we tried to recover it by 'distraining' on Irish imports into Britain. Could we have done nothing, especially in view of the fact that Mr. Cosgrave's Government had regularly paid over the money? In any case the point is not so much in the policy of retaliation as in its spirit. It is not, in the average Englishman's eyes, a demonstration of enmity. He does not *want* to hurt the Free State, to deal it a 'blow', to engage in a 'tariff war'. If it could be honourably done, he would be glad to settle, even at a financial sacrifice, an affair which seems petty and sordid against the black background of world politics to-day.

It is much the same with the abolition of the oath or with any unilateral violations of the letter or spirit of the Treaty. To many, probably to most Englishmen, it does not seem quite 'playing the game'. 'Why not negotiate?' they would ask: 'we should try not to be unreasonable.' But, in any case, we are not going to get excited about it. Even a Republic—but more of that presently.

It is probably too much to expect that Irishmen in the South should understand all this. What about the 'loyalists'? What about the North? No one, of course, can fail to sympathize with the changed fortunes of the Anglo-Irish Unionists or at least with those of them who did not ridicule or vilify the national aspirations of the majority of their countrymen. Even though the Fianna Fail Government seems inclined to continue the tolerant policy of its predecessor, it is no happy fate for them to watch in impotence the breaking of ties and traditions that have made up so much of their life. But they cannot, indeed they do not, expect England to go crusading for them. And, as for the Protestant North, while it can safely count on aid to defend any part of the United Kingdom in the improbable event of serious attack from without, Englishmen are incapable of sharing its feelings towards the South. It is easy, no doubt, for Englishmen to take a high moral line about 'communal' strife in Ireland as in India, though the Gordon Riots were only a hundred and fifty years ago and sectarian disputes can still be acid enough to-day; but wars of religion, such as are waged from time to time in the streets of Belfast, do seem out of date, and the unification of Ireland, however long it may take, does seem the right and natural thing in the end.

No; however you look at it, the picture of England still trying to 'oppress' Ireland, of a 'fight' for Irish freedom, is a fantasy.

6

If only something could be done to destroy this illusion, it might go far to expose the whole tragic futility of the Anglo-Irish quarrel. But what? Nothing, it seems, is to be expected from the Irish side of the water, North or South. Is it for England to make yet more concessions? Might they not prove as useless for our purpose as the Treaty? Would it hurt us, on the other hand, to make them? Should we be worse off than we are now if they failed?

The difficulty of concession on the annuities dispute is painfully obvious; and yet one cannot contemplate its dragging on indefinitely with an easy mind. Not only does it so blatantly encourage the false idea of a hostile, fighting England: it is so clearly out of harmony with all the international idealism which figures so often in our statesmen's speeches. No doubt it was forced on us. No doubt our case in law or in plain common sense is strong. And yet, behind it all, lurks Irish history. We smile when Mr. de Valera begins every controversy by going back to Cromwell or even Strongbow. We smiled when he assessed our real debt to Ireland at an astronomical figure. That sort of thing is not business. Practical politics must have a Statute of Limitations. And yet, on second thoughts, and especially on a question of money, it is not easy to wipe out of our minds and off the slate the old historical facts of mercantilism in the eighteenth century.

But the annuities dispute, irritating as it is, seems at the moment overshadowed by the 'fight for a Republic', and on that major issue what concession is conceivable?

Can any really impartial student of the situation doubt

that the final conversion of the Free State—it cannot be all Ireland—into a Republic, its formal secession from the Commonwealth, would be a deplorable thing? It could only injure Ireland. It would make her disunion almost irretrievable. The economic opportunities of the Free State, its financial strength, its credit would be weakened. Its people would lose the advantages—and they are not insubstantial — which a citizen of the Commonwealth carries with him all over the world. And a host of personal difficulties, practical and sentimental, would be created. Irish servants of the Crown, in the British army and navy, in Whitehall, in the Indian or Colonial civil services, administrative, medical, and the rest, who were born in what is now the Free State, would have to sever their connexion either with the Crown or with their homeland. Surely the break would be felt, too, by the millions of Southern Irishmen who have made their homes in the Dominions. They know what Dominion Status means and are content. Would they think it a little thing that, merely for a figment, for a name, their old homeland, which they love as only Irishmen can, should sever its connexion with their new homelands: that those who live in it and their children should become, so to speak, strangers and out-siders, like Belgians or Danes? And something more precious than political threads would be cut. British history, after all, has been also Irish history. Uneasy though the partnership has been, Ireland, South as well as North, has taken a noble share in it. Look at the military record: the place which the British Isles have won and held in the world through a century and a half of wars is largely due to Irish daring and Irish skill. It is the same with the arts of peace. Statesmen, orators, writers, poets—the roll of honour is bright with Irish names. And the great story of adventure and achievement overseas belongs

to Ireland as well as to Britain. She, like Britain, has been
a 'mother-country', peopling new lands with her sons. If
the Second British Empire has done better than the First,
not only in the field of colonial settlement but in its treatment of backward peoples also, the credit of it and the
pride in it are for Irishmen to share, if they will, with us.
Has there been no spiritual value in this partnership in
making history? Will not some virtue fade out of Irish life
if the major part of the country cuts itself clean off from
that historical tradition?

The break would also injure Britain, not very much,
perhaps, in material things, but in spirit and in sentiment.
It would be a blow to our prestige, a final proof of our
incapacity to solve the Irish Problem, a witness to the
world that somehow or other, by misunderstanding perhaps as much as by misconduct, we had alienated Catholic
Ireland just too much for reconciliation to be possible. And
it would wound our feelings, too; for, despite the age-long
friction, the physical nearness of Ireland and the common
history of the British Isles have linked her with British
sentiment as no foreign country could be linked. Sisters
can quarrel and not forget their sisterhood. Personal ties
without number have been woven across the narrow gap.
And, if most Englishmen are now more or less indifferent
to what happens in Ireland, they would regret, when it
came to the point, the formal and final rupture. Some of
them might reflect, moreover, that their desire to be free
of Irish entanglements might be less easily fulfilled if
the unnatural frontier between North and South divided
foreign states, not fellow-members of the Commonwealth.

And the Commonwealth itself would suffer. It is possible,
doubtless, to exaggerate the effect on its unity and strength
of the Free State's secession. Intelligent observers in all
parts of the Empire recognize the peculiarities of the Irish

F

people and the Irish Problem. As the situation in Ireland is unprecedented, so its development should set no precedent. And yet surely the *fait accompli* of secession would encourage those disruptive forces which, though they may not be at present very formidable, exist in various quarters of the Commonwealth as in all political societies. The irreconcilable minority in South Africa would cling more stubbornly to their dream of restoring the old Republics or of severing the whole Union from the Crown. And in India, where the course of Irish nationalism has been closely watched, the 'extremists' would acclaim the rupture as a proof that no nation which has been conquered into the Commonwealth can ever rest content within it. Injury to the Commonwealth, moreover, would be felt beyond its borders. The world sees in it the greatest practical example of international co-operation. A breach in its unity—explain it away as you will—would be a loss to the whole cause of internationalism, a gain to the unsociable, self-assertive nationalism which is pushing the world to the edge of ruin.

Ireland, Britain, the Commonwealth, the world — all would suffer, it seems, in some degree from the fulfilment of Mr. de Valera's purpose. And what would he purchase at that price? The Free State would not be a jot more free as a Republic than it is now. It would be less free, indeed, from the external pressure of the world outside the Commonwealth than it is inside it. And would a Republic's relations with its nearest neighbours, Northern Ireland and Britain, be more profitable after the breach? 'We cannot remove our respective sections from each other,' said Abraham Lincoln to the Southern Secessionists, 'nor build an impassable wall between them. . . . They cannot but remain face to face, and intercourse, either amicable or hostile, must continue between them. Is it possible, then,

to make that intercourse more advantageous or more satisfactory after separation than before?'

7

On this issue there can be no agreement. A settlement of
the annuities dispute is just conceivable. The abrogation
of the oath and minor amendments of the constitution are
not vital questions. But an actual secession, an establishment of a Republic—in that we can never concur.

Can nothing be done, then? Is it impossible to 'eliminate
the imperial factor' from Irish politics? Must Irish passions
still be stirred by the illusion of a fight with England? Is it,
after all, an illusion?

It is—for the simple reason that, though we think the
secession of the Free State would be a disastrous mistake
for all concerned and cannot, therefore, agree on it, we do
not intend to resist it by force. How can we? Is it possible
for us to violate the spirit of the Covenant, whatever be its
letter, within our own more intimate league of nations? Is
it possible for us, signatories of the Kellogg Pact, to resort
to war as 'an instrument of policy' against the Free State?
And, beside those ties of honour, is it imaginable that the
British electorate would acquiesce in British soldiers being
sent again to shoot or be shot by Irishmen? Surely not.

Two points, no doubt, must be guarded. Obviously we
should have to use force, if it were needed, to repel an
assault on Northern Ireland. Obviously, too, it would be
difficult, since another European war is unhappily not impossible and, if it occurs, may well begin with a surprise
attack, to withdraw our 'care and maintenance parties'
from the watch they keep over two or three strategic points
on the Irish coast. But Mr. de Valera might acquiesce in
that. It is said, indeed, that he still clings to the alternative

treaty he drafted in 1921, the famous 'Document No. 2', which accepts those coastal posts. And, if he refused to acquiesce, we should be justified in defending them in virtue of the Treaty: nor could the most malign imagination represent purely defensive action of that kind, on the coast or on the Northern frontier, as fighting to prevent the establishment of a Republic.

If, then, subject to these safeguards, we have no intention of using force in our dealings with Irish Republicanism, why not say so? Opinion in Dublin regards the establishment of a Republic sooner or later as virtually certain. It also assumes that Britain will resist it, though nobody seems to visualize what form the resistance will take. Suppose the British Government, taking its cue from some public utterance in the Free State on the 'fight for a Republic', were to point out that the Irish people were being seriously misled: that two parties were needed for a fight: that Britain, while it would deplore the secession of the Free State, could not forcibly resist it: that, in fact, the unity of the Commonwealth being based on consent, the people of Southern Ireland were free to choose their destiny—might not such a declaration have a startling effect? The 'fight' idea would be exploded. The full freedom of Dominion Status would be proved beyond a doubt. The material disadvantages of secession from the Commonwealth could be considered without the passion of a 'war mentality'. Republicanism would be put morally on the defensive. It would have to demonstrate its value to Ireland and the world. The very idea of a Republic might lose a little of its glamour when it was known that it could be had without a blow. It does not seem quite impossible that a majority of the people, assured of their freedom of choice, might choose right.

And what an opening it would make for that 'supreme

act of statesmanship' which at each of its critical phases in
the past the Irish Question has demanded, and always in
vain! No more could be asked of Britain: it would be
Ireland's turn to give. If only the North could offer the
South some sort of federal union if it chose to remain
within the Commonwealth! If only Mr. de Valera could
feel convinced that now at last the Free State was really
free—as General Hertzog felt about South Africa after the
Declaration of 1926—and, turning his back on the barren
past, could call on his people to make the first use of their
freedom to achieve a free and final reconciliation with their
ancient enemy! The far-reaching effect of such a great
decision can scarcely be in doubt. Could the North be
wholly unresponsive? Would the hope of an ultimate Irish
union be still so desperate? In Britain, at any rate, the
response would be immediate: passive indifference would
quicken into positive good-will. There would be the same
relief, the same good-will in the Dominions. And even in
the outer world the dramatic example of injured Ireland
choosing under no constraint to be Britain's friend and
partner might not be altogether without influence on other
nations nursing an historic quarrel with their neighbours.
Mr. de Valera, indeed, would have a chance of proving
himself what his younger admirers believe him to be, a
Man of the New Era. More than that, though the fruits of
his decision would take time to mature, he might go down
to history as the statesman who solved the Irish Problem.

Probably this is the sort of fantasy to which minds un-
used to Irish air are said to be liable. If the free choice
were offered—and that is what an intimation of non-
resistance to the establishment of a Republic would be in
effect—it seems more than likely that Mr. de Valera would
choose a Republic and that the majority of the electorate
would follow his lead. None the less, the intimation would

still have served a purpose. It would at least have chilled the atmosphere in which the blunder of secession was committed. It would have stripped it of the false emotion bred of battle-cries. It would have made it harder for Republicans to pose as the only patriots, the only Irishmen brave enough to defy the might of Britain; harder too for them 'to gloat over their victory', to quote a clear-sighted Irishman, 'as though the giant-killer had brought the giant to his knees, even as though it were the victory of Good over Evil'. 'And what could be more harmful than that,' he added, 'either to the morale of our people or to the future relations between your people and ours?'

VI

THE MEANING OF THE EMPIRE

1. THE COMMONWEALTH OF NATIONS [1]

I

ON the third of next September a century and a half will
have elapsed since by the signature of the Treaty of
Versailles the thirteen seceding colonies were finally acknowledged to be 'free, sovereign, and independent states'.
One is sometimes tempted to try to imagine how differently
the course of those intervening years might have run if the
breakdown of the First British Empire could have been
averted: but it is not very profitable to speculate on the
impossible. In the circumstances of 1775 the problem of
imperial unity could not be solved. A federal parliament
at Westminister was impracticable. The only other solution was for British statesmen to adopt the new American
conception of inter-imperial relations. 'All members of the
British Empire are distinct states, independent of each
other, but connected together under the same sovereign.'
Nothing less would have served in the long, or indeed in
the short, run. The thirteen colonies were already fairly
old-established communities; their population had passed
two millions; and the spirit of nationalism was already
doing its double work, fusing the jealous provinces together while it severed them from their mother-country.
Nothing less would have served than the acceptance of
something like 'Equal Nationhood', endowed (since the
Stamp Act had forced this issue) with its ultimate attribute

[1] University of Toronto, April 11, 1933.

of equal legislative authority; and, far as the British negotiators, striving for peace too late, were willing to go in permitting legislative independence in domestic policy, the notion that an American legislature could be conceded a completely equal footing with the Imperial Parliament at Westminster would have been almost passionately rejected even by such enlightened imperialists as Burke or Chatham. No: the American Revolution was inevitable. Even if the problem had been less crudely handled after 1763, if the quarrel had been evaded and postponed, yet, sooner or later, by force or acquiescence, the schism would have come. The growth of the American people, in politics, in economics, in national self-consciousness, in the need for self-government, had outstripped the development of imperial theory; and to square their claims at any stage after 1763 with the unity of the Empire would have required an inconceivable precocity of statesmanship. It would have required that Lord Durham's ideas should have prevailed in Burke's day, and Lord Balfour's in Lord Durham's.

That history has not repeated itself, that a second British Empire exists to-day, is mainly due to the fact that time was given for the growth of theoretical ideas side by side with the growth of practical needs.

Both in theory and in practice the Second Empire may be said to have been born when the United Empire Loyalists crossed the border into this province of Upper Canada; when they petitioned for 'the blessings of the British constitution'; when Grenville drafted the Canada Bill of 1791 on the principle of 'assimilation', despite Thurlow's previous warning that its application would convert the British Empire into a group of sovereign independent kingdoms; when Pitt introduced the Bill as intended to give Canada 'a free constitution in the British

sense of the word' and 'as near as the nature and situation
of it would admit to the British constitution'; and when
Dundas, Pitt's shrewdest colleague, interpreted his leader's
phrase as meaning that the Bill would 'lay the foundation
for the same constitution when increased population and
time shall have made the Canadians ripe to receive it'. The
Act of 1791 was certainly no more than a foundation, no
more than representative government, very little more in
itself than the pre-Revolution system; but it fitted the
needs of the time, it went far enough, it ignored the
pessimistic logic of Thurlow and reaction. And happily
it was not for nearly half a century, not till liberalism had
revived in England, till the Reform Bill had been passed,
till the conceptions of freedom and self-government had
been freed from the inevitable constriction of war-time,
that the next test came. And then, between 1837 and 1849,
there was another conflict of ideas and another victory for
the wiser ones. Again the theory of 'assimilation' was pursued, but not too far. Again the reactionaries prophesied
doom. 'Local responsible government and the sovereignty
of Great Britain', said Wellington, 'are completely incompatible.' 'Responsible government', said Gladstone, not
yet M.P. for Oxford University, 'means nothing more
than an independent legislature.' And this time the logic
of disruption was preached by no less liberal-minded a
man than Russell. 'Concede responsible government only
if and when you must', was the line he took; 'but realize
that you are giving 'sovereignty' and 'independence' with
it. "Since there's no help, come, let us kiss and part."'
But again it was the practical liberal-minded men, not the
reactionaries or doctrinaires, it was Durham and Elgin
who prevailed—Durham whose 'foresight enabled him to
base his policy on those principles on which the coming
age of the world will be ruled', and Elgin who believed

that the colonies, 'without severing the bonds which unite them to Great Britain . . . may attain the degree of social and political development to which organized communities of free men have a right to aspire'. So it was that the idea, whose birth had heralded the schism of the First Empire, could be born in Canada under happier auspices —the idea that a contiguous group of British colonies could constitute a nation without breaking their allegiance to the Crown. So Durham could write as early as 1838 of 'a great and powerful people with a nationality of their own'. So Macdonald at Quebec could hail the scheme of Federation in 1865 as enabling the Canadians to build up 'a great nationality, commanding the respect of the world', and Carnarvon at Westminster could bless it 'as laying the foundation of a great State'. So Laurier in 1900 could look forward to 'a nation which will be foremost among the great powers of the world'. So Borden in 1915 could speak of 'the manhood of a young nation' vindicating 'her patriotism and her national spirit' on Flanders' fields. And all the growth in strength and freedom which these sayings implied was achieved without any serious straining of those 'uniting bonds'. On the contrary, it was evident that the sense of unity was deeper than before. The pessimists had been wrong. Thurlow's and Russell's bogeys, it is true, had materialized, but they had lost their terrors in the process. The erstwhile colonies had grown into 'free, sovereign, and independent states': but 'sovereignty' and 'independence' no longer meant in the twentieth century what they had meant in the eighteenth. They did not mean 'separation'. King George was still king in North America.

Thus, when the long process of 'assimilation' reached its end, when the question of legislative equality was raised, not abruptly and tumultuously as in 1775, but gradually and quietly and in its natural place, when the Statute

of Westminster completed in 1931 the scheme of inter-
imperial relations which Jefferson and Franklin and their
colleagues had long ago envisaged, there was something
almost of an anti-climax in the ease and brevity of the
procedure, in the stillness of the air. The British people
watched without enthusiasm (for they are imbued with a
deep sentimental conservatism) but without antagonism
(for they are a sensible people, quite able to understand the
patent fact that a Canadian is the equal of an Englishman)
the spectacle of the Mother of Parliaments divesting herself of those quasi-celestial powers which, though to Burke
they had seemed eternal, had long withered in her hands.
The old vaticinations were still audible, but what a feeble
echo of Thurlow or of Russell! I trust nobody in Canada
imagines that the few politicians who attacked the Statute
mainly owing to the peculiar implications of the peculiar
Irish Question, or the few lawyers who seemed to think
that forms can still be useful when they have lost all
relation to facts, represented anything but a negligible
body of British opinion. It is worth, perhaps, observing the
contrast between 1931 and 1849. On the issue of Elgin's
attitude to the Rebellion Losses Bill—the issue which
closed the question of responsible government—no less
than 150 votes to 291 were cast in the House of Commons
against Elgin and no less than 96 to 99 in the House of
Lords. The Bill which became the Statute of Westminster, on the other hand, passed its third reading in
both Houses without a division. Only those, indeed,
whose minds are still in the eighteenth century can suppose that the Dominions' request for the Statute should
have been refused. Twentieth-century Englishmen know
better.

To those of you who believe as I do in the value of the

British Empire to its members and to the world, it must be a matter of deep satisfaction that the process of 'assimilation' or 'equalization' has come so smoothly to its end. But we must not be surprised if our satisfaction seems a little paradoxical to observers who know nothing of our history and do not understand our way of doing things. The whole process, after all, looks very like a process of disintegration: and in its later phases, especially since the War, all the stress seems to have been laid on loosening ties, not strengthening them, on autonomy or independence, not unity, on the Nations rather than the Commonwealth. Some foreign critics, indeed, lacking the knowledge and insight of Professor Yandall Elliott, for example, or M. Chevallier, are frankly sceptical. While we have been congratulating ourselves on a great achievement of co-operative statesmanship, they have been smiling at our limitless capacity for self-deception. 'Be logical', they seem to say, 'or even cynical; drop your cant and confess that this so-called rebirth of your Empire is really its euthanasia. Your declarations and statutes are only *camouflage* to hide the inevitable repetition in a less unpleasant form of the American Revolution. Unwrap the legal parchments and you will find a corpse.' Nor is it to be wondered at if among our own peoples the younger, the post-War generation do not feel quite the same quick satisfaction that we feel who have watched the evolution of the Commonwealth for the last twenty or thirty years. They cannot, of course, make the foreigner's mistake: their acquaintance with fellow-citizens of the Commonwealth from other nations than their own forbids it. They know that the Empire is alive, that only Imperialism is dead. But they are not so ready to take its value for granted. The mark of this post-War age is a question-mark. Every institution however venerable, every convention however sacrosanct, every imperative however categorical, must demonstrate its truth and its utility. For my part I welcome the application of this questioning spirit to the Empire. It has nothing to fear from enquiry. Ignorance and indifference are its worst enemies. And the franker, the more realistic the questions, the better. There has been so much dressing-up and play-acting on the imperial stage in the past, so much rhetoric and false sentiment, so much partisan exuberance, that it is rather refreshing to hear a young voice from the gallery asking 'What is your old Empire anyway? And what is it for?'

2

It is to those questions that I propose to address myself in these lectures: and to-day I will take that part of the Empire to which I have so far been mainly referring—the British Commonwealth of Nations: what is it and what is it for?

Of the meaning of half the phrase—apart from the question of the difference between a 'nation' and a 'state' —there can be no doubt. In the familiar italicized words of the Balfour Committee of 1926, the Nations of the Commonwealth are *autonomous communities within the British Empire, equal in status, in no way subordinate one to another in any aspect of their domestic or external affairs*: to which the rider was added, 'Every self-governing member of the Empire is now the master of its destiny. In fact, if not always in form, it is subject to no compulsion whatever.' And all subsequent developments have been directed to making the 'form' coincide more closely with what on major points was already the 'fact' in 1926 and had indeed been the 'fact' since the meetings of the Imperial War Cabinet and of the Paris Peace Conference. Nor, I think, is that side of the business so little understood in the outer world as it was ten years ago. The election, for example, of Canada and the Irish Free State to represent the smaller nations on the Council of the League shows that the autonomy of the Dominions is recognized at Geneva.

It is the other side of the matter that puzzles European logic, the other half of the phrase that poses our real question; and any attempt to answer it may well begin from the same historic definition. Those autonomous communities (the formula runs on) are *united by a common allegiance to the Crown, and freely associated as members of the British Commonwealth of Nations*. 'Common allegiance' and 'free association'—these are the constituents of the Commonwealth, these make it a Community.

The supreme position of the Crown in the whole structure of the Commonwealth is significantly attested in the Statute of Westminster itself. The preamble (you remember) contained what may be described as a declaration of constitutional usage. 'It would be in accord', it ran, 'with the established constitutional position of all the members of the Commonwealth in relation to one another that any alteration in the law touching the Succession to the Throne or the Royal Style and Titles shall hereafter require the assent as well of the Parliaments of all the Dominions as of the Parliament of the United Kingdom.' No one who knows anything of our traditional constitutional practice will doubt the potency of this declaration. One might more easily doubt the need of it. For the Crown is so much more than (to quote the preamble again) 'the symbol of the free association of the Members of the British Commonwealth of Nations' that any variation in the succession to it as between those Members would *ipso facto* dissolve the 'association'. Nor is it only a matter of the personal loyalty to the King which, I believe, is more deeply felt to-day than it has ever been since the later

years of Queen Victoria's reign. The Crown is stamped on
all the Dominion constitutions; and in nothing is the new
status of equality so effectively realized in practice, in
nothing does form so solidly agree with fact, as in the independent existence of His Majesty's Government in each
of the Dominions as well as in the United Kingdom.
Dominion ministers now enjoy, and have exercised on
several occasions, the right of direct access to the King.
They can advise and they have advised him face to face
without any intermediary. And, of course, as laid down in
another of our declarations of usage, in 'any matter apper-
taining to the affairs' of their Dominions 'it would not be
in accordance with constitutional practice' for ministers
in the United Kingdom or (it is implied) in any other
Dominion to tender contrary advice.

Nor—of course again—is the operation of His Majesty's
Government in any Dominion limited to its internal or
domestic concerns. It operates in all that field which is
common ground for the Commonwealth: it operates as
freely in the world at large as that of any foreign state: and
that means in technical language that in these common
or external affairs also its ministers can advise the King.
That raises the kind of issue which delights the academic
controversialist. 'What will happen', he asks with gusto,
'when in these matters of common concern the advices of
ministers from different parts of the Commonwealth conflict? Can the deadlock be resolved except by the King
choosing between them? And will not such acts of choice
be executive decisions of the first importance, bringing
the Crown into the political arena from which in these
modern days the wisdom of our monarchs and our statesmen alike so carefully secludes it? Will it not lower its
prestige and even endanger its existence?' The answer is
simple. Obviously, the offer of conflicting advice to the

King creates an unpleasant dilemma; and obviously, for that very reason, ministers will never offer it, *provided that they wish to maintain the Commonwealth at all*. Indeed the constitution of the Commonwealth is so loose that it can only be worked by good-will: it provides the wrecker with endless opportunities of mischief: and the fact that Mr. de Valera has been recently exploring some of them has induced a little doubt as to his ultimate intentions.

The next concept to 'common allegiance' is 'free association', and that leads at once to another of those speculative disputations. What about the 'right of secession'? Those of us who have been nourished on an old-fashioned political philosophy are apt to be cautious about 'rights'. We have been taught to think first of the duties which the rights imply. Secession, we should say, might conceivably be a duty and be justified as such, like a rebellion or a revolution. And in law, of course, it would be a revolution. As General Smuts once pointed out, a Dominion possesses no legal right to convert itself into a Republic: so radical a change in its constitution is a revolutionary act. But to most British minds this question of secession is not so much a question of ethics or of law as of practical politics, a matter of power rather than of right; and it would not be denied, I think, that any Dominion has the power to secede in the sense that, if secession were the manifest desire of its people, it would not be forcibly resisted. Was that not admitted in the words of the Declaration of 1926 which we have taken as our text? When Britain and the Dominions are described as 'freely associated', does that not imply that they are free to disassociate? And, when in addition they are said to be 'masters of their destiny' and 'subject to no compulsion whatever', does that not mean that none of them will be compelled to remain in the Commonwealth against its will? I suppose—but how speculative all this is!—one should guard oneself by some such proviso as 'in normal circumstances'. If, for example, another war were to engulf the world, enforcing its inexorable rule of 'safety first', there is no saying what would happen to the freedom of nations as of individuals. The free secession of one nation of the Commonwealth in the middle of a war might conceivably involve the other nations in defeat and subjection. But, apart from that, I cannot imagine the dominant public opinion in any quarter of the Commonwealth recidivating to the philosophy of Lord North. What value in our unity can be preserved by force? It has no moral value without consent, nor material value without good-will.

One more academic issue must be dealt with. It is sometimes asserted that, in the event of the King declaring war, any one of his Governments, not content with the admitted right of 'passive belligerency', should have the right to be neutral. But is not the very conception of neutrality fast getting out of date? All the members of the Commonwealth have signed both the Covenant and the Kellogg Pact. Do any of them propose to ignore the Covenant? Do any of them take the implications of the Pact more lightly than Mr. Stimson? Except on the assumption that a member of the Commonwealth were to be the villain of the piece, the law-breaker and war-maker, it seems hard to imagine how the issue of neutrality can arise unless the world slips back into the international anarchy of pre-War days. And in any case the moral aspect of the claim seems a little lop-sided. Can a member of the Commonwealth enjoy the benefits of partnership in peace-time, and, when the other partners are involved in the dangers and losses of war, be justified in withdrawing from the partnership 'for the duration', in refusing even the lesser hardships of a 'passive belligerent', in maintaining

G

such intercourse with the enemy as neutrality permits or requires—with the pleasant prospect of resuming the partnership when the trouble is all over? Surely that is not only not good morals, it is not good sense. Surely a declaration of neutrality in war-time by Britain or a Dominion could only be regarded as a declaration of secession. I couple Britain with the Dominions in that sentence because, though the point is usually ignored in this discussion, she must clearly enjoy the same 'rights' of secession or neutrality as the Dominions. A painter can be cut from either end.

But I must spend no more time on those speculative questions. I have only mentioned them because I thought you might expect me to give my opinion on them for what it is worth. Frankly I find them boring. They seem to have so little practical importance. Discrepancies in logic and anomalies in law are as impotent to disrupt the Commonwealth as niceties in either are to maintain it.

Let us next consider how this 'free association' operates, how in fact the members of the Commonwealth do associate one with another. The primary instrument of association has already been mentioned—the King in contact with his Governments. The second is the regular quadrennial Imperial Conference, supplemented between its sessions by an unceasing flow along the cables and through the air of information and discussion on all questions of common concern. The third is the special Conferences, summoned to deal with particular matters, and the various Committees for co-operation in technical affairs. The fourth is the collocation in certain places of other representatives of the Governments—political and commercial agents in London and the Dominion capitals, diplomatic agents at three or four of the chief foreign capitals, members of the Council and Assembly of the League and in three cases a resident representative at Geneva. This is such familiar ground that I will not linger on it except to make two passing comments. Observe, first, the difference between the League and the Commonwealth machinery. Just as the members of the Commonwealth are not bound to co-operate as between themselves by any Covenant, so their method of co-operation is simpler and looser. Unlike the League, the common organ of discussion and decision is unicameral. We have only a Council, not an Assembly. And, unlike the League, we have no permanent Secretariat. Secondly, I would suggest that the existing system of representation overseas could profitably be extended: that political agents of each of His Majesty's Governments should be accredited to *all* the others, and that diplomatic agents of each should be appointed in *all* the greater or more important foreign States.

But my main object in this lecture is not to discuss machinery. Its importance is obviously great but too much stress can be laid on it. It is far more important to make quite sure what the machine has got to do; and it is our British way—one cannot help repeating it—to fashion our institutions to meet practical needs as they arise. Clearly, then, the prior question is one of function. What is this system of inter-imperial co-operation to do? What is the Commonwealth for?

3

It is sometimes forgotten that the Commonwealth does something by its mere existence. The association of its nations and the common allegiance of its peoples make war between them impossible. The King cannot declare war on himself. On the outbreak of such a war the Commonwealth has ceased to be. The only possible settlement of an inter-imperial dispute is by conciliation or arbitration or reference to a suitably constituted court. More than that, such a war is really 'unthinkable'. You cannot imagine Britain fighting Canada or Australia fighting New Zealand. Nor is the Irish Free State in fact an exception. The British people are never again going to make war on the Irish people. The Commonwealth, in fact, is a league of nations, with an unwritten, yet inviolable covenant, making peace certain for a section of the world. If it ceased to exist, the world would suffer. Its disruption would strengthen all the forces of nationalistic reaction and weaken all the hopes of a new international order. For, if the nations of the Commonwealth, with so many of the advantages which make concord and co-operation easy, with so much common sentiment and common tradition, cannot live and work together, what chance is there for France, Germany, Russia, and the rest? It is at least as obvious a truism now as it was twelve years ago that, if the British league of nations dies, no other league can live.[1]

But this essential peacefulness and friendliness of the Commonwealth is only, so to speak, a passive or negative function; and, to quote again the Report of 1926, which was partly drafted (it is understood) by Lord Balfour but adopted (it is well to remember) by the representatives of all the Dominions, 'The British Empire is not founded upon negations. It depends essentially, if not formally, on positive ideals.' And among the common objects aimed at, Lord Balfour and his fellow-signatories enumerated 'peace, security, and progress'. Let us briefly examine these objectives in their application, first to the inner life of the Commonwealth and then to its relations with the outer world.

Between the members of the Commonwealth, as I have just pointed out, Peace is assured as long as the Common-

[1] See p. 13 above.

wealth exists; and as to Security, one of the most obvious
functions of the Commonwealth is that of common defence
against external attack. Of the value of that co-operation
the War was proof enough. Each and all of us would be
worse off now if the Dominions had not leapt to arms in
1914 to share with Britain in resisting Prussian militarism.
Without those million soldiers from overseas the War
could not have been ended as and when it was. Again and
again, indeed, their swift and steady convergence on the
battlefields of Europe—one of the most impressive spec-
tacles in history—is cited as proving the inherent stability
of the Commonwealth. 'Do not worry', it is often said,
'about its future unity. If 1914 is ever repeated, you will
see the same sight again. Blood is thicker than water. If the
mother-country is in danger, she can always count on her
sons.' Now, I do not question for a moment the sincerity or
strength of that sentiment. The sense of kinship is un-
doubtedly one of the strongest links that holds the Commonwealth together. But to-night I am deliberately playing
the sceptic's part: and you will not, I think, misunder-
stand me if I make some comments on the attitude of mind
I have just illustrated. The first is this. That rally of 1914
was not only to help the mother-country, not by any
means. Nor was it only to defend the integrity of the
Commonwealth as a whole. Its vigour and persistence
were mainly inspired by the fact that the Dominions had
separately and severally made the common cause their own.
Each was fighting for its national ideals. Secondly, in the
case of many individual citizens in all of the Dominions
and of a majority in South Africa and of a great majority
in Southern Ireland, there is no question of a 'mother-
country'. Only those whose ancestors lie buried in the soil
of Britain can feel the call of the blood, and even for them,
as the generations hurry by, the call must needs get

fainter: while for those who have come to the Dominions from foreign lands, and still more for those like the French Canadians or Dutch South Africans or Southern Irish, who, whether lately or long ago, were conquered into the Commonwealth, not bred or settled in it, there is no call at all. It is as natural as it is significant that most of the talk about the right of a Dominion to be neutral in war comes from the Union and the Free State. And lastly, one may ask, apart from the sentiment inspiring it, is that function of mutual defence enough of itself to keep the Commonwealth together? Even those who put little faith in the League of Nations are as anxious as the rest of us to get rid of war altogether; and, whether that be possible or not, we may hope at the very least that the intervals between the greater wars may not be shorter than they were. What happens, then, to the Commonwealth in a period of peace, which conceivably may last for ever, if its main function is mutual defence, if its strongest sense of community is only evoked by war? I do not know how you feel in Canada, but, speaking for myself and probably for many other Englishmen, I have been conscious for some time past of a certain feeling of reaction from the great experiences of War-time. One can never forget that brotherhood-in-arms. But little by little, ever since then, those fellow-members of the Commonwealth who stood so close beside us in those grey days have seemed to be drawing away. We have had no real peace yet in Europe. And we have no real friends there, at any rate among the stronger Powers. Year after year we are confronted by jealous or mistrustful neighbours. At times the strain seems scarcely less burdensome, the outlook scarcely less anxious, than in 1914. And we are facing it by ourselves —or so it seems. One wonders, indeed, now and then, whether the Dominions have any interest left in Europe except to keep out of it. Is it only the reassertion of the fact of distance? 'The ocean remains; you cannot pump it dry.' Or did something of the spirit of comradeship fade away with the smoke of the home-going transports? Is England more alone in the world than she was?

The second object, Progress and Prosperity, in its internal aspect raises at once the question of economic co-operation, which is so controversial and has been so fully discussed of late that I will only say two things about it. First, I would ask to be allowed to think that the efforts we are making to strengthen and expand inter-imperial trade are good in themselves. I cannot understand the view that 'buying British' is in itself immoral. My conscience does not prick me if, rather than order my tea from some strange emporium in London, I buy it from my friend the village grocer or direct from my cousin in Ceylon. Secondly, the Ottawa Conference has proved that the potentialities of economic co-operation, though greater than it was thought in some quarters, are less than it was thought in others. If indeed the assertion were true that the Commonwealth can *only* be saved from disruption by a network of preferential duties, then the gathering at Ottawa might be regarded by future historians as scarcely less portentous in its way than the 'Boston tea-party'. But it is not true. It would be truer to say that the Commonwealth would certainly disrupt if its unity depended *only* on commercial interests, if internal economic co-operation, however important, were its *only* function. It would be truer, again, to say that, valuable as the Ottawa agreements may prove to be in their inter-imperial aspects, their higher value lies elsewhere: that in attempting to temper the rigours of economic nationalism, to lower tariffs rather than to raise them, to establish the principle of 'reasonable competition', Ottawa has not only marked out the path of progress for the members of the Commonwealth, it has given the world a lead. Indeed, the more one considers the problem, the more one is drawn to the belief that the greatest function of the Commonwealth and its strongest bond of union are concerned with its external rather than its internal relations.

4

It is not pessimism, still less 'defeatism', to face the black facts of the world to-day. After all its centuries of travail since the Dark Ages, after all the human effort and suffering it has involved, after all its hardly won and not inglorious achievements, modern civilization is in danger of destruction. Everyone who is close to the heart of things knows that. And even if all the efforts now being made to lessen the danger—to strengthen the 'collective system', to promote disarmament, to restore the flow of trade—are more successful than we can dare to hope, that is only the beginning of recovery; that only gives the world a breathing-space; and it will need all the energy and all the virtue of a generation to win back for civilization the strength and faith, the stability and momentum, it possessed in the nineteenth century. For the old mainstays of its political and economic life are not what they were. All have been undermined: some have collapsed. Democracy, the unimpeachable dogma of Victorian days, is widely discredited. In the greater part of Europe it has been discarded; and, where it survives, it is under a double attack, from Caesarism on the right and Sovietism on the left. Capitalism, similarly, is on the defensive. It is confronted by the growing forces of Socialism and Communism, and for all its great inherent power it has already been compelled, here and there, to make concessions to 'the spirit of the time'. Nor are these political and economic conflicts merely national and domestic ailments: they infect, they may poison, the whole body of the world. We may most of us feel confident that, sooner or later, somehow or other, the world will roll on into clearer weather and that civilization will not go down in a hurricane of war or revolution; but such confidence may be too easy. It is common sense, not panic, to admit that chaos will come again if enough men and women do not work hard enough to prevent it. And there are other possibilities than chaos. Civilization might survive, but so changed as to have lost its spiritual value, so mastered by material ideals, so shorn of all we mean by 'freedom'. If the British Commonwealth can help to save mankind from that, need we ask a greater function for it?

But perhaps you will say: 'What can Canada do? We are so far away from the centres of the world's unrest. We know so little of Europe's diplomatic tangles. And the atmosphere of the Old World is not ours. It still believes, it seems, in force. It even contemplates another war. Will it not be better for us and for the world if we stand aside, keeping our hands clean and our ideals unsullied, till the fever of Europe has burnt itself out?' I can appreciate the attractiveness of such an argument: but surely it is based on an illusion. Canada cannot stand aside in safety. If the storm breaks, it will sweep the whole world. To suppose that any nation, however powerful or however sequestered, can hide behind its frontiers and escape the deluge is as barbarous an anachronism as the Great Wall of China at this moment. Remember, too, what we ourselves would sometimes like to forget—that Britain is in Europe: for, if you remember that, you will not paint the whole of Europe black. Whatever you may think of some other Powers, you know that Britain does not want another war. We suffered from it more than you did. We are at least as anxious not to repeat the experience. We are as loyal as you are to the obligations of the Covenant and the Kellogg Pact. Too much attention has been given by the newspapers to the recent resolution of the Oxford Union; but strip it of its provocative phrasing; interpret it, as most of its supporters interpreted it, as no more than a reaffirmation of the Pact; and the vast majority of Englishmen would vote for it.[1] But I am wasting words. You cannot doubt that the cause of peace means as much to us as it does to you. Do you realize, though, that we need your help in its defence? The smaller democracies of Europe, it is true, are often ranged on our side: but, unless more is happening behind the scenes than on the stage, our kinsmen and partners from oversea seem usually rather silent and aloof. Canada has a larger population than Belgium. Canada and Australia together are greater than Czechoslovakia. I should like to hear the voice of Mr. Bennett in the councils of Europe as often as the voice of M. Benes. I should like to see the New World not only criticizing the Old, but helping to put it straight. I do not mean that you should concern yourselves overmuch with the narrower, the more local European issues: Britain herself is trying to hold aloof from them. But on the fundamental questions which affect the whole world—on the authority of the League, on the need for disarmament, on the removal of obstacles to trade—the very fact of your remoteness from local quarrels would add weight to your opinions. Why should not the candour and vigour of your idealism make the same sort of impression on the higher politics of Europe as your young manhood made on its battlefields?

But is co-operation for the maintenance of world peace,

[1] The wording of the resolution was 'That this House will in no circumstances fight for its King and Country'.

it is sometimes asked, a function of the Commonwealth? Could not its nations do their duty to the world as well or even better if they were separate? What can they do as members of the Commonwealth which they cannot do as members of the League?

It might be more difficult to answer those questions if the world were some decades or generations older, if the League had stood the test of time and become not only all-embracing but universally recognized and trusted as the indispensable foundation of world society, if in fact the relations between its component states had grown more like the relations between the nations of the Commonwealth. As it is now, the Commonwealth is far the stronger institution. The reciprocal attitude of its members is more intimate, more fraternal, more generous-minded than that of any foreign states. Not by any superior virtue, but as the natural outcome of its history, it has attained a higher plane of internationalism. It sets a standard to which all nations must aspire if the world is ever to be really united. Surely, then, it cannot seriously be maintained that the stronger league should be dissolved and absorbed into the weaker. It would do the latter no service. As I have already suggested, the moral effect of the Commonwealth's disruption would set back the cause of internationalism throughout the world.

A more positive argument can be advanced for our nations working for the world through the Commonwealth and the League rather than through the League alone. The contribution each has to make is more practically effective. Truth and wisdom, whosoever the hands that offer them, will prevail, one hopes, as a rule and in the end; but their prevailing is a matter of discussion and persuasion, and the place where the real decisions are made is the inner chamber of the League Council or the Inter-

national Conference. It is the few men gathered there who
have to be persuaded; and, whether in Council or in Conference, the statesmen of the Dominions have more opportunity of making their case and winning it than those of
most other nations. As regards the Council, one Dominion,
it is never likely to be two, may be represented as a smaller
Power—or may not. But in any case all the Dominion
representatives can and should be in close contact and
discussion with one permanent and potent member of the
Council, the representative of Great Britain. To a large
extent, indeed, the delegates of Britain and the Dominions
at Geneva are continuing the function of the Imperial
War Cabinet and the British Empire Delegation at Versailles. And, of course, in an International Conference the
procedure adopted at Paris and afterwards at Washington
—a procedure which the Governments of the Commonwealth should insist on maintaining—admits the representatives of the Dominions on an equal footing with
those of all the Great Powers concerned. Those are not
negligible aids to the practical effectiveness of a nation's
policy.

And by effectiveness I do not mean a blind adherence
to Britain's policy! There are bound to be, there have
already been, differences of opinion on foreign affairs. But
it is far easier to discuss and compose those differences
round the table of the Imperial Conference than in the
Assembly at Geneva, and far easier for a Dominion than
for a foreign state to persuade Britain she is wrong! It is
an open secret that Canada changed Britain's mind on
the question of the Anglo-Japanese alliance in 1921. Could
she have done it if her voice had been a foreigner's? But
in general, surely, agreement is likelier than disagreement.
Our ideals and our interests in the world are so much the
same. Geography, it is true, gives a different weight to

different issues in different regions of the Commonwealth. Britain, for example, is part of Europe, while Canada is part of North America and looks over the Pacific. But just as the peace of Europe is really as much Canada's interest as Britain's, so friendship with the United States is really as much Britain's interest as Canada's. Indeed it is the supreme necessity of British foreign policy. And, as to the Far East, Britain and Canada must needs agree in principle. We are equally committed to maintain the integrity of China. We equally desire its prosperity. Hong-Kong, for whose safety Britain is responsible, is nearer to Japan than Vancouver; and the volume of British trade with China is five times that of the Canadian.

If, then, as a rule, we find ourselves agreed in principle and can by frank discussion agree also, as a rule, on policy, consider with how much greater force it comes to bear on world opinion within and without the League as the concerted policy of the Commonwealth. It was John Stuart Mill, no 'jingo' imperialist but the greatest liberal thinker of his day, who saw in the continued unity of the Empire an 'advantage specially valuable at the present time', namely, that it strengthened 'the moral influence and weight in the councils of the world of the Power which of all in existence best understands liberty'. That was written in 1861. Nowadays we should write it a little differently. We should more clearly associate the Dominions with Britain in the understanding of freedom and in the task of its protection. But is not the advantage Mill spoke of at least as 'specially valuable' now as it was then? Can any democrat assert that now when the future of democracy is at stake is the time to disrupt our league of democracies? Will you get closer to other friends of freedom, to France, Czechoslovakia, Scandinavia, by getting farther from Britain? Is it easier to resist the influence of Fascist Italy or Nazi Germany or Soviet Russia as separate republics than as a united commonwealth?

The answer to those questions is the answer needed to complete this lecture. The nations of the Commonwealth can serve the cause of peace and freedom in the world more effectually through their free association than in any other way. That is the primary function of the Commonwealth: that, above all else, is what it is for.

But I seem, as I finish, to have forgotten my realist's rôle. 'You have missed your cue,' you will say. 'You are talking about service to the world. But all nations are selfish, including Britain and the other members of the Commonwealth. Just look at them.' Well, I admit, of course, that national altruism in any full sense of the word is too much to expect. Yet is not the state of the world to-day almost forcing the realists into idealism? Internationalism *must* be more than a fashionable cult or so much pious cant; the nations *must* make just that amount of sacrifice that is needed for the common weal; for otherwise our civilization is doomed. And, paradoxical as it may sound, I believe that beneath the surface of self-centred nationalism, in every or almost every country, a new post-War sense of the world's unity and its claims is stirring. In Britain I am certain it is so. There is more international idealism among the younger generation than there has ever been before. I do not mean 'hot-air' and 'uplift': I mean a quiet conviction that 'patriotism is not enough'. And you will tell me, I know, that the same is true of Canada. Those 'great open spaces' we hear so much about in little England must be good for growing better things than wheat. And this Canada, now that she has attained her adult nationhood, now that those visions of 'a great and powerful people, commanding the respect of the world' have come true, can never be content to limit her national ambition to the service of herself alone. Not hers the national watchword of *sacro egoismo*—words that on Christian lips are literally blasphemous. Hers, rather, the doctrine of a greater Italian: 'Your liberty will flourish, protected by God and by men, so long as you regard it as the right to choose freely and according to your special tendencies a means of doing good'.

VII

THE MEANING OF THE EMPIRE

2. INDIA

I

'DEPEND upon it, this business cannot be indifferent to our fame. It will turn out a matter of great disgrace or great glory to the whole British nation. We are on a conspicuous stage, and the world marks our demeanour.' The speaker of those words was Burke, the subject British rule in India, the date 1783. They occur in the historic speech wherein was first enunciated the doctrine of 'Trusteeship' as the governing principle of the relations between the British people and those weaker and politically more backward peoples with whom the pursuit of trade had brought them into contact; and, as you know, that idea of 'Trusteeship' started a new development in India just as the idea of 'Assimilation' started a new development in Canada. Together they inspired what I have described elsewhere [1] as the 'Imperial Revolution' which brought to birth the Second British Empire. In the last lecture we considered what has been the outcome of 'Assimilation', into what sort of association the relationship between Britain and Canada and the rest of the self-governing part of that Second Empire has grown in the course of a century and a half. To-day let us consider what has been the outcome of 'Trusteeship'; let us see how that 'business' of British rule in India has in fact 'turned out': let us ask the same

[1] *The American Revolution and the British Empire*. London, 1930.

104

questions—what *is* the present-day connexion of India with the Empire and what is it *for*?

One striking fact confronts us at the outset. The two fields are no longer so distinct as they were a hundred and fifty years ago. Contacts and reactions between East and West have gone far beyond the realm of trade. The differences that remain, both material and spiritual, are very great; but there is much that the East has accepted and absorbed from the West. India, like Japan, has adopted the forms of European industry; and India, unlike Japan, has adopted the forms of British politics. Its constitutional development has gradually assumed a parallel course with that of Canada. Internally, it is already equipped, as to two-thirds of its area, with provincial parliaments and governments, and it is contemplating in the immediate future an All-India Federation with a federal parliament and government at its head. Externally, its eyes are fixed on the same goal of free and equal partnership in the Empire which the Dominions have recently attained. 'Trusteeship' in a word, has found its ultimate expression in 'Assimilation'.

Surely that turning-out of the business is one of the most remarkable things in all the history of politics. In view of what he said, Dundas ought perhaps to have imagined—a reactionary like Thurlow did vaguely imagine —the possibility of something like the Statute of Westminster of 1931; but neither Burke nor any of his contemporaries could conceivably have imagined anything resembling the 'Proposals for Indian Constitutional Reform' submitted by the British Government for the consideration of Parliament in 1933. A federation of that vast sub-continent on a basis of parliamentary government! An approximation to Dominion Status for India! Inconceivable in 1783, that prospect is startling enough to

H

many Englishmen to-day—startling to those who find it hard to believe that other peoples, especially Oriental or coloured peoples, can be entitled to an equal footing in the world with themselves; and startling, too, to those who admit the claim to equality in principle but were not prepared to have it thrust on them in practice quite so swiftly. But most of us, I think, have recovered our breath by now and realize that nobody ought to have been taken by surprise. Indian history for at least a century has been moving steadily towards this climax. The situation in which Britain and India find themselves to-day is not really a sudden and fantastic novelty, fabricated by accidental or transient forces. It is the product of evolution, not of revolution. It is the logical, one is tempted to say inevitable, result of forces set in motion when the first Englishman landed on the Indian coast.

Let me expand and illustrate that assertion. Let us watch the present situation growing out of the past. Thereby we shall find the answer to the first question of this lecture—what *is* India's place in the Empire?

2

There is nothing new in the idea that British rule in India, like Roman rule in Britain, would some day come to an end. Burke, it is true, when he defined it as a 'trust' and declared that any trust should cease as soon as it varied from the purpose—in this case the good government of India—for which it was established, was only concerned to secure its stricter execution at the moment. He probably never asked himself whether one of its results might not be to qualify the Indians to execute it themselves; whether sooner or later the ward might not grow out of tutelage. It is true, too, that, for years after Burke was dead, public opinion was too much preoccupied with the struggle with Napoleon and the internal state of England to speculate about the future overseas whether in India or the Colonies. But when the long strain was over, when the doctrine of 'Trusteeship' in India, like the doctrine of 'Assimilation' in Canada, was revived and confirmed, the question was soon raised as to whither it was leading. And it was answered. British officials in India were not afraid to contemplate, like British officials in Africa to-day, a time, however distant, when India would be 'able to stand by herself'. In 1824 a remarkable minute was drafted by one such official in which he tried to predict 'the final result' of British rule on the character of the Indian people, and he concluded it as follows:

We should look upon India, not as a temporary possession, but as one which is to be maintained permanently, until the natives shall in some future age have abandoned most of their superstitions and prejudices, and become sufficiently enlightened to frame a regular government for themselves, and to conduct and preserve it. Whenever such a time shall arrive, it will probably be best for both countries that the British control over India should be gradually withdrawn.

The requisite advance in Indian thought and custom, he went on, would be a long process, but there was no reason to despair.

If we pursue steadily the proper measures, we shall in time so far improve the character of our Indian subjects as to enable them to govern and protect themselves.

Twenty years later another civilian defined in similar terms the aim and end of British rule.

We cannot expect to hold India for ever [he wrote]. Let us so conduct ourselves in our civil and military relations as, when the connexion ceases, it may do so not with convulsions

but with mutual esteem and affection: and that England may
then have in India a noble ally, enlightened and brought into
the scale of nations under her guidance and fostering care.

The men who thought like that a hundred years ago were
not idealogues nor 'defeatists'. They were clear-sighted
men of action than whose no names stand higher on the
great roll of India's public servants—Thomas Munro and
Henry Lawrence.[1]

There were certain issues of practical policy, moreover,
which were bound to raise that ultimate question. When
Indians, for example, were encouraged to aspire to a share
in the administration, when a clause in the Act of 1833,
confirmed in 1853 and 1858, prohibited the maintenance
of a 'colour bar' for any public office, when after the Act
of 1861 Indians began, in free competition with Englishmen, to enter the highest administrative service, the I.C.S.
itself, a process had obviously been started, the 'Indianiza-
tion' of the bureaucracy, which was certain to continue at
an accelerated pace—to what final goal? Still plainer, if
more general in its bearing, was the issue raised by the
deliberate decision to improve and extend the facilities for
Indian education. There were still some survivors of the
eighteenth century in England who saw what that meant
and dreaded it, dreaded the education of Indian subjects
for much the same reasons as they dreaded the education
of the English poor. But their opposition was brushed
aside. Speaking in the House of Commons in 1853 Sir
Charles Wood, then President of the Board of Control and
soon to become the first Secretary of State for India and
the first Viscount Halifax, expressly repudiated the opinion

---

[1] Cf. Tom Hughes, author of *Tom Brown's Schooldays*, writing to
Lord Ripon about India in 1885. 'I am sanguine that we may see it
yet a self-governing country and an integral and satisfied branch of
the Empire of the future.'

'that we ought not to promote the education of the natives as tending to diminish our hold on India'. And he was echoed in characteristic antitheses by Macaulay: 'I will never consent to keep them ignorant in order to keep them manageable or to govern them in ignorance in order that we may govern them long'.

No honest man could have interpreted the duty of Trusteeship in any other terms; but Wood and Macaulay can scarcely have realized how quickly their decision in the field of education would take effect in the field of politics. Within a single generation it created a movement which could have no other logical end than the termination of the Trust. By the 'eighties the expansion of higher and secondary education, the multiplication with government aid of schools and colleges and universities, had brought into being a new and fast-growing class of educated Indians, whose education had been mainly a literary education, mainly conveyed to them in English. Inevitably, therefore, they had acquired a knowledge of English ideas, and particularly political ideas, since by no accident the classics of English liberty are among the classics of English literature. Young Indians came to know more of Milton, Burke, Shelley, Byron, than most Englishmen of their age. They studied with a more personal zest the works of John Stuart Mill. They watched at least as keenly the course of Gladstone's last crusade. And, if the depths of English political philosophy remained as much a mystery to them as the depths of Hinduism to Englishmen, two plain facts could not escape them: and the first was this—that Englishmen not only took their own national independence for granted but were the traditional, if sometimes ineffective, champions of other nations 'struggling to be free' from alien rule—of Poles, Magyars, Greeks, Italians, and even, when one party was in power, of Irishmen. The idea of

Indian nationalism, for good or ill, was one of England's gifts to India.

An Indian nation? A generation earlier, Indians themselves could not have dreamed of applying the term to the diverse peoples of their huge multifarious sub-continent; but in 1885, when the Hindu National Congress first met, if an Indian nation was still far from a reality, it was at least an aspiration. And that it could be so was another fruit of British rule. Three things had happened. The whole of India was now as it had never been before, not even in the greatest days of the Moguls, directly or indirectly under a single 'Raj'. The building, secondly, of a network of railways, roads, and telegraphs had provided for all quarters of India an equally unprecedented facility of intercommunication. It might still be difficult, but it had been made infinitely easier, for a Madrasi, say, to realize that the Punjab was part of India. And, thirdly, educated Indians, many of whom had hitherto been unable to speak each other's language, now all possessed in English one common second tongue. Thus, mild though its mood might be compared with that of its descendant to-day, the first meeting of the National Congress was a portent. Its discussions could not have been held, its very name could not have been invented, in any earlier age.

To a student of history the sequel seems almost automatic. The idea of national unity is inseparable in any subject people's mind from the idea of national independence: nationhood, like manhood, seems robbed of 'half its virtue' if it is not free: and the National Congress had not long been born before the movement for 'Swaraj' began. It was a quiet beginning. The leaders of the movement were content to accept the theory of a British 'trust' under which their countrymen could patiently prepare themselves for freedom. Unfortunately, just at this period, the 'trustees', in England or on the spot, had lost interest in their ultimate objective. It was not unnatural. The time when men think most about the purpose of a job is when they first undertake it. Once hard at work on it, they tend to forget the morrow in their concentration on the duties of the day. No doubt, if questioned, most Englishmen concerned with India would still have accepted Munro's goal, but all the years that had passed since Munro's day had brought no nearer the prospect of its actual attainment. On the contrary, as the vast task of Indian administration expanded, as government became more complicated and technical and efficient, it was progressively more difficult for its authors and managers to imagine the safe transfer of it all to inexperienced Indian hands. So, when the question of self-government was raised anew, not this time by themselves from above but by Indian nationalists from below, on the whole their response was neither quick nor warm. Again it was not unnatural. Only a cowardly or incompetent ruler enjoys the thought of abdication; and the more honest a trustee, the more he wishes to be certain that his trust is really fulfilled before he surrenders it. Naturally, too, this hesitant attitude reacted ill on Indian nationalism. There was a swing to the 'Left'. An extremist faction took the field, vilifying the British and all their works, denouncing the 'Trust' as a figment of imperialist hypocrisy, preaching hate and sedition and even murder. The stage seemed set for tragedy on a great scale—a conflict of irreconcilable forces, not to be resolved but only hardened and embittered by an alternation of rebellion and repression, and drifting in the end into a chaotic revolution more damaging materially and morally, whatever the result, to both contestants than the Revolution of 1775.

So far this tragedy has been averted, and I would suggest

—we stand too near the scene to dogmatize—one or two reasons for this good fortune.

In the first place the case for Nationalism in general and for Indian Nationalism in particular was greatly strengthened by the course of events in the world during the first thirty years of the 'Swaraj' movement. The Russo-Japanese War in 1904 showed that the claims of nationality long admitted in Europe could not be denied to Asia on the plea that Nature had doomed the coloured races to be eternally inferior to the white. Ten years later the World War brought India on to the international stage, fighting side by side with other nations, sharing in their suffering and achievement, acquiring a new consciousness of nation-hood and a new claim to its recognition. Was not the War regarded by the victors as a struggle for the rights of weaker nations? Was not 'national self-determination' one of their battle-cries?

Secondly, it is not, I hope, mere arrogance to claim that there is something in the British temperament and tradi-tion which moderated the inherent difficulty of the Indian crisis. The British people, despite their occasional aberra-tions and excesses, are at heart a tolerant folk. Given time and good leadership, they are able to do justice to other people's opinions. 'Live and let live'—that motto might be written over most of our domestic history; and, paradoxical as it may seem, I believe it has become applicable also, in the long run, to our relations with those millions of other people on whom we once imposed our rule. The idea of forcing our will, even with the best intentions, on subjects who resist and resent it has somehow become distasteful to us. I think, too, that Englishmen—and not least those whose interest in a question is primarily material—are usually able to assess fairly coldly and shrewdly the limits of what force can do. Chatham was more English than

North in his attitude to the American insurgents. 'If you conquer them, what then? You cannot make them respect you. You cannot make them wear your cloth.' Beside 'Live and let live' I should like to write a typically English proverb, 'You can take a horse to water but you can't make it drink'. It is mainly, I suggest, the English gift of political realism that explains why, when the century-old idea of a self-governing India freed from our control was taken from the shelf and thrust in our teeth, it proved not impossible, the time and the good leadership happily being given, for us to conquer our first instinctive hesitations and to swallow it.

There remained, of course, the difficulty of putting our concession of the Indian claim to freedom and equality into practice—a difficulty so great that it is hard to conceive how it could have been met in any other sort of Empire. But in the British Empire—and this is my third point—there was a notable precedent for dealing with a situation which for all the differences of circumstance was the same in principle. The root of the difficulty was the need for 'gradualness'. To lift India at a stroke from dependence to full partnership was out of the question. Nobody imagined that every vestige of British control could be at once withdrawn from Indian government and every British soldier and official at once evacuated from Indian soil without precipitating a catastrophe. Yet, as long as any alien authority were exercised, as long as any 'garrison' remained, how could Indians be convinced that their claim had really been conceded, that they were not to be kept for ever in a state of modified dependence, that the only hope of achieving the fullness of their nationhood was not, after all, an attempt, however desperate, however destructive, to break the tie with Britain? To this question, as you know, the evolution of our Commonwealth of

Nations gave the answer. The process of 'Assimilation' had been a gradual process. Stage by stage, as they became 'ripe to receive it', the younger nations had acquired an equal measure of self-government with that enjoyed by Britain. In 1914 the process was still not quite complete. Canada, for example, had no share in shaping a foreign policy on which her fate depended. There was a brigade of British troops in South Africa. But no one doubted that such symptoms of inequality were transient. Long before 1926 and 1931 the culmination of the process was a certainty. Here, right to hand, then, lay the obvious method of trying to solve the Indian crux. Here was a policy which not only prescribed the gradual means but also guaranteed the end. Let 'Trusteeship' be merged in 'Assimilation'. Let India take her place in the historic march of the overseas nations of the Empire—not yet abreast of the Dominions, but on the same road and moving to the same goal.

It was an Indian who first pointed out this way of meeting the aspirations of Indian nationalism. One of its wisest exponents, Mr. Gokhale, defined its objective in 1905 as 'a form of government . . . similar to that which exists in the self-governing colonies of the British Empire'; and the acquisition of Dominion Status remains to-day the policy of Mr. Gokhale's successors—those 'moderate' Indian statesmen who desire to free their country from British domination without depriving it of British partnership. And the British people for their part—I assert, you see, that the people are behind the Government and Parliament on this great issue—have responded in word and deed. In 1917 the famous Declaration initiated a 'gradual' policy of which Dominion Status was then implicitly and is now explicitly 'the natural issue'. And to-day the Government has submitted to the judgement of Parlia-

ment a constitution which invests India not indeed with
full and final Dominion Status—a difficult 'transitional
period' has to be traversed before that—but a status comparable with that, say, of Canada in 1868 or South Africa
in 1910. Is it too much to hope that the dream of Lawrence
and Munro is taking solid shape at last this side of the
horizon?

3

Dominion Status, as every student knows, has nothing
to do with a Dominion's internal or domestic constitution.
It is only concerned with the position of the nations of the
Commonwealth in respect of one another. It is a question,
so to speak, of international relations. If Canada were
governed by a dictator or Australia by a *soviet*, they could
still be Dominions as long as they were willing to share
with their fellow-nations in a common allegiance to the
Crown. And India similarly could attain to full national
self-government under any form of constitution which
observed that one condition. But, just as each of the
Dominions possesses a democratic parliamentary system
of government, so the constitutional scheme now proposed
for India approximates not only externally to Dominion
Status but also internally to a parliamentary and mainly
democratic system. At first sight, as I suggested at the
outset, the latter development seems at least as surprising
as the former; but closer study shows the one, I think, no
less than the other, and in India not so very much less than
in the Dominions, to be the natural outcome of history.
'Assimilation' was bound to operate in the internal as well
as the external field.

Let me take you back again just a century, back to the
Indian Charter Act of 1833. That Act was one of the first-
fruits of the bloodless revolution in England which had

ended the long dominion of the Tories and started a new era of Reform. It was the child of a Whig Ministry born on the morrow of its victory. The traditional champions of parliamentary government stood round its cradle. And yet there was little evidence in the Act of new or liberal ideas. Its main intent was the winding-up of the commercial side of the old East India Company: it left the system of government, improved in detail but unchanged in principle. But why, you will ask, were the Whigs so fearful of their faith in this one field? Let the most famous of them answer. 'We have to solve', said Macaulay, then a member of the House of Commons and associated with India as secretary to the Board of Control, 'one of the hardest problems in politics . . . to give a good government to a people to whom we cannot give a free government.' It would be easy enough — it is the Whig politician speaking—if representative institutions were possible in India, but James Mill himself, then a clerk at the India House, had confessed that they were 'utterly out of the question'.

This, then, is the state in which we are. We have to frame a good government for a country into which by universal acknowledgment we cannot introduce those institutions which all our habits, which all the reasonings of European philosophers, which all the history of our own part of the world would lead us to consider as the one great security for good government. . . . The light of political science and of history is withdrawn; we are walking in darkness; we do not distinctly see whither we are going.

Macaulay went on to describe the system of government which had grown up in this darkness and was to be improved by the Bill: a bureaucratic system with the supreme executive and legislative power over all British India in the hands of the Governor-General and his Council of British

officials — the executive government of the Provinces[1]
similarly wielded by Governors and Councils, to whom
local legislative power was also accorded by the Bill—the
higher ranks of the administration occupied by British
officials for whose better selection and training the Bill
provided—an efficient, honest, tolerant, just government
—a despotism, if you will, but far better than any other
despotism in the world—in fine, the best government
which India was at that time capable of possessing. Nor
was it to be wholly devoid of 'self-government' in the sense
of government by Indians. From the beginnings of British
rule a host of subordinate officials had been perforce recruited from the natives of the country; but it was now
to be enacted that no native 'shall by reason only of his
religion, place of birth, descent, colour, or any of them be
disabled from holding any place', however high, in the
administration. But, while Macaulay stresses and praises
that famous clause, his liberal instincts are unsatisfied; a
bureaucracy manned entirely by Indians would still be a
bureaucracy; and in his peroration he hints, and obviously
he also hopes, that India may one day attain the better
government, the fuller liberty, which in his opinion only
representative institutions can provide.

It is difficult to form any conjecture as to the fate reserved
for a state which resembles no other in history. . . . It may be
that the public mind of India will expand under our system
till it has outgrown that system; that by good government we
may educate our subjects into a capacity for better government; that, having become instructed in European knowledge,
they may in some future age demand European institutions.
Whether such a day will ever. come I know not. But never
will I attempt to avert it or retard it. Whenever it comes, it
will be the proudest day in English history.

[1] They consisted at that time of Bengal, Madras, and Bombay, and
were called 'Presidencies'.

Thus, within a decade of Munro's forecast of Indian independence comes Macaulay's forecast of Indian democracy. How bold they seem to us now, looking back across a hundred years! Most of those years, indeed, were to pass before they were remembered and repeated. While Munro's idea, as we saw, soon dropped into the back of the British mind, Macaulay's dropped out of it altogether. As a matter of fact, the subsequent constitutional development of British India might well be described in the very terms he used; yet, strange as it now seems, that was never realized, still less admitted, till near the end. At all stages except the last British statesmen in England and their colleagues in India were still walking in darkness, not distinctly seeing whither they were going, still declaring that no political precedents could apply to a state which 'resembled no other', still paradoxically encouraging the growth of institutions which seemed 'out of the question' in India.

The process began in the Indian Councils Act of 1861. The Mutiny had shown that the Government of India, however benevolent its intentions, had been deplorably out of touch with Indian opinion; and it seemed unwise, to quote Sir Bartle Frere, to continue 'to legislate for millions of people with few means of knowing except by a rebellion whether the laws suit them or not'. Accordingly, a few 'unofficial' members were nominated to sit on the Governor-General's Council and on the Provincial Councils, and in the latter case they were mostly natives of India. But the function of these enlarged Councils was strictly limited to legislation; indeed they were expressly forbidden to discuss anything not concerned with a legislative measure. They were to be nothing more than 'committees for the purpose of making laws'. They could not criticize nor even discuss the executive government. They were akin to

the *durbars* by means of which Indian princes from time
immemorial had acquainted themselves with their subjects' opinions.

The next stage was the Indian Councils Act of 1892.
The experiment of 1861 had proved successful. The 'unofficial' members had admirably served their purpose. It
was felt that legislation had benefited by Indian criticism
and advice, that it might now be extended to permit discussion of, though not resolving or voting on, the budget,
the mainspring of government, and that it would be still
more helpful if the critics and advisers were themselves in
closer contact with the people. It was decided, therefore,
that some of the local bodies or corporations which had
been growing up in India—municipalities, chambers of
commerce, universities—should be invited to select or
delegate representatives of themselves and their opinions,
and recommend them to the Government for nomination
among the 'unofficial' members. But care was taken again
to guard against misconception. The principle of election
was not conceded. The candidates would only be 'recommended'. And Lord Dufferin, who was Viceroy when the
measure was under discussion, declared that it would be
'very wide of the mark' to conclude that 'they were contemplating an approach . . . to English parliamentary
government and an English constitution'.

So thought the Viceroy: but what were the Indians
thinking—the Indians whose opinions he was anxious to
consult? One thing was certain. Since 1861 they had begun
to think about politics as they had never thought before.
Doubtless this new political interest would have developed
in some degree whatever the form or the flag of India's
government; the ideas of nineteenth-century Europe could
no more be kept out of Asia than the products of its
factories; but the process was greatly stimulated and

hastened by the spread of English education of which I spoke just now. I said, you remember, that there were two things about English political life which no English-educated Indian could miss, and that the first was that Englishmen took their national self - government for granted. The second is equally obvious—that to Englishmen the particular form in which they had learned to govern themselves seemed incomparably the best form in the world. Now, at this period, outside the inmost circle of Hindu conservatism, there was little, if any, distrust or dislike of British rule or British ideas. Indians, it was thought, could best learn to equal Englishmen by imitating them. Were they not bound, then, especially to imitate their politics in the hope that some day they might be qualified to share in the good things in which their rulers —who were also their tutors—took such conscious and vocal pride? Representative institutions, moreover, were no longer a mystery in India. If a little time were needed to prove that the new 'recommendations' for the Legislative Councils were virtually 'elections', already the policy of local self-government initiated by Lord Mayo in 1873 and extended ten years later by Lord Ripon, had established the regular holding of elections, pure and simple, for Municipalities and Rural District Boards: though, it may be observed in passing—and again how strange it seems!— Ripon himself, despite his political descent from Macaulay, expressly disavowed the intention of introducing 'a representation of the people of an European democratic type' or of 'imposing an English system on India'. And that was not all. In natural concomitance with the development of education and local government an Indian Press was growing up, freed from official control by the repeal of the Press Act in 1878 and showing an increasing vigour and courage in political discussion and an intimate knowledge of English parliamentary practice and the doctrines of English publicists.

In such a *milieu*, it seems obvious now, the Councils Act of 1892 could only be a temporary palliative; and close on it followed that uneasy period in which Indian nationalism became more urgent, more impatient of tutelage, more violent. Never since the Mutiny had there been such widespread unrest in India as that which confronted the new Liberal Government of 1905. The Secretary of State for India was John Morley, disciple of Mill, lieutenant of Gladstone, *doyen* of Victorian Liberalism. Barren repression was to him unthinkable, and he tried to check the rising tide of anti-British nationalism by giving one more Liberal twist to the existing constitution. The Act of 1909 enlarged the size of all the Councils. In the Governor-General's Council the 'official' majority was retained. As to the Provincial Councils, not only was 'election' now legally admitted as well as 'nomination', but the 'official' majority was abandoned. In all of them the nominated *plus* the elected members outnumbered the officials. In Bengal the elected members alone had a clear majority. At the same time the power to discuss the budget was extended to cover all matters of public importance, and to include the right of moving resolutions and voting thereon. . . . Nothing revolutionary in all that? No change of principle? So, clearly, thought Lord Morley. The new measures, he explained, were meant to enhance 'the strength and steadiness of the paramount power'. He agreed with the Viceroy, Lord Minto, in 'repudiating the intention or desire to attempt the transplantation of any European form of government to Indian soil'. 'If it could be said', he declared outright, 'that this chapter of reforms led directly or indirectly to the establishment of a parliamentary system in India, I for one would have nothing at

I

all to do with it'. That must seem, I think, especially to Canadians, a more startling attitude of mind than that of 1861 or 1892. Morley, who knew so much other history, can have known little Canadian history. Otherwise, surely he must have seen that the constitutional development of British India from 1861 to 1907 had followed, at a slower pace, the precedent of Canada between 1774 and 1791, that the first Council Act was akin to the Quebec Act and the last to the Constitutional Act, and that he had now created in Bengal—and the other Provinces were soon bound to obtain the same status—precisely the constitutional situation which led first to the deadlock of the 'eighteen-thirties' in Canada, and then, in the next decade, since only so could the deadlock be resolved, to responsible government. So, at any rate, it was. At once in Bengal and sooner or later in all the Provinces, equivalent in size and population to great European states, an executive, responsible ultimately to the Secretary of State and Parliament in England, was to be confronted with a legislature the majority of whose members were not amenable to its control. Morley had crossed the Rubicon. He had conceded real representative government in the Provincial field. And since the new generation of Indian politicians still regarded the British parliamentary system as their model and goal, and soon proved that they could imitate its practices as accurately as they remembered its precedents, the eventual establishment of that inconceivable, 'out-of-the-question' form of Indian constitution was henceforth—so now it seems—only a matter of time.

No further step was possible, you see, along the old vague track which sought a middle way between a *durbar* and a parliament. To give a bit more than Morley gave, to make all the Councils wholly or overwhelmingly elective, would merely give to Indian politicians the power of paralysing government unchecked by the responsibility of ever having to govern themselves. The only practicable policy was Durham's policy—to rationalize and stabilize representative government by making it also responsible government. And that policy, as you know, was adopted. When the War came, when democracy was linked with national freedom as the cause for which the Allied and Associated nations, India among them, fought, when it was recognized that the Indian claim for another constitutional advance could not be withheld, the British Government defined its aim in India as 'the progressive realization of responsible government'.

The sequel is too recent and familiar for me to dwell on it. You know how that famous definition cleared the air for anyone who knew what responsible government meant, how at last we emerged from Macaulay's darkness and saw distinctly whither we were going, but how difficult we found it to start in that direction, how much more difficult to do in India in 1919 what had been done in Canada in 1846—how the problem was solved for the moment by 'dyarchy', a variation of Durham's device of dividing the field of government, and how cumbrously perhaps but effectively it served its temporary purpose—how swiftly then, with all the winds behind it which the War had set loose in the world, the tide of Indian aspiration and agitation rose once more, and how, long before anyone had expected, the whole system of government was under reconsideration by a Parliamentary Commission, and representatives of all India, Indian States as well as British Provinces, were sitting round a table in London to shape the framework of a constitution for an All-India Federation—and how now, after three or four years of intense hard work, a scheme is awaiting Parliament's decision which establishes responsible parliamentary government, subject to the Governor's right of intervention for certain specific purposes, in every Province and a similar federal government for all India, with similar 'safeguards' and with the reservation of such subjects as foreign policy and defence to the Governor-General's control, the whole structure in the Provinces and two-thirds of it at the centre to be based on the voting power of a widely extended Indian electorate—a scheme, in a word, which offers India a constitution, unique in many of its features because India is unique, but roughly comparable with the constitution of Canada at the outset of confederation.

And now that we reach the end of the story, does it not seem, as I said at the beginning, as if it was bound to turn out as it did? To those of you, indeed, who know little of India, the puzzling thing must be not so much the evolution of the British form of government as the recurrent refusal of British statesmen to recognize it as such, still less to welcome or assist it. Why, right on into the twentieth century, did they shut their eyes to the prospect of democracy in India? Why was Morley's faith in the universal value of representative institutions apparently so much less robust than Macaulay's? Why are there still so many critics who maintain that parliamentary government cannot work in India? The answer, though plain enough, is complex. (1) The India of 1909 or 1933 was not very different except on the surface from the India of 1833. Its town-bred English-speaking *intelligentsia* had come into being in the interval, but that constituted less than one-tenth of the population. The real India was still the old village India wherein nine-tenths of its people dwelt, simple peasants for the most part, wholly illiterate, and, if not quite so poor as they had been, still miserably poor. To provide primary education for so vast a multitude—there are roughly 250 million 'ryots' in British India to-day—had hitherto proved beyond the resources of governments more immediately concerned with the costly duties of defence and material development. Where, then, was the electorate for a full-grown representative system? Could democracy be built on such a swamp of rural ignorance? Could parliamentary government be anything but an urban oligarchy in thin disguise? (2) Democracy assumes a relatively homogeneous society. It can only settle differences of political opinion by the vote because all the members of the community are just sufficiently alike in traditions and outlook and standards of conduct to acquiesce in the principle of majority rule. But India? Could a society more diverse be imagined? A society divided first between the Provinces of British India with their western-minded politicians and their half-western forms of government and the ancient Oriental autocracies of the Indian States, still only tempered here and there by the beginnings of liberal institutions—divided, secondly, by sharp differences in all or most of the attributes which hold men together in any form of society, differences in race, language, tradition, creed, differences between Bengalis, Mahrattas, Tamils, between Sikhs, Parsees, Christians—divided, thirdly, as to its major part, by the Hindu caste system, itself to all appearances a stark negation of democratic principles—divided, lastly, by the deep chasm which separates most Moslems from most Hindus so widely that in their recurrent spasms of hate and strife their common Indian motherhood seems forgotten. The real India has not changed so very much since Macaulay's day, and in that day Macaulay denied the possibility of Indian democracy at least as vigorously as Morley denied it in his.

Well, then, you may ask, was not Morley right, if not in his policy, at least in his principles? Would it not have been better for India if he had more whole-heartedly applied those principles, if he had stood firm on the constitution of 1892 and maintained an 'official majority' in all the Councils, or, if some advance could not be avoided, divined a path which would lead not to the alien and uncongenial goal of British parliamentary government but to something grounded in old Indian tradition, better suited to Indian conditions, more earthy of Indian soil?

Yes, but what? . . . The truth is there was no alternative. The form of freedom, the kind of self-government, that the politically minded Indians wanted was a parliamentary system—and nothing else. You remember Burke: 'If any ask me what a free government is, I answer that for any practical purpose it is what the people think so; and that they, and not I, are the natural, lawful, and competent judges of the matter'. Can you imagine that any British statesman could regard it as practical politics to attempt the forcible imposition on the Indian people of some other constitutional device than the one they desired? It would be a different matter if the monarchies of the Indian States had been retained in British India or if the old system of village self-government had not been neglected or smothered by the zest for direct, efficient, centralized administration. Then possibly British officials could have done in India what they are doing in Tropical Africa. The monarchies might have been supervized, purified, and gradually converted into constitutional governments. The village-councils might have been tutored and strengthened and correlated to form the basis of democracy on an ever-widening scale. But neither of those experiments was possible in our time. The materials for them were no longer there.

Let us face the fact, then, that India is committed for the most part to democracy in its British parliamentary form. Let us admit it to be, considering the vastness and variety of

India, the boldest political experiment in history. And then let us take heart and not too lightly doom this work of ours to failure. For it is our work. It is we who planted the flower of British liberty in India and consciously or unconsciously fostered its growth; and it ill becomes us to wither it now with our distrust. Are we only proud of our liberty because it is only ours? Do we really believe, whatever the portents of the moment, that only Anglo-Saxons and perhaps Frenchmen and a few Swiss or Scandinavians are fit for freedom and that the rest of mankind must be content to serve a Caesar or a clique? Do we maintain that Asiatics are inhibited by some biological or climatic law from possessing or acquiring the mental and moral habits on which democracy depends for its success? Do we think that democracy *must* fail in India just because it is so foreign? If it lives at all, it will soon lose something of its strangeness. India will adopt it and breathe her spirit into it and mould it to her nature. Delhi will be no mere replica of Westminster or Ottawa. And, if it can thus survive and be acclimatized, may not democracy do for India something akin to what it has done in the West? It will betray, no doubt, the same sort of weaknesses as it betrays in Britain or in Canada. Not all its practitioners will be honest or selfless men, nor all its elections fairly fought, nor all its newspapers above reproach. It may have to live through and live down a period of perversion. But may it not also prove in the long run that government by discussion is better than government by force? May it not help those millions of simple peasants, so powerless now and easy to exploit, to stand on their feet and look after themselves and their neighbours, inspire gradually a wider and deeper sense of public service, undermine the old traditions of intercommunal strife, draw the peoples of that whole vast land closer together, and so 'enable them', more effectually, perhaps, in the end than anything but democracy could, 'to govern and protect themselves'?

4

I have tried to answer our first question—What is the connexion of India with the Empire?—and to show that the external status of India is now in process of assimilation to that of Canada and that, though in theory the one is not necessarily bound up with the other, in fact a like assimilation is taking place in the internal constitution of India. Now for the second question—What is the connexion for? What is its purpose, its value?

To-day there is, and for many days to come will be, one obvious answer. The main reason why India has not yet acquired, nor will under the 'White Paper' scheme at once acquire, complete Dominion Status is that the Indian people are not yet able to defend themselves unaided. There are now some sixty thousand British troops in India; the Indian army is still officered mainly by Englishmen; and for the lives of these British soldiers the British Parliament must remain in the last resort responsible. Genuine efforts are being made to train a wholly Indian army controllable by an Indian ministry and legislature, but they will take time to achieve their end. You cannot improvize a General Staff, for example. And, meanwhile, it is the British connexion that makes it possible for India thus to arm herself in safety. Her frontier, I need not tell you, needs more defence than Canada's. Beyond it lies one of the world's most restless and intractable areas. Leave its mountain gateways open, and the peaceful plains of Northern India are at once exposed again to the fate they so often suffered before the British came.

Nor is the guarding of the frontier the only service that British troops can render in the period of 'transition' to full Dominion Status. Among the gains to India which on any fair view must be set against the losses inherent in alien rule, one gain stands easily supreme. The *pax Britannica*, it is true, was largely imposed by conquest; but almost every stage of it was relatively quick, clean and not unmerciful; and the completion of the process gave India a permanent relief from large-scale internal strife. It made possible, as we observed just now, the impossibility of a united Indian nation. But that unity, so much more precious to India than anything else, is by no means yet assured. It has been gravely impaired, indeed, by the new stimulus given to old jealousies and hates by the recent discussions of constitutional change. Its loss is far the gravest risk which the new *régime* will run. Without it no constitution will be worth the paper it is written on. Without it democracy will prove a dangerous illusion. And nobody doubts that the best guarantee for its maintenance at the present moment is the British Army.[1]

But the help which Britain can give to India in the years that lie immediately ahead is not military only. Remember again the difficulties of the experiment on

---

[1] Sir P. Chetwode, the Commander-in-Chief in India, in the course of a speech explaining the cost of defence in the Council of State at Delhi on March 19, 1934, said: 'In France, in Germany, in Russia, in Italy, wherever you like, when their armies go to war, they have only to think of the enemy without. I have to look as much behind me, if my troops are on the frontier, as I do in front. That's the pity of it. And I would venture in all earnestness to suggest that, if Indian politicians would pay less attention to how much Sikhs, Moslems, Hindus, caste and untouchables and all the rest of them, are going to get out of this and out of that and more attention to making India into a nation, it would not only be better for their political future but it would almost immediately reduce the cost of Indian defence. As it is now, I have only to suggest to a Governor-in-Council that I propose to remove one battalion of "internal security" troops or reduce them permanently for an immediate protest to be made to the Government of India.'

which India is embarking. They are obvious enough in the large to anyone, and still more obvious in detail to those who know the country. It is proposed to establish a single federal system, based on parliamentary government, for a sub-continent not much smaller than Europe and at least as variegated, with a population of 360 millions, increasing at the rate of about 3 millions a year! The problems of Canadian federalism, formidable though they may be, are dwarfed to littleness by this. Even the great achievement of the United States seems small, simple, easy, compared with it. And nobody who wishes it success, whether he be English or Indian, doubts that the administrative co-operation between Indians and Englishmen which has gone to make the new machine must be continued for a time in the working of it. The retention of an adequate number of first-rate British civil servants seems scarcely less essential than the retention of the British army; and that is not because, with all their merits, these officials are 'heaven-born', but because they know, as Indians cannot yet know, by experience and by inheritance—it is in their blood, it infuses their way of life—what self-government means, and also because, by merely being British, they can regard those obdurate conflicts of communities and creeds which most imperil the success of the new *régime* with a more effortless impartiality than can any Indian.

Clearly this continued co-operation is desirable, indeed essential, but it is not so easy as it might seem. For it demands of Englishmen higher qualities than were needed in the old days of the 'Raj'—a gift for aiding rather than ruling, a more sensitive understanding of Indian psychology, a quicker appreciation of the best in Indian life, a capacity not only for the equal comradeship implicit in a common duty and allegiance but also, at need, for sub-

ordination and self-effacement, a readiness to serve India
by serving Indians. And from Indians still more is required. The presence of British officials in their motherland is a constant reminder of past subjection to alien
rule. More than that, it signifies that India is still unable
to stand quite alone. Is it to be wondered at if Indian
patriots, afire with the achievements and hopes of the new
era, should accept with reluctance and suspicion the service of their old masters and impatiently await or even try
to forestall the day of their dismissal? And, if that be their
mood, will not the Englishman's task be made yet harder?
Can he, indeed, be expected to go on shouldering it? . . .
The difficulty, then, is patent: but it can be overcome if
Indian pride will face the facts, and especially if it will
perceive and admit the fact that these Englishmen are not
staying in India in order to keep in their clutch the last
vestiges of imperial power, but simply and sincerely to
help the new India to make its freedom a reality. And that
is not asking the impossible. It has happened elsewhere in
recent years—on the far smaller and simpler but not
wholly dissimilar stage of Irak. 'The Arab Government
is gaining ground,' wrote Gertrude Bell in one of her
fascinating letters; 'and people begin to see that we really
intend to do by it all we say.' May not the same thing
happen in India? Our intention is no less real; and 'plain
good intention', in Burke's familiar words, 'is of no mean
force in the government of mankind'.

5

Aid of a similar sort, military and civil, was once
rendered by the mother-country to the Colonies in
the course of their development towards national self-
sufficiency; and, if all goes well, India, like the Colonies,
will some day outgrow the need of it. In her case the

difficulties and dangers of the 'transitional period' are clearly greater; but if and when in course of time they are surmounted and India attains Dominion Status and becomes a full member of the Commonwealth, what then? What more than 'transitional', what lasting purpose is served by the association? Do the answers I suggested in the preceding lecture with regard to the other Dominions apply to a Dominion of India?

The first of those answers clearly does apply. There is the same mutual advantage in India's case as in that of any Dominion in the peace the Commonwealth maintains between its members and in the common defence it offers them in time of war. The strategic value of India to the Empire can hardly be exaggerated, especially in the coming age of air power. If it is hard enough as things are to bridge securely the gulfs that separate Britain from Australia and New Zealand or Malaya and Hong-Kong, it would be far harder if India were a foreign country, and well-nigh impossible, I imagine, if her coast were occupied by a hostile naval power. And will not the connexion be as valuable to India? However adequate her own national forces may become in course of time for her military defence in normal circumstances, it would profit her, surely, to be able to confront the incalculable dangers of the North with the assurance that at need her partners in the Commonwealth would rally to her side. And, of course, it is not by land only that India is more exposed to risk than Canada. In the greatest days of the Mogul Empire India never mastered the sea as the Arabs, for instance, mastered it in earlier days: and the immense cost alone makes it improbable that she would attempt the creation of a first-class modern navy. Would she be safe, would she be really independent, then, unless, like Australia or South Africa, she could rely for her protection on the combined

sea-strength of the whole Commonwealth? 'Swaraj India',
writes one of the ablest and most experienced of Indian
nationalists, 'may prove to be an idle dream, even though
the British Raj were to come to an end. The Pax Britannica
may be superseded by a Pax Japonica.'[1] The situation
would be different, of course, if a collective system for the
maintenance of international peace and justice were firm-
set and effectual throughout the world; but that—it becomes
clearer every day—is going to take time; and meanwhile
there is no reason to suppose that India would find in the
League of Nations a surer shield from external interference
and spoliation than China has found in it.

In the economic field, likewise, the possibilities of co-
operation for mutual advantage are the same for an Indian
Dominion as for the others. The Indian market for Western
manufactures is not what it was last century when, for
example, the value of cotton piece-goods it absorbed from
Britain rose from £1 million in 1830 to £14 million in
1880. For India, like the Dominions, has been 'assimilated'
economically as well as politically. Like Canada and the
rest she has developed, though still on a relatively small
scale, her own industries, and like Canada and the rest she
protects them against British competition—for, under the
'convention' established in 1921, she already enjoys something like a Dominion's fiscal autonomy. But in 1930
Britain's exports to India were still nearly 10 per cent of
her total exports; and, if the Dominions' trade with India
has hitherto been relatively meagre, the Ottawa agreements, negotiated on India's behalf by her own representatives and freely adopted by the majority of the Indian
Assembly, may generate a steady and substantial increase.

And there is much to be set on India's side of the
account. The dust and clamour of political conflict have

[1] S. K. Datta, *Asiatic Asia* (London, 1932), p. 170.

obscured the fact that her gravest problem is economic. Her people under the existing system are not misgoverned, but they are underfed: and it must be the first, as it will be the hardest, task of a free India to raise her myriad peasantry above the level of bare subsistence at which most of them are living. There is more than one way, of course, of doing that. It ought not to be impossible to revivify village life, to loosen its subjection to urban politics and finance, to restore something of its old self-rule and self-possession, to improve its agriculture and reorganize its handicrafts, to create a new atmosphere, a new 'will to prosperity'. But the dominant, the essential factor in any solution of the agrarian problem in India is a bigger market for her agrarian products—her cotton, rice, tea, jute, oil-seed, wheat, and the rest. And will not that be found for her most easily by co-operation within the Commonwealth? Isolation, indeed, seems as hazardous for India in economics as in politics. We have entered on an age of desperate international competition, and India, like every other nation, is already feeling its effects. Japanese imports into India, which only began in the period of the War, have already proved more formidable rivals to the products of Indian industry in its home market than British imports. And it is the same in the overseas markets. Nothing, for example, could have seemed more solidly established than Indian trade with Arabia and East Africa: it goes back beyond the beginning of recorded history. But the trade figures at the two chief ports of entry reveal how gravely it is now imperilled. At Zanzibar and even more at Aden during the last decade the volume of Indian imports has been steadily falling and that of Japanese imports rising. It seems, indeed, as if India will grow still poorer than she is unless something is done by international agreement to keep her ancient footing in the markets of the Indian Ocean. And in that delicate and sometimes rather formidable business of bargaining surely again it would be worse for India if she had no partners at her back.

But there is a higher value in maintaining the connexion of India with the Commonwealth than accrues from the advantages, great as they would be, of political and economic partnership. India would be more than just another Dominion. Her association with the rest would mean more than just a widening of the circle. It would mean that its circumference had been extended beyond the world of European race and civilization to embrace a part of Asia—that a coloured people had linked its destiny with white peoples—that all the gulf which Nature set between them and all that history has done to deepen it had not prevented their final union in a common cause. What that might signify for the welfare of the world is more than one can measure. If European civilization survives its present crisis, if it succeeds in adjusting the international relations of the European peoples without disaster, it will still have to endure a second and perhaps more rigorous ordeal. It will have to come to terms with other civilizations. There must be peace and harmony, political and economic, between races as well as nations if any social order worth the name is anywhere to survive. No collective system can endure which does not sooner or later collect on a common basis of mutual respect and profit not only Europe and America and Australasia but also Asia and Africa. We are beginning dimly to perceive the difficulty of that task in Africa. In Asia it has struck us in the face. The strongest Asiatic nation, in an access of militaristic nationalism, is deliberately widening the gap between the races. She has turned her back on the whole structure of international ideas and practices built

up so precariously in war-worn Europe. She preaches a
'Monroe Doctrine' for Asia. She is even suspected of
hoping some day to unite the power of a submissive China
with her own in antagonism to Europe and America. We
cannot foretell the issue, but that it will be affected this
way or that by the attitude of India is obvious. And, while
it is easy for Indians to remember all that Asia has suffered
from Europe, may it not be easier for Indians than for
Chinese or Japanese to remember also something of what
she has gained? History has given them a longer and more
intimate connexion with the West. Is it too much of a
paradox to suggest that a people who have actually been
subjected to British rule may be better able than a people
who have never known it to discard the old tradition of
distrust? Indians know our virtues, for what they may be
worth, as well as our vices. They have watched not a few
Englishmen dedicating their lives to the welfare of India.
They have made many close friendships with them. They
see them now for the most part acquiescing in the process
of India's emancipation from their rule; and, even among
the minority who deplore and resist it, they know there
are some who are mainly influenced by the fear that it
will injure India. Surely it ought not to be impossible, if
the record of the British connexion is read as a whole
and pondered over, for Indians to desire to continue it
and make the most of it when it no longer means subjection but free and equal partnership. And, if that indeed
be their attitude, it might go far to prevent an irreparable
schism between East and West. The second largest country
in Asia, her immense number of Asiatics second only to
the number of Chinese, if India chooses to throw the
political and economic weight of her new nationalism into
collaboration with the Commonwealth and its international
ideals, she will break the 'common front' of Asia and do

more than anything else could do to transform it into a 'common front' of the world. Would not the example of India, an unimpeachable authority on the nature of 'imperialism', help China to realize that her worst suspicions are now out of date? Might not the sight of India, finding it not only tolerable but profitable to live and work with Western nations, awaken in Japan a new belief in interracial co-operation?

Is that a dream? If so, it is at any rate an Indian as well as an English dream. Speaking at Simla some ten years ago, Mr. Srinivasa Sastri, one of India's most eminent 'elder statesmen', declared his belief that 'the connexion of India with England is somehow intended to fulfil some high purpose for the benefit of the world'. And he suggested that that purpose might be to prevent the possibility or at least to limit the effect of a future clash between Asia and Europe, 'marked by the shedding of more blood and the destruction of more human happiness than any clash in the history of our planet. . . . The British Commonwealth stands unique in the world for the reconciliation of East and West.'[1] Will that be the ultimate attitude of India? It would be if we could make it so. The day on which free India takes her equal place in the councils of the Commonwealth will be indeed our 'proudest day'. It will mean that we have done our part in achieving the hardest task ever set to a ruling people. *Regere imperio populos* —it was a great gift Rome gave her world; but, because she could give no more, the Roman Empire fell. If the British Empire stands, it will be mainly because we have come to believe that, for others as much as for ourselves, freedom is as desirable as unity, and in that faith have tried to reshape our old imperialism into something nearer the world's need.

[1] *The Times*, May 15, 1922.

K

VIII

INDIA AND DOMINION STATUS[1]

I

INDIAN nationalism is a revolt against alien rule, and the common objective of all its exponents is a united Indian state, as fully self-governing as any other state, taking its place on equal terms in the world society of states. But Indian nationalists differ as to the means of attaining this objective. The Extremists hold that it can only be attained by severance from the British Empire. Even if they could be convinced that this is untrue, many of them would probably still desire to break away. There are Indians, as there are Irishmen, who have inherited or acquired a dislike and distrust of any association, however free, with Britain and the Dominions. They want India to stand alone in the world, like China or Japan, at whatever risk to its internal harmony or to its relationships, political and economic, with other states or to the cause of international and interracial concord. The Moderates, on the other hand, wish to obtain free and equal nationhood for India within the Empire. Thirty years ago Mr. Gokhale, their greatest leader, advised them to seek this goal along the lines of 'colonial self-government'; and when, as a result of the War, 'colonial self-government' completed the last stage of its long development and became 'Dominion Status', this advice seemed justified. For the essence of Dominion Status is the full national equality it establishes between all

[1] October 1934. For a note on the meaning of Dominion Status, see p. 275 below.

the 'autonomous communities', including Britain, which are associated, in common allegiance to the Crown, in the British Commonwealth of Nations. They are 'equal in status', runs the famous definition of 1926, 'in no way subordinate one to another in any aspect of their domestic or external affairs'. If the Dominions had been denied this full equality, no bonds of sentiment or common tradition or consciousness of kinship in race or civilization would have availed to keep them in the Empire: sooner or later they would have followed the old American example and taken their chance outside it. And this applies with still greater force to India. At the end of the masterly survey of the Indian scene which constitutes the first volume of the Simon Report, 'We should say without hesitation', wrote its authors, 'that, with all its variation of expression and intensity, the political sentiment which is most widespread among all educated Indians is the expression of a demand for equality with Europeans and a resentment against any suspicion of differential treatment. . . . It is a great deal more than a personal feeling; it is the claim of the East for due recognition of status.' Anyone who has been in India or China knows how real this 'revolt of Asia' is, how passionate the repudiation of inferiority by individual Asiatics. Canadians or Australians may have sometimes felt a trifle warm on the question of their manifest equality with Englishmen; but Indians—it is easy to understand it in the light of history—are on fire. For them in an even deeper psychological sense than for the Dominions the test of any tolerable place within the Empire is the prospect it offers of ultimate equality.

The process of constitutional development which enabled those overseas colonies, which had been settled by British colonists or after French and Dutch settlement had been conquered and annexed by Britain, to grow to their

full political stature without breaking the tie which linked
them to Britain and to one another, was described in its
early stages—by Simcoe when he introduced representative government in Canada and by Elgin when he advanced
it to responsible government—as a 'great experiment'. It is
a still greater experiment to apply the same process to
India, a huge and multifarious country, occupied and controlled but never colonized by Britain, peopled by Asiatics
whose numbers will probably exceed 400 millions in
twenty years' time. It is indeed a strange contrivance of
history that a country so different from any of the
Dominions should follow the same track of political development; and, while it seems to have been the almost
inevitable result of its inclusion in the British Empire and
its contact with British ideas and institutions, it is not
altogether surprising that British political opinion should
have been slow to acquiesce in it. As a matter of fact
British policy was committed to Dominion Status as its
ultimate goal by the Declaration of 1917. For 'the gradual
development of self-governing institutions with a view to
the progressive realization of responsible government' in
India implies the progressive elimination of British control,
and its climax will mean that India is no longer in any way
subordinate to Britain, which is, it may be repeated, the
essence of Dominion Status. But for one reason or another
several years elapsed before this interpretation was officially
accepted. It was not, as some Indian critics seem to have
supposed, that British statesmen refused to contemplate
the ultimate emergence of India from all British control.
The authors of the Declaration clearly looked forward to
a day, however distant, when India would be fully self-
governing. The royal proclamation on the passing of the
Act of 1919 spoke of it as 'pointing the way to full responsible government hereafter'. But it is one of the most

characteristic habits of the British political mind to make
future commitments as vague as possible, to avoid cut
and dried plans, to keep free to adjust policy to changing
circumstances. Despite, moreover, the honesty of the intention, there may well have been a reluctance to discuss and
define the precise form of its final fulfilment for fear of
encouraging in India too sanguine a view of the time it
would take to reach it. To-day, the practical possibility of
an Indian Dominion, though still some distance off, seems
nearer than it did in 1917. In those days, too, the status
which the Dominions had in fact attained was not widely
understood: it was not authoritatively defined till 1926.
And even after 1926 there were some who supposed that,
because the national governments of all the Dominions are
parliamentary, a promise of Dominion Status would com-
mit India, at the Centre as well as in the Provinces, to
parliamentary government more strictly than the promise
of Responsible Government; whereas, of course, the truth
was the other way about, since Responsible Government
in its scientific and historical sense must be parliamentary,
and Dominion Status has nothing to do with the internal
constitution of the country concerned except in so far as
it precludes external interference therein and requires
allegiance to the Crown. But probably in most Englishmen's minds the main reason for hesitating to apply the
Dominion precedent to India was simply, as suggested
above, a vague recoil from its strangeness. It was difficult,
it is still none too easy, to conceive India, if only because
of its huge population, as a fellow-member of the Commonwealth with New Zealand.

But the evasion and its reasons are now of merely
academic interest. The matter is settled. 'In view of the
doubts which have been expressed both in Great Britain
and India', said Lord Irwin in 1929, 'regarding the

interpretation to be placed on the intentions of the British Government in enacting the Statute of 1919, I am authorized on behalf of His Majesty's Government to state clearly that in their judgment it is implicit in the Declaration of 1917 that the natural issue of India's constitutional progress, as there contemplated, is the attainment of Dominion Status.' Lord Willingdon declared in 1933 that his purpose was 'to help forward India to the goal of absolute equality with the other Dominions within the Empire'. And in the course of his exhaustive evidence before the Joint Select Committee in 1934, Sir Samuel Hoare described the 'White Paper' proposals as having in them 'the seeds of growth into Dominion Status, assuming that the distinctive conditions that separate India from the rest of the Dominions are eventually removed'.

Dominion Status is the goal, then; but in accepting it in that last-quoted sentence the Secretary of State was weighing his words. The existence of those 'distinctive conditions' in India is undeniable. And because of them the manner of India's progress to the common goal is necessarily different from that of the Dominions. Their progress, for example, was seldom marked by legislative enactments. It was mostly the outcome of a gradual change of custom, often so unobtrusive and informal as scarcely to be noticed. There was nothing remotely comparable with the forthcoming Government of India Act and the intensive and protracted work that has preceded it. There are features, again, of the 'White Paper' proposals which have no precedent in Dominion history. Indeed, the analogy seems at times so faint as to be no analogy at all, and the difference of approach so wide as almost to negate the identity of the goal. But it is clearly as undesirable to exaggerate the difference as to underestimate it; and it may therefore be worth while to compare India's present constitutional position with that of the Dominions in the past and to measure the length of the advance proposed towards the final status they now possess.

2

C'est le premier pas qui coûte, and it always takes less time to follow precedents than to make them. None the less, the length of the advance already made in India in the short time which has elapsed since the whole process began is remarkable. A few Indians were nominated to sit on Provincial Legislative Councils as early as 1861. Other Indian members were 'recommended', and so virtually elected, by constituent bodies after 1892. But it was not till 1909 that, under the Morley-Minto Reforms, one Indian province, Bengal, obtained real representative government such as that which the British North American Provinces obtained between 1758 and 1791; in other words, the majority of the members of the legislature were now openly and directly elected. In the other Provinces there was an unofficial majority in the legislatures after 1909, but the elected members were outnumbered by the officials *plus* the members nominated by Government until 1919. In Canada, upwards of fifty years elapsed before the next stage was reached—the advance from representative to responsible government in the domestic field. In India, responsible government for the control of a large and important part of the domestic field but not all of it was conceded to the Provinces by the Montagu-Chelmsford Reforms in 1919, *i.e.* only ten years after the initiation of representative government in Bengal and concurrently with its initiation in the other Provinces. At the same time the central government became representative, but not responsible.

Moreover, India was represented at the Imperial Conference from 1917 onwards, and, like the Dominions, took part in the Paris Conference, signed the Treaty of Versailles, and became one of the original members of the League of Nations. This new international status was, of course, an anomaly. India does not stand in the League on the same independent footing as Canada, since her external relations are under the control of the British Government and her representatives at Geneva are therefore appointed by the Secretary of State and the Government of India. But her membership of the League was far from meaningless. It brought Indian statesmen into the centre of world politics: it ensured that Indian opinion should not be overlooked: and it was in itself a sort of guarantee that full Dominion Status was the ultimate objective.[1]

A further marked advance was quickly made. Canada obtained fiscal autonomy in 1859, some fourteen years after the introduction of responsible government. India obtained something very like it in 1921 when a 'convention' was established which precluded the Secretary of State from interfering in the regulation of the Indian tariff by the Government of India, provided the latter was in agreement with the Indian Legislature. The honesty and value of this convention have been proved in practice. In determining its fiscal policy the Government of India has put Indian interests first, and in this field, therefore, it has usually been supported by the Legislature.[2]

Thus, in the twelve years between 1909 and 1921, India

[1] Similarly, India was represented from the outset at the International Labour Office, and as one of the eight leading industrial countries she obtained a permanent seat on its governing body. Its elected chairman in 1933 was an Indian (Sir Atul Chatterjee).

[2] The *de facto* fiscal autonomy of India has been recently demonstrated by the presence of an Indian delegation at the Ottawa Conference and the confirmation by the Indian Assembly of the agreements there concluded between India and the nations of the Commonwealth, and by the negotiation and conclusion in India of a commercial

covered a stretch of ground not altogether incomparable with that covered by Canada in the sixty-eight years between 1791 and 1859.

The 'White Paper' scheme goes a long way farther. In the briefest terms, it extends responsible government in the Provinces over the whole domestic field: it unites the Provinces and the Indian States in an All-India Federation: and it renders the Federal Government responsible to a Federal Parliament except as regards defence, external affairs, and ecclesiastical affairs—the last being only concerned with the provision of Christian ministers for the British troops and officials in India—which are still 'reserved' to ultimate British control. Two primary points of comparison with the Dominions are at once to be observed. First, whereas Canada had to wait over twenty years and Australia over forty years before the scope of their responsible government was widened from a provincial to a national scale by federation, responsible government in India is to become 'nation-wide' in some sixteen years after its partial establishment, and actually at the same time as its complete establishment, in the Provinces.[1] Secondly, it cannot be argued that the reservation of

agreement with Japan. Two other analogous minor developments may be mentioned here. (1) In pursuance of the Act of 1919, a High Commissioner for India resident in London was appointed by the Government of India in 1920, charged with similar functions to those of the High Commissioner for Canada, first appointed in 1879. Since 1922 the High Commissioners have been Indians. (2) In the controversy arising from the residence of many Indians in South Africa, the Government of India has dealt directly, and with the warm support of the Legislature, with the Union Government, and, as a result of an intergovernmental conference, an Agent-General of the Government of India has been posted in South Africa since 1927. The holders of this office have been Indians.

[1] On this point it should be remembered that Canada and Australia had no central government at all during those years, whereas India has had a strong central government for a long time past.

defence and external affairs keeps India far back on the path to Dominion Status. Those were the last two fields to be 'transferred' in the Dominions. If Canada assumed full responsibility for her local defence as early as 1871, she left her foreign policy in British hands till 1917.

Comparison with the Dominions should serve, then, to correct the view that the advance proposed by the 'White Paper' is not substantial. A little further examination will show that it stops where it does for the time being in accordance with Dominion precedent. The same practical and constitutional facts necessitated a 'transitional period' in the Dominions before the final goal was reached.

The crux of the position is the admitted fact that India is at present dependent for the defence of her frontiers and in the last resort also for the maintenance of internal order on a force which is partly composed of British troops and partly of Indian troops with British officers. Steps are being taken to train Indian officers with a view to creating as soon as possible a wholly Indian army, capable of maintaining external and internal security unaided. But, until that object is achieved, the control of defence cannot be 'transferred' from the Governor-General responsible to the British Government and Parliament to an Indian minister responsible to the Indian Legislature. British soldiers are enlisted by the British Government on the understanding that anyone charged with their welfare and safety will be accountable in the last resort to that Government and to Parliament. It is constitutionally and morally impossible, except at such emergencies as may require in time of war that one commander should control the combined forces of allied nations, to put the lives of British soldiers at the ultimate disposal of any other Government than the British, however experienced and trustworthy it may be.

Since this crucial principle is not always understood, it may be useful to illustrate it from Dominion history. British troops were retained in New Zealand for sixteen years after the introduction of responsible government, in British North America for twenty-six years (including four years after Federation), in British South Africa for forty-nine years (including twelve years after Union). The control of them in each case, whether they were employed in native wars or in suppressing civil disorder, was retained by the British authorities.

In New Zealand, this constitutional principle was emphasized by the number of British troops required and the losses suffered by them in the Maori wars; and there was never any question that, though the New Zealand Government was a responsible government in all its domestic affairs, the use of the British troops was wholly 'reserved' from ministerial control. The Duke of New-castle, Secretary of State for the Colonies, instructed the Governor, Sir George Grey, in the following terms in 1863:

You would be bound to judge for yourself as to the justice and propriety of employing and the best mode of employing Her Majesty's Forces. In this matter you might of course fortify yourself by taking the opinions of your Ministers, but the responsibility would rest with yourself and the Officer in Command.[1]

The same instructions were repeated by the Duke of New-castle's successor at the Colonial Office, Mr. Cardwell.

In Canada, one of the first measures undertaken by the Federal Government created in 1867 was the reorganiza-tion of its military forces, for which purpose a Militia and Defence Act was passed in 1868. For three years, during which this Act was being put into operation, British troops

[1] Parliamentary Papers, 1863, xxxviii, No. 177, p. 16.

remained in Canada, and in 1870 the Dominion Government requested the British Government to permit them to be used in conjunction with Canadian militia for the suppression of the Red River rebellion. The following is an extract from a Minute of the Dominion Cabinet:

It is obvious that the expedition must be undertaken, organized, commanded, and carried through under the authority of Her Majesty's Government.[1]

This authority was exercised in the event through the Governor-General, Sir John Young and the Commanding Officer, Colonel Wolseley.

The most recent case is that of South Africa. Like the Dominion Government in Canada, the Union Government in South Africa, created in 1909, soon set about reorganizing its military forces. The South Africa Defence Act, establishing permanent and 'citizen' forces, reserves, and a South African military college, etc., was passed in 1912, and thereupon the previously existing forces were disbanded. When, therefore, in 1913, as the result of an industrial strike, disorder broke out on the Witwatersrand so serious that the police force was inadequate to cope with it, the military force at the disposal of the Union Government was, to quote the official report on the disturbances, 'in a transition state'.[2] The Government was thus obliged to ask for the assistance of some of the British troops which had been retained in South Africa after Union with the Government's full consent. The request was granted, and

---

[1] Public Record Office, C.O. 42/684. Until recently, the words 'Her' or 'His Majesty's Government' were only used of the 'Imperial' Government. One of the titular changes resulting from the attainment of Dominion Status has been the use of the words to denote the Governments of all the members of the Commonwealth. Thus H.M.G. by itself is, in strict form, incorrect: it should be H.M.G. in the United Kingdom or H.M.G. in Canada or H.M.G. in Australia and so forth.   [2] [Cd. 7112], p. 59.

the disorders, which owing to the large native population
on the Rand might have become very grave, were quickly
suppressed.

The constitutional principle was stressed on this occasion by the fact that the action of the Governor-General,
Lord Gladstone, was criticized, both in South Africa and
in England, in quarters which were sympathetic with
the strikers. Lord Gladstone, it was said, by granting the
Union Government's request for the aid of British troops,
had taken sides in a domestic dispute which lay outside his
constitutional orbit—a charge which implied, quite cor-
rectly, that Lord Gladstone had been free to refuse. For
though, at this late date, South Africa had nearly acquired
de facto the full Dominion Status of to-day, there was no
question at all that British troops could only be used under
British authority. They were so used under the authority
of the Governor-General and the General Officer in Command (Sir R. C. Hart), who were instructed by cable from
the Secretaries of State for the Colonies and for War. The
following extracts from the relevant documents illustrate
the position:

TELEGRAM: Smuts to Gladstone, *June 30th*, 1913. Owing to
sudden and very serious development of strike on East Rand
have found it necessary to ask General Hart send 500 infantry
to Benoni. Trust Your Excellency will confirm action.[1]

MINISTERS' MINUTE, No. 666. *July 3rd*, 1913. . . . Ministers
have to inform His Excellency the Governor-General with
much regret that the conditions on the Witwatersrand have
materially changed for the worse. . . . Ministers have the
honour, therefore, to request that His Excellency will approach
the General Officer Commanding His Majesty's Troops for
the purpose of securing the services of 1000 more soldiers to
assist the forces now engaged.

[1] Lord Gladstone was away at Durban. He confirmed Hart's concession of Smuts' request and at once returned to Pretoria.

MINISTERS' MINUTE, No. 677. *July 4th*, 1913. . . . Ministers beg to express their appreciation of the readiness of the Imperial authorities to come to their assistance.[1]

Small detachments of British forces are still stationed to-day on 'Dominion' soil. In South Africa, by agreement with the Union Government, Simonstown is maintained and garrisoned as a British naval base: and in the Irish Free State, in accordance with the Treaty of 1921, British warships are stationed at Berehaven, Queenstown, and Lough Swilly and 'care and maintenance parties' are occupying the harbour defences. In both cases, of course, the naval and military units are under the sole control of the British Government.

These precedents have been cited at some length because the maintenance of British troops in India is the cardinal point of the whole constitutional position. It marks the limit to which the scope of Indian self-government can be extended at the present time. It necessitates the 'reservation' of Defence, and that in turn necessitates the 'reservation' of External Affairs, since soldiers are the instruments and may be the victims of foreign policy. And since, apart from the minor matter of the 'ecclesiastical establishment', External Affairs is the only field 'reserved' besides Defence, it follows that the 'White Paper' proposals, as far as the scope of self-government is concerned, do not, as some of their critics have declared, needlessly withhold from India powers she is already qualified to exercise, but, on the contrary, offer her the full maximum that is possible as long as she is unable to provide her own defence. In having to traverse, moreover, a 'transitional period' in which this self-defence is being organized, she will be doing what the Dominions did. Here, as elsewhere, the analogy, of course,

[1] [Cd. 6941] pp. 1-5.

is not exact. Externally, the Indian frontier is not only the one dangerous frontier in the Empire, but it is always dangerous; and the geographical position of India, midway between Europe and the Far East and straddling the route by sea and air from Britain to Malaya and Australia, makes its protection from foreign invasion and occupation more vital to the British Empire as a whole than that of any other part of it save only the British Isles. Internally, the question of order and security is far graver than in any Dominion. The number of British troops, therefore, now stationed in India is far higher than was required in time of peace in any Dominion. The Governor-General, moreover, will be more actively and continuously employed in the administration of the 'reserved' field: he will be served by organized 'departments'; and in order to ensure the due discharge of his responsibilities in this field he will be given powers of executive and legislative intervention, if the need should arise, in the wider field 'transferred' to his Indian ministers and the legislature. But, whatever the differences in circumstance and method, the position in India is similar in principle to that in Canada, say, before 1871 or in South Africa before 1914.

On this question of defence and foreign policy, however, it is important to remember that Dominion Status, being a characteristic product of British political life, is not a cast-iron, immutable thing. It arose from circumstances, and circumstances may change it. It took its present shape at a time when another world war, if not inconceivable, seemed only a very distant possibility. Already the atmosphere has worsened. Instead of a new age of international harmony, we may be entering a long period of international discord and tension. If that be so, and in view of new developments in methods of warfare, especially in the air, it seems possible that the nations of the Commonwealth may draw nearer to each other under pressure from the outer world. The safety of the whole Commonwealth may come to be regarded as so essentially the common concern of all its members that their co-operation, both in the conduct of foreign affairs and in the organization of defence, may become closer and more constant than it is at present. And in that case the security of any vulnerable part of the Commonwealth might be regarded as a matter for concerted and combined action, on a basis, of course, of free agreement, rather than as the sole and unaided responsibility of the Dominion immediately concerned.

3

Apart from the extent of the field in which self-government is conceded to India under the new scheme, there is the question of its quality or the fullness of its power. In this respect, Dominion self-government during the last stage before it achieved full Dominion Status was limited in law first by the superior authority of the British Parliament and secondly by the Governor-General's power act, in both the executive and legislative fields, without or even against the advice of his Dominion ministers and under instructions from the British Government. In fact these legal rights were rarely exercised, and most, though not all, of them had become obsolete through disuse before they were finally discarded between 1926 and 1931.

In principle again, the position under the new scheme in India is the same. The British Parliament's power to legislate for India is not questioned, and the Governor-General and the Governors of the Provinces, who continue to be responsible to the British Government and Parliament, are enabled at need to override their ministers and to act at their own discretion, both legislatively and executively. But there is a striking change of form. Instead of leaving this power of intervention undefined, unlimited, and even unstated as it used for the most part to be left in the case of the Dominions, certain particular matters, besides those which affect his control of the 'reserved' field, are to be enumerated in the Act, as the Governor-General's 'special responsibilities', and for the due discharge thereof the Act is to empower him, after consultation with his ministers, to act as he chooses, subject to any directions which the Secretary of State may give him. The Governor-General is also charged with discretionary powers of intervention in legislation similar to those once exercised by Governors-General in the Dominions. Furthermore, in the event of an emergency arising when the Legislature is not in session, the Governor-General may legislate by Ordinance if his ministers are satisfied that such action is necessary, or on his own initiative if his 'special responsibilities' or 'reserved' subjects are involved. And, lastly, if a general breakdown should occur making it impossible to carry on the government in accordance with the constitution, he may assume such powers as he thinks necessary by proclamation. Similar special responsibilities and powers are committed to the Governors of the Provinces.

These, of course, are the famous 'safeguards' on which so much controversy has centred. It is here that India seems to diverge most widely from the path trodden by the Dominions, because it is here that 'the distinctive conditions which separate India from the Dominions' have most weight. In any case the 'breakdown' and 'emergency' powers can scarcely be called in question: the latter would normally require ministerial assent for its exercise: and as to the former, every Government possesses the right to save the State if its constitution fails, and in India in whom

L

else could it be vested than in the Governor-General? But the 'special responsibilities', it must be admitted, are unknown to Dominion history and can only be explained or justified by the special circumstances of India. In no Dominion, not even in the Irish Free State, is there such acute and deep-seated antagonism between different communities as in India, and nowhere, therefore, is 'peace or tranquillity' so easily menaced or so hard to preserve. No Dominion, again, runs the same risk of losing the financial confidence of the world at large as India runs in the early years of this great constitutional advance, and none needs, therefore, such convincing guarantees for the maintenance of its 'financial stability and credit'. Even in the Dominions financial 'safeguards' of a sort have not been entirely dispensed with. Clauses in their constitutions require that the interest on all public debts existing at the time of their enactment should be charged on the Consolidated Fund. It was not till 1910 that the control of Canadian currency was 'transferred' to the Dominion Government.[1] And, in order to obtain for their domestic loans the high credit attached to British Trustee securities, the Dominions submit to a measure of British control, direct or indirect, over legislation affecting such loans.

Special protection of 'the legitimate interests of minorities' and 'the rights of any Indian State' is similarly necessitated by Indian conditions. Both the minority communities and the States demanded it. Without it they would have refused, it appears, to acquiesce or co-operate in the new constitution. And here again there is something analogous, in principle at any rate, in the Dominions. Special protection is given in the Canadian constitution

[1] A Canadian Act was disallowed in 1851 on the ground that it interfered with British control of currency which was specifically recognized by a Dominion Act of 1871.

to the rights of denominational schools on behalf of the Protestant or Roman Catholic minorities in the Provinces;[1] and the South African Constitution safeguards the continued enjoyment of the parliamentary franchise by those natives or coloured persons who fulfil the qualifications previously required.[2]

Special provisions for maintaining the rights and interests of the Public Service may likewise be found in Dominion constitutions;[3] but there are two unique proposals in the 'White Paper' scheme, arising from the unique character of the partnership between India and Britain. There is no Dominion parallel to the retention of civil servants, other than the Governor-General's personal staff, to be recruited or secured by any other authority than that of the Dominion Government; nor is there any provision in Dominion constitutions for preventing 'commercial discrimination' otherwise than by the operation of ordinary law or by reciprocity and good-will.

For most of the 'safeguards', then, analogies may be found in the Dominions, but they are not close analogies, especially inasmuch as the power of intervention to be maintained for the present in the ordinary operation of responsible government in India is to be exercised under the ultimate authority of the British Government and Parliament. This power is apt, however, to seem more formidable and more derogatory to the status of India on paper than it is likely to prove in fact. Its obvious purpose is to prevent things being done which in the interests of India quite as much as, if not more than, in those of Britain ought not to be done. It is to be expected, therefore, that Indian

---

[1] Section 93.

[2] Sections 35 and 152.

[3] *E.g.* the South African, Section 143; Irish Free State, articles 77 and 78 and subsequent Acts.

ministers will not desire to do them; and if by inadvertence or under political pressure they are tempted to do them, the Governor-General or Governor will presumably point out to them that such action will involve his 'special responsibilities', and he will only use his power of intervention in the last resort if he fails to persuade his ministers to take the requisite course themselves. This important point was clearly made by the Secretary of State before the Joint Select Committee. In answer to a question by Mr. Jayakar with regard to the powers of intervention, Sir Samuel Hoare said:

'I am hoping that there would be a great deal of previous consultation between the Governor and the Ministers; and I am hoping that, as a result of that consultation, those powers will very seldom be exercised. The Governor would, I presume, call the attention of the Minister or the Government to some case that is likely to lead to an infringement of the special responsibilities, and I would have thought that, if things were working well, the Ministers and the Government would welcome the opportunity of removing the cause of the trouble, and that the Governors therefore would never have to intervene.'[1]

Indeed, since the purposes of the 'safeguards' are generally admitted to be just and in Indian interests, it ought to be possible for ministers so consistently to avoid provoking their use as to render them in course of time as obsolete as the similar, though unspecified, powers once possessed by Governors-General in the Dominions.

One last point should not be overlooked. Over against the potential infringement by the 'safeguards' of full responsible government may be set the guarantee of its operation as the normal procedure in all save the 'reserved' fields—a stronger legal guarantee than that enjoyed by the Dominions. Responsible government was introduced in

[1] Q. 5978.

the colonies by nothing more than dispatches from the Secretary of State enjoining Governors to act normally on their ministers' advice. Such orders were never incorporated in the formal instructions, even after responsible government was extended from a provincial to a national scale. Its continued operation was dictated merely by convention, just as in Britain whence it originated. Even in 1926 it was only laid down in a political agreement of the Imperial Conference that the Governor-General, like the King, acts on the advice of responsible ministers. With the sole exception of the Irish Free State, no Dominion constitution contains any reference to the matter. It is simply taken for granted. Under the new Indian scheme, on the other hand, the formal Instructions to the Governor-General and Governors will enjoin them to be guided by their ministers' advice in all other than those specified matters in which they are to exercise personal responsibility and discretion.

4

The conclusion, then, reached by a comparative examination is that in its broader aspects the measure of self-government contemplated for India under the new *régime* roughly corresponds with that of the Dominions in the penultimate stage of their advance to Dominion Status, but that certain restrictions, most of which are only distantly or in principle analogous to Dominion precedents, are to be maintained for the present on the operation of responsible government. While, however, such comparisons may serve to clarify ideas about the theoretical framework of the Indian problem, they are, when all is said, an academic business. The chief test, indeed, of Indian statesmanship in the coming years may well be its capacity to recognize that its path to Dominion Status is more a question of practice than of precedent. The length of the 'transition' to the final goal cannot be determined by analogy. It varied in the Dominions as regards different fields of government and as between different Dominions. It was determined in all of them, as it will be determined in India, by circumstances. Nothing is to be gained, therefore, by a political pedantry that thinks more of forms than facts and strives to imitate minutely a model which fits the case in principle but not in detail. The only way to shorten the 'transitional' period is to remove the 'distinctive conditions' which make it necessary. That work is mainly for Indians to do. When it is done, the path to full free nationhood is open.

IX

THE MEANING OF THE EMPIRE

3. BRITISH TROPICAL AFRICA [1]

I

CONSTITUTIONAL developments in the Commonwealth of Nations and in India have occupied so much of the public stage since the War that the main facts and problems of those two sections of the British Empire are relatively well understood. But there is a third section which is not so often in the limelight and about which most people in Great Britain know little and most people in the Dominions (so I am told) know scarcely anything at all. Yet it is a world in itself, this 'Colonial' or 'Dependent' Empire: it covers more than three million square miles, a bigger space than Europe; it contains over sixty million inhabitants, six times the population of Canada: and among them are representatives of most of the varied races which make up mankind—white men, black men, brown men, yellow men, Europeans, Africans, Arabs, Indians, Malays, Chinese, Polynesians. Scattered over continents and oceans, its manifold and diverse communities have nothing to unite them, nothing in which they all share, except their common allegiance to the British Crown or their common subjection in different degrees and ways to the ultimate control of the British Parliament.

It is this part of the Empire with which our young post-War critics are apt to be most impatient. They can tolerate

[1] University of Toronto, April 12, 1933. *University of Toronto Quarterly*, October 1934.

the Commonwealth. They can digest the meaning of our connexion with India. But as regards our so-called 'tropical possessions' the old prejudices die hard. Many high-minded people are still inclined to regard these 'colonies' of browns or blacks in much the same light as Cobden regarded white colonies in Canada and elsewhere a century ago—as disreputable relics of the *ancien régime*. You remember how Cobden, writing in 1836—he was then just thirty-two—classed the Colonies with the army and navy, the church, and the corn laws as 'impurities' belonging to 'aristocratic government' of which John Bull had got to 'purge his house'. For 'aristocratic' read 'capitalistic', and the old clap-trap seems curiously modern. But the reiteration of other and older people's formulas can scarcely be congenial to the rising generation, and for this section of the Empire, as much as for the others or more so, they will want, I expect, to examine the facts afresh and to ask those primary questions—what *is* it and what is it *for*?

2

To deal with those questions except in very general terms over the whole field of the Colonial Empire would be impossible in a single lecture: so I propose to limit myself to one part of it—the group of territories under British rule in mid-Africa, that huge belt of country between the Sahara and the Zambesi. Conditions in that part, of course, are different from conditions in other parts: it is Africa, the others are not: but, since they are all (except the naval stations like Gibraltar, Malta, or the Falkland Isles which are a class by themselves and need not concern us now) in tropical or subtropical areas, all inhabited mainly by coloured and politically more or less backward peoples, and all under British rule, the dominant facts and ideas

about them are broadly the same. The situation in British
Malaya is not so very unlike that in British Tropical Africa.
Though more than gulfs of space divide them, British rule
in Nigeria or the Sudan cannot be something quite different
in principle from British rule in Fiji or Guiana. If, therefore, I attempt an interpretation only of that African part
of the Colonial Empire, it can be applied, in essentials and
mutatis mutandis, to the whole.

What, then, *is* British Tropical Africa? In the West,
it consists of the colonies of Nigeria, Gold Coast, Sierra
Leone, and Gambia, with adjacent protectorates and strips
of mandated territory. In the centre of the continent,
secluded from the sea, there are in the north the Sudan
(which is under an Anglo-Egyptian 'condominium') and
the Uganda Protectorate; and in the south the Protectorates
of Northern Rhodesia and Nyasaland. In East Africa there
are Kenya Colony, the Kenya, Somaliland, and Zanzibar
Protectorates, and the Mandated Territory of Tanganyika.
The total area of all these units together is roughly $2\frac{1}{2}$
million square miles, and their total population roughly
45 millions. But they do not constitute a single connected
area like India. The West African section is divided in
itself and cut off from the Central and Eastern by territories under French and Belgian rule; but all the rest,
except Somaliland, is contiguous; the eastern section links
the two central sections; the spread of British rule, mandatory or otherwise, is unbroken from the Upper Nile to
the Upper Zambesi.

The form of government in all this area is more or less
uniform. It is what is called 'Crown Colony government',
which, as you know, was the kind of government with
which most of the white colonies of the Empire began their
political life and under which, roughly speaking, British
India was still living some thirty years ago. Each territory

has its Governor, who represents the King and whose authority cannot be questioned by anyone within it. For executive purposes he is advised, but cannot be overridden, by an Executive Council, usually constituted of officials only, and his orders are carried out by a civil service, in which the higher posts are almost exclusively filled by Europeans, mostly recruited from Britain but to some extent also from the Dominions. For making laws the Governor is advised by a Legislative Council, which consists partly of officials and partly of unofficial members nominated by the Governor. In Kenya, Northern Rhodesia, Nigeria, and the Gold Coast, in addition to the nominated members, there are other unofficial members elected by constituencies. But in every Legislative Council the officials are in a majority, and they are bound to vote, if need be, as the Governor bids them. Clumsy as it may seem, this official majority is a vital element in the whole system. It is essential that the Governor's will should in the last resort prevail in everything, not indeed in order to make him an unfettered autocrat, but, on the contrary, to make him an effective instrument of another and, paradoxically enough at first sight, a democratic authority. The sovereign of British Tropical Africa is the King-in-Parliament; it is Parliament's will that must prevail; and this would not be achieved if the Governor were not free to carry out the orders of Parliament's agent, the Secretary of State for the Colonies, who drafts the Governor's commission and instructions, supervises, directs, or vetoes his policy, and can advise his dismissal as he advises his appointment.

This 'Crown Colony government' is in force throughout the area, with a few exceptions or modifications. In the administration of the mandated territories—Tanganyika, Togoland, and the Cameroons (of which the two latter are united for governmental purposes with the Gold Coast and Nigeria)—the freedom of the Governor, as of the Secretary of State and Parliament above him, is limited by the specific obligations of the Mandate, for the due fulfilment of which the British Government has to render account every year to the Mandates Commission of the League of Nations. In one or two protectorates such as Northern Nigeria or Ashanti the Governor legislates without a Council. In the Sudan the Governor-General is appointed by and responsible to the British and Egyptian Governments jointly, and is advised both for executive and for legislative purposes by a single Council.

So much for the system of government. It is not a perfect system, and there are some who think that it calls for reconsideration and reform: but it is reasonably efficient and not ill staffed. No 'anti-imperialist' is likely to grudge the tribute which is paid by everyone who knows them and has seen them at work to the honesty and energy and public spirit of the Colonial Services.

3

But to what end, our critics ask, is this government directed? Do these zealous officials realize what they are doing? They keep the peace, they try to deal justly with the native peoples, they wish them to be contented; but for what other purpose than to smooth the profitable path of British trade? They attend to their wards' material needs, they try to improve their environment and protect them from disease; but is it because the welfare of these poor Africans is an end in itself, or are they only being multiplied and fattened up to be the more productive serfs of European capitalism? Is it pretended that we went into Africa or are staying there now for anybody's advantage but our own? Are not the only really candid people those who for fifty years past have described these tropical countries as 'our imperial estates' to be exploited for the profit of those who 'possess' them? Is not all the talk about 'trusteeship' merely *camouflage* or cant?

Some of those questions are answered by history. Since the days of the abolition of the British Slave Trade and of British Slavery—of which latter event we are celebrating the centenary this year—the humanitarian tradition has been a persistent and potent factor in all our dealings with backward races. Consider the extraordinary power which Wilberforce and 'the Saints' exercised over Parliament and public opinion. Consider the significance of Livingstone— his whole-hearted devotion to the Africans, his immense prestige in Britain, his triple doctrine of Christianity, commerce, and colonization as the means of civilizing Africa. Read the record of territorial expansion, and observe, as you will, that economic interest was not the only motive which impelled reluctant British Governments to occupy and annex the country. There was first, in almost every case, the certainty that if Britain did not do it, a rival nation would, and there was secondly, in many cases, the conviction that only by the establishment of European control could the natives of the country be rescued from slave-raiding and slave-trading and the endless disorder and destruction caused thereby. It is true, of course, that the process of occupation required as a rule the use of force—more force, probably, than would be needed nowadays with our better knowledge of native custom—but, except when it was resisted by relatively strong and well-organized armies like those of the Khalifa or King Prempeh, the actual bloodshed was very slight. It is true, again, that during or after occupation in certain cases grave injustice was done to native rights: but, if you look at the field as a whole, you will find that those cases occurred only in the relatively very small area which was suitable for European settlement.

But to assert that British rule in Tropical Africa was not precipitated solely by material greed, that on the whole it was humanely established, that on the whole it has been justly exercised, is not, of course, to deny the existence and persistence of the economic motive. Europe demands the economic development of Africa. Europe desires its copper, its tin, its gold. Europe can scarcely do without its cocoa, coffee, rubber, cotton, vegetable oils, fruits, cereals. And Europe greatly needs its market for manufactured goods, a market already substantial but capable of almost indefinite expansion. Nor is Europe only in the picture. America and Asia are scarcely less concerned in tropical exploitation. No more than the other continents can Africa escape from the economic network which now binds all the world together. But, while I admit that the economic development of Africa is inevitable, I do not for a moment abandon the principle of 'trusteeship'. The admission defines the trustee's duty. It is our business to see to it that economic development does no more injury to Africa than it has done to Europe. Wisely planned, firmly controlled, it might well do less! I do not suggest it is an easy business. The forces of Mammon are always in the field, and it is deplorably easy for the white man to take advantage of the ignorant black man. But, if it is a difficult, it is not an impossible task to plan and control the economic process in the common interest of both races. And I believe that British public opinion, with our inherent sense of fair play and our great humanitarian tradition behind it, will do its best to achieve it. I believe, too, that British philanthropy will find a colleague in British commercial sagacity: for it must be clear to any far-sighted business man that methods of exploitation so hasty or so unmethodical or so unjust that they injure, impoverish, and antagonize the African producer and the African consumer are bound in the long run to defeat their own end.

No: if watched and safeguarded as it must be, the exploitation of Africa's wealth *need* not harm the Africans. On the contrary it *ought* greatly to help them. For it will mean more money in their pockets, and that again will mean two things: first, a higher standard of life, a chance of providing themselves with better food and lodging and with pots and pans and furniture and bicycles and what not—all the things for which, by the way, Europe wants a market at least as much as it wants raw materials—and secondly, and more important, a higher public revenue to pay for all the assistance they require from the State for building up a healthy and progressive African society.

4

But the economic interrelationship of Africa and Europe is only part of a wider problem. In many other places than the minefields and plantations, in many other ways than the intercourse of trade, European civilization is 'up against' African life. On the result of that contact or conflict *as a whole* the fate of Africa depends. And one cannot indulge in any casual or complacent optimism about it. If the process were more gradual, it might seem less risky: there would be more time to study and perhaps to regulate it. But the dominant, the unprecedented aspect of it is its speed, a speed still increasing year by year. No more than half a century ago the map of all midland Africa was only just beginning to be filled in by the intrepid explorations of Livingstone and his contemporaries. There were no roads, still less, of course, a railway: nothing but native footpaths

winding from village to village through the 'bush'. Movement was infinitely slow. Goods were transported almost
exclusively on human heads. But now the whole vast area
is intersected by a network of roads, good, bad, and
indifferent, but mostly capable of carrying motor-cars
and lorries except in the rainy season. A few years ago
I motored over ground in Tanganyika and Northern
Rhodesia in less than six days which sixty years ago took
Livingstone more than six months to cover. And, of
course, there are railways now, thousands of miles of them,
from the coast on east, west, and south to the very heart of
the continent, with their sleeping-cars and dining-cars and
long lines of goods waggons. And for passengers, if not yet
for bulky goods, there are swifter means of transport than
the rail. Every important African centre can now be reached
by air. It only takes a week to fly right down the backbone
of the continent from Cairo to the Cape. . . . And it is only
half a century or so since Livingstone was asking that
Africa should be 'opened up'!

By all these means of transport Europe has descended
upon Africa. In 1873 only a minute minority of mid-
Africans away from the coast had ever seen a white man.
To-day there is an equally minute minority that has not at
one time or another enjoyed or suffered that experience.
European merchants, in big trade and small, are coming
and going everywhere. In one or two highland areas
European colonists have come to stay. The whole land is
dotted with European missions. And omnipresent ever,
whether herded with their files in an imposing urban
Secretariat or speeding singly about their rural 'districts',
revolving the wheels of government, tax-collecting, keeping the peace, judging, supervising, teaching, healing, sur-
veying, building, researching, are the European officials in
their thousands. Nor, of course, is it only by direct contact

that this great alien invasion impinges on the African. Stories of the white men pass from mouth to mouth—their bearing and behaviour, their strange ideas, the meaning of their presence in the country: and it is easy nowadays for the native who has learnt his lesson in a European town or on a European farm to pass it on to the villagers at home. It is not only the white man who moves more quickly now in Africa. Not long ago most natives spent their lives within a narrow circle round the village: but now thousands of natives own bicycles, and many own cars; and those who cannot afford such luxuries may be seen packed tight and careering at reckless speed down the roads in the covered motor-lorries which are increasingly playing the part in Africa of the ubiquitous motor-omnibus in Europe.

Directly and indirectly, then, the African is being confronted with European civilization in most of its diverse aspects. He observes its virtues and its vices, its energy, its forethought, its self-control, its persistence, its zest for individual responsibility, its loyalties and disloyalties to its Christian faith, its arrogance, its stolidity, its hardness, its greed. He sees the church, the school, the race-course, the cinema, the gin-shop. He hears a multitude of doctrines, all of them, high or low, alike in their conflict with the traditional ideas which have hitherto ruled his life. His mind is stirred as it has never been stirred before in the history of his race. Ancient custom is no longer quite so sacrosanct. He dreams new dreams of what he might make of his life. And inevitably these new ambitions, at any rate in the young, are imitative. What must impress the African most is not the goodness or the badness of white men, but their power, their magical mastery of nature, their irresistible mechanical force and the wealth they have attained thereby. If Africans could learn to think and act as those white men do, might not they too become like gods?

There, it seems to many who know Africa, the greatest danger lies. It is bad enough that the African should so easily acquire our vices: it would be tragic if he suffered also from a too hasty and indiscriminate attempt to assimilate what he thinks to be our virtues. Christianity itself cannot lightly, in a moment, be so well digested as to provide as strong and lasting sanctions as the old beliefs, however primitive and superstitious. Education can as easily unfit a man as fit him for the life he has to lead. Social and political ideas and institutions which flourish on British soil may lose their practical value if too thoughtlessly or hurriedly transplanted to the Tropics. Is it not possible that too swift and drastic a process of assimilation might disintegrate the whole traditional basis of African society without providing a firm or durable substitute and so leave the native deracinated and unbalanced, with no solid ground to stand on as the steadily mounting tide from the outer world sweeps over Africa?

5

Fortunately this danger has been detected, and a policy has been framed to meet it—a policy which seems to me to find its natural place in the general readjustment of the Empire to suit the conditions of this post-War age.

Its central idea is to try to keep the African rooted in Africa and to help him to become the best possible kind of African, not something half-and-half or hybrid, still less a synthetic European. Do not misinterpret that idea. It does not imply any futile attempt to shut out European influences. The African will get what he wants from Europe by hook or by crook whatever we do or leave undone. Our task is to make it as easy as we can for him to want and to get the best that Europe can give him; and,

M

meantime, to help him, wherever possible, to retain what is best in his African birthright and to deepen and enrich it so that it can absorb the new and alien elements without losing its own natural strength and value. To change the metaphor, it is not a matter of planting a new tree, roots and all, but of feeding and pruning an old tree and grafting new shoots on its stem. Nor, again, does our central idea imply an effort to impose on Africans what we happen to think is good for them whether they like it or not. Nothing effective can be done without the consent, the cordial agreement rather, of African opinion. Already, indeed, it appears that some of the West African *intelligentsia* suspect our motives and imagine that we want to hold them down to their African past, almost to keep them primitive, for fear lest they become too like ourselves and challenge our superiority! But I do not think that such distrust will last. I believe the more thoughtful African will understand what we are after: and, if he understands, can he fail to approve? His native instinct, his love of all that Africa means to him, his natural pride of race will compel approval.

Let me now attempt a brief description of the manner in which this 'African' policy is applied first to the educational and then to the political or administrative field.

Until a very recent date education in British Tropical Africa was not very different in aim and matter from education in England. Above the elementary stage, where the teaching was necessarily in the native tongue and the subjects of the simplest, it concerned itself, broadly speaking, with the rudiments of European culture. It taught the African to speak, read, and write English. It provided him with what he could digest of an English schoolboy's fare, mostly by means of English text-books written from the English standpoint. It was, with a few notable exceptions, a literary, not a vocational education; and, while it fitted Africans for a limited field of lifework, in backward areas to be clerks in Government departments or business offices, in advanced areas to be lawyers and journalists and schoolmasters, it did not fit them, it often unfitted them, for the life which the vast majority of them would have to lead—in the villages, on the farm, in the workshop. It tended, therefore, to create a similar class of literate unemployed to that which a similar concentration on literary and English culture has created in India. It tended, also, to foster that break with nature and the past, that deracination, of which I spoke just now. The new policy seeks to avoid that danger. I wish I could discourse on it at large. It could scarcely fail to interest you. But I must be content to quote a summary definition of it from the memorandum drafted by the Advisory Committee on African Education at the Colonial Office.

Education should be adapted to the mentality, aptitudes, occupations, and traditions of the various peoples, conserving as far as possible all sound and healthy elements in the fabric of their social life; adapting them where necessary to changed circumstances and progressive ideas. . . . Its aim should be to render the individual more efficient in his or her condition of life, whatever it may be, and to promote the advancement of the community as a whole through the improvement of agriculture, the development of native industries, the improvement of health, the training of the people in the management of their own affairs, and the inculcation of true ideals of citizenship and service.

That statement was made ten years ago, and much has been done in the interval to put its principles into practice in the readjustment of curricula, the training of teachers, the composition of new text-books, and so forth. Professional critics may even grumble that the new doctrine has been a little over-stressed. But that fault, if it exists, is on the right side, and already a useful corrective is observable in the attention now being given not only to saving the best of what is African but to discovering the most effective methods of 'putting across' the psychological gulf between black and white the best of what is European.

But the most striking application of the principle of an 'African Society' is in the political field and is known as 'Indirect Rule'—a method of government which is now in operation in the greater part of British Tropical Africa. It originated in no sudden inspiration. It had nothing to do with theories or principles. It was just a practical contrivance for meeting the needs of time and place. When the territories were first occupied, it was obvious at the outset that the British occupants, who were now responsible for their administration, could not possibly undertake it all themselves. The area to be administered was far too vast. It would have needed a host of officials and a huge revenue to pay them. Inevitably, therefore, the aid of the native inhabitants was enlisted for the task; and where, as in Northern Nigeria or Uganda, an organized system of native government existed, attracting the natural or traditional loyalty of the people, this system was maintained under the supervision, guidance, and, at need, control of British officials. In other areas where there was no large-scale political organization but only a congeries of more or less independent tribes, this 'indirect' method seemed at first inapplicable. In such areas, therefore, government was more completely centralized. The major functions of administration, including all finance, were kept in the hands of British 'district officers', who gave orders to the tribal chiefs. But, observe, even under this 'Direct Rule', the chief was a necessary part of the system, if only as a channel for communicating the Government's will to the

tribe and helping to get it executed. And in such an area
as South-east Nigeria, where political organization was
confined to groups of villages or clans or families and there
were no tribal chiefs, the office was artificially created by
the appointment under warrant of the native who seemed
most suitable. So far, it may be said, policy had been
dictated by convenience: it was a matter of improvisation
to meet the immediate need of efficient administration. It
was not till a later stage that, under the impact of the
War and of developments in India and East Africa, the
new ideas of an African Society emerged; and then it
seemed clear that, whereas Indirect Rule accorded with
those ideas, Direct Rule did not. The North Nigerian
Emirates, the kingdom of Buganda, these were African
institutions, capable under careful supervision and encouragement of preserving and strengthening the political
capacity of the people, deepening their sense of public
responsibility, and developing in course of time on natural
lines to accord with the growth of education and progressive ideas of government. But the 'direct' method seemed
to lead in the opposite direction. Chiefs under a British
official's orders would be necessarily regarded not as the
trustees of African tradition, interpreting their people's
laws and customs and commanding their innate respect,
but as the instruments of an alien and unnatural authority;
and they themselves and their advisers among the people,
possessing no real power in any but minor matters, would
tend steadily to lose their sense of responsibility, their
initiative, even in the end their interest in public affairs.
Direct Rule, moreover, however hard its British agents
tried to understand the Africans, was bound to be on
British lines, and would therefore tend in the long run
to wean the natives' minds from African ideas and institutions and push them, as their education deepened

kindling new desires, along the uncertain path of political imitation.

In the last few years, accordingly, an attempt has been made to convert Direct Rule in the tribal or unorganized areas into Indirect, first by making sure, as far as possible, that the chief is in fact the rightful ruler by native custom and where necessary (as in South-east Nigeria) restoring in place of the chief we had artificially created the old traditional governing body, and then widening the powers and responsibilities of those truly 'Native Authorities' to the fullest practicable limit.

6

To anyone who has never been in Africa—and I expect that covers most, if not all, my present audience—the things I have been saying in the last few minutes must have seemed somewhat academic and unsubstantial. Let me try, therefore, to give you a concrete illustration. And for locality I will choose Tanganyika Territory because I was able myself to observe the new policy in operation there five years ago.

In Tanganyika the contrast between the new policy and the old is sharpened by the change-over from German to British control. The German Government found the occupation and pacification of the country no easy task. For some twenty out of the thirty years of its rule there was constant fighting. As a result many of the chiefs were deposed or executed, and over a large part of the country the tribal system was broken up. Where it survived in strength, the Germans governed through it. But elsewhere they acquiesced in the collapse of tribalism—in some cases they confirmed it by splitting up tribal areas into different administrative districts—and governed 'directly' through native agents or Akidas, chosen for their personal capacity without regard to their previous standing among the people. The British policy, inaugurated by Sir Donald Cameron in 1925, aimed, on the other hand, at trying to save and revive what was left of the old tribal system. Careful enquiry revealed that in most cases the chiefs deposed by the Germans or their heirs had still commanded in hiding or retirement the furtive allegiance of their tribesmen. When their restoration was suggested and the ideas behind it explained, the general satisfaction—to put it mildly—was unquestionable. 'The people conceive', to quote an early official report, 'that the policy of indirect rule implies that they are to be governed by their traditional rulers, and they will have none other.' So far, so good. The next step was to endow these Chiefs-in-Council (for nowhere in Africa is monarchy absolute) with the requisite powers of local self-government more or less on the lines of the first edition of Indirect Rule as established in Northern Nigeria or Uganda. Education, medical and veterinary services, roads and buildings, agricultural development, afforestation, anti-tsetse and anti-vermin operations—these 'departments' were established, on a local scale of course, and subject to the supervision and assistance of the Government Departments operating in the Territory as a whole with their staffs of British officials. Secondly, since in African tradition executive and judicial functions are seldom separated, the Chief-in-Council was constituted a 'Native Court' with authority to try cases below the major level of importance in accordance with native law and custom—its decisions, again, being subject to scrutiny by the British district officer and to the right of appeal to his and higher courts. Thirdly, as to finance, the hinge of all administration, while the power of taxation was at present reserved to the Territorial Government, a portion of the taxes it levied on the people concerned—on the average about a quarter—was deposited, together with the yield of sundry local fees, in the 'Native Treasury' at the disposal of the local authority for the payment of fixed salaries to the Chiefs (in lieu of the old irregular tribal tribute) and to the other administrative and judicial personnel and to meet the cost of the local services. Let me quote you some items from one of the annual budgets of those 'Native Administrations' as they are called—that of Unyanyembe for 1928-9. Out of a revenue of £6740 (of which £5150 comes from the tax rebate and £500 from court fees and fines), £1700 is allocated to the Paramount Chief's salary, and roughly another £2000 to the salaries of various sub-chiefs, headmen, clerks, overseers, messengers and medical 'dressers'. On roads £300 is to be spent, on buildings £50, on dispensaries £90, on a leper settlement £120, on the tsetse-fly campaign (observe its great importance) £400, on the purchase of seed £50. Another 'N.A.', with twice the revenue, estimated to spend some £1200 on its schools. But I must not linger over these little budgets, fascinating as they are. I have cited enough of them to show you that the system affords a real training in the responsible management of public money.

Indirect Rule, then, is founded on local self-government in accordance with native tradition. That is its strength. Its foundations are laid so firmly on African soil that they ought to be able to bear whatever structure may be built thereon in future. And that structure is already beginning to rise. In order to adjust the relationships between one 'N.A.' and another and to enlarge the administrative opportunities of the smaller units, a process of amalgamation and federation is at work in Tanganyika. Again it depends on the consent of the people concerned, and again this consent has been forthcoming as soon as the advantages of co-operation were made clear, especially the power it gave to small units to provide public services in common which were too expensive for their separate revenues. Let me quote some examples:

In Bukoba, where the chiefs were as jealous of their independence as they are proud of their ancient and common lineage, a Council of Chiefs has been created representing some 200,000 inhabitants and disposing of a joint revenue of £28,000 a year. In Mwanza Province, two areas, each of which was until recently divided between half a dozen chiefdoms, have of their own motion formed themselves into two Native Administrations under two paramount chiefs, each of whom now rules over some 170,000 inhabitants. . . . The chiefs of Kilimanjaro, who for centuries and until the establishment of European rule made ceaseless warfare on each other and who five years ago would scarcely meet, are now grouped in three Councils, each of which has a common treasury and is constituted as a court of appeal. . . . One of the most pleasing effects of our policy has been a revival of ancient ties, the effacement of old animosities, and the union of sections which by nature belong to the same stock, the creation of wider interests, and a new spirit of unity and co-operation. . . . As yet this development is in its infancy, but there is every prospect that closer union will spread until all of those groups which have a common custom and language will be united in some form of tribal amalgamation.[1]

That was written five years ago. The process of unification is steadily continuing, and, if nothing happens to check it or break it down, it ought, one would hope, to go on until in the distant future the bounds of local speech and usage are overpassed and all the peoples of the Territory are united for its common purposes under a single representative federal organ. There will be difficulties, of course. One of them, no doubt, will arise from the adjustment of relations between the Native Administrations and

[1] *Report to the Council of the League of Nations on the Administration of Tanganyika Territory for 1927*, p. 98.

the European and Asiatic colonists in the Territory: but at present the numbers of the latter are small—about 8000 Europeans and 30,000 Asiatics against 5,000,000 Africans —and relatively small, too, are the areas suitable for further European settlement in a country greater in size than Germany and the British Isles together. Other territories will have their own problems. In Kenya there is the same question, in a more acute form, of the immigrant communities. In Northern Rhodesia there is the 'copper belt'. In Nigeria the Native Administrations vary so much in character—the Northern Emirates, the Yoruba States, the village groups in the South-east, the 'sophisticated' Colony and other urban areas—that ultimate union will be a more complex matter than in relatively homogeneous Tanganyika, more like the problem of Indian federation. But everywhere, it may be hoped, in the long run—a very long run, perhaps—the new policy will fructify in the co-ordination of local administrations in a single territorial or quasi-national structure.

And what then? Until it has reached its final stage, of course, the development of Indirect Rule will have been not only supervised but controlled by the British Government, whether or not the precise forms of 'Crown Colony' administration are maintained. So only can Parliament fulfil its trust. But does not this final fulfilment imply its termination? Does it not mean the conversion of trusteeship into partnership? Before the War, I imagine, few, if any, people interested in Tropical Africa contemplated the day when it would govern itself. But the War forced us in every quarter of the Empire—in the Colonies as in the Commonwealth and in India—to look beyond present preoccupations to ultimate ends, and brought to the front of our minds ideas which, I think, were already implicit in our pre-War policies. In due course, for each quarter, those ideas were formulated. For the Commonwealth at the Imperial Conferences of 1917 and 1926; for India in the Declaration of August 20, 1917; and for Tropical Africa in the Peace Treaty itself. Article XXII of the Covenant of the League of Nations declares that the ex-German colonies, being 'inhabited by peoples not yet able to stand by themselves under the strenuous conditions of the modern world', are to be handed over as 'a sacred trust of civilization' to Mandatory Governments. Those words, no doubt, are familiar, but have you realized all that is in them? Do they not imply that these peoples some day *will* be able to stand by themselves and that it is the Mandatory's main duty to help them so to do? And is it not morally impossible for any Government to pursue a different aim in the similar territories it ruled before the War from that which it has undertaken to pursue in a territory now entrusted to it under mandate? The British Government, at any rate, has admitted the necessity. It declared in 1923 that 'the principle of trusteeship for the natives' was no less unassailable in Uganda or in Kenya than in Tanganyika.

So in the meaning and purpose of the Empire British Tropical Africa and in due time and method the rest of the dependent territories fall into place. They are beginning in their own native forms a similar process of assimilation or equalization as that now consummated in the nations of the Commonwealth and nearing its consummation in India. It will take different lines, no doubt, in different areas. In East Africa it may be complicated, though it need not be perverted, by the growth and character of non-African communities.   But over the vast field as a whole there seems to be no intrinsic reason why it should not go on smoothly to its end. A Dominion of Nigeria, for example? Why not? May we not hope that those black peoples of Africa, gradually learning to govern as well as to produce, may lessen the difference which the conditions of their past environment have created between their rate of progress and our own until, one far-off day, they too may be 'masters of their destiny', sharing on equal terms with other peoples in the life of the world, making their own African contribution to its common weal? If that day ever dawns, it ought surely to be another proud day for us. When the British record comes up for final judgement at the bar of history, 'the glories of our blood and state', the triumphs of our material wealth and strength, will not go far to win a favourable verdict. It will help us more if it can be pleaded that, whatever its origin and character in earlier days, our Imperialism came in the end to mean an honest attempt, both in our dealings as between the different branches of our own stock and in our treatment of the weaker peoples whom circumstances had put in our power, to fulfil the common need for freedom and unity on earth.

AFRICAN SNAP-SHOTS[1]

1. CONTRASTS IN KENYA

DAWN off Mombasa at the end of June—the monsoon blowing over the island—the Indian Ocean breaking in surf on its white beaches and low ruddy cliffs. At the south-east corner the sea, purple on the horizon and grading thence into deepest blue, sweeps over a coral reef in bands of incredibly pale green. Here the Kilindini inlet opens—a broad channel of surf-fringed blue between green island and green mainland. A creek winds southward through dense groves of coconut-palms. Follow it up round that next bend, and surely you will slip in a moment out of the world you know and be lost in the wild loneliness of Africa. To the new-comer, indeed, this first impression is almost absurdly romantic. The sea, the surf, the low early sunlight, the palms, the green plain behind rising into darker uplands—it is so like the Tropics of the explorers and the story-tellers. You think of Livingstone and Kirk landing seventy years ago at the mouth of the Zambezi.

But you have shut your eyes to one or two intrusive things that break the spell. There, on the mainland, lies the terraced garden, the broad 'loggia', the tiled roofs of an Arab aristocrat who might well have been ruling this slice of Africa in Asia's name if Europe had never come. And here, on the island, the low line of cliff is dotted with

[1] *The Times*, October 2, 3, 5, 1928; February 13, 14, 15, 1934.

European bungalows. Only Europe could have built that lighthouse gleaming white on the point. And those long strips of bright green along the cliff reveal themselves, as slowly you draw nearer, to be a golf course.

A little farther and the whole scene is changed. Kilindini Harbour, the finest on the coast, spreads out before you. H.M.S. *Effingham* is at anchor, and near her a couple of heavy British cargo boats and two or three more from foreign ports. Made fast alongside the stone-faced deep-water quay is the French 'packet', an up-to-date liner of some 12,000 tons. Along the quay stand eight electric cranes. Behind them is a long two-storeyed warehouse; boxes and bales lie heaped within its open doors; one heap is fringed with a tangle of creamy cotton, shining like silk. Is this mid-Africa? It seems more like Bombay.

Behind the warehouse and the Customs office are the terminal sidings of the Kenya-Uganda Railway—rows of big open trucks and metal goods waggons. There, or at Mombasa Station, a mile away, you can board the passenger train which leaves every afternoon for the interior. It is the most modern of trains, built on the pattern of the Continental *wagons-lits*, and you sit at ease in your *coupé* while the engine, driven at choice by coal or oil, draws you over the long steel bridge, beside the half-finished causeway which is to carry the trunk road to the mainland, and then steadily upwards through dense coconut groves with here and there a clearing and a cluster of native huts.

The sun sets about 6 o'clock; and it is at sunset, on your return journey, that you may see, if the weather favours you, one of the grandest sights in Africa. Away on the southern horizon, some fifty miles off, a vast faint-blue mountain mass towers up over 19,000 feet into the sky. Kilimanjaro! There are no other mountains near it, nor any lofty foot-hills. It stands alone and gigantic, scaling heaven. Its huge rounded snow-cap glows golden in the dying sunlight; now it is flushed with rose, and now the whole unearthly picture fades into the dusk. . . . When night has settled down and the stars are out you make your way to the restaurant car to eat a five-course dinner, as good as any meal you have had on any railway in the world. Ablaze with electric light, the long clattering train, Europe's vehicle, cleaves through the heart of the African darkness. It seems unbelievable that within living memory scarcely a single white man had set foot upon this land. Nowhere else in the world, nowhere else in history, have such changes come so fast.

By 9 o'clock next morning you have climbed above 5000 feet and are nearing Nairobi. On your left lies the great Masai Reserve, where those pastoral aristocrats, who hold their finely modelled heads so high that they seem always to be looking down on 'lesser breeds', graze their big herds of cattle. On your right is an area of white settlement. That rounded hill over there shelters a couple of prosperous farms which supply Nairobi from their scientific dairies with rich, pure milk that many English towns might envy. And now you are traversing a game reserve—open grass-country, sprinkled with thorn-bushes and low trees. A hundred yards off, unruffled by the train, stalks a file of four ostriches. A troop of zebra wheel round and watch. A herd of antelope graze gracefully, their single sentinel thrown out on guard, or, taking fright, speed, leaping high in the air, across the plain. A couple of warthogs go paddling along, tusks showing, tails in air. If there are some high trees about and you are lucky, you may see a giraffe. And then a few minutes later you are in Nairobi, a bustling young town, with its banks and shops and news-paper offices and motor-cars and clubs, where nearly 4000

Europeans and more than twice as many Asiatics are at work.

The Kenya highlands, eighty miles north of Nairobi, 8000 feet above sea-level. You arrived at dusk after twenty miles of skidding over earth roads turned to slime by rain; and you warmed yourself at the big wood fire, and were glad of several blankets on your bed. You are out now, before breakfast, for a first look at this new country. An unforgettable hour. It is brilliantly fine weather. A few fleecy clouds are sailing over the blue. The climbing sun is pleasantly warming. The air has an alpine sting in it. Behind the solid wooden 'home-made' farm-house the valley rises to a wooded *col*. Down it, just below you, hidden by orchard trees, runs a rippling stream with trout in it. You are in Devon. In front, a mile to your left, a long shoulder of grassy downland slopes to the plain. Flocks of sheep are grazing on it, cloud shadows chasing over it. You are in Sussex. A mile to your right the tree-clad face of the Aberdare mountains climbs steeply for 2000 feet or so. You are in Scotland. But look ahead due northward, and you are nowhere but in Africa.

Broadening to twenty miles or more, the upland plain sweeps into the far distance, one vast level stretch of green, broken only by the gleam of a lake half-way down it, walled on one side by the Aberdares, on the other by a curving range of blue and purple hills, closing in to rim the faint horizon forty miles away. The sense of space, the blended colours, the soft transparent morning light, the vast range of vision—you are lucky if, wherever you have wandered, you have seen a lovelier sight.

Here and there, at the foot of the Aberdares, or out on the plain, a wisp of smoke betrays the site of a settler's farm. But they are few as yet and several miles apart. And though the wheat-fields or the sheep on the down or the cattle at pasture or the nearer landscape may seem so English, you know at once that you are far from England. Why? Chiefly because you see no villages. Not one church spire rises from all those level leagues. There is no place within miles where men may congregate, no institute or hall or market or cinema, no rustic 'pub'. In rainy weather, moreover, it may be almost impossible to traverse, except on foot, the sodden miles which divide a settler and his wife from their nearest neighbours. Nor is there anything in that paradise of nature to remind them of their human associations—no visible symbols of the old traditions and ideals of their race, no monuments of its history, not even that one church spire. As pioneers have always been, they are very much alone—alone with themselves and with savage Africa.

The Equator, after all, is only thirty miles away. The plain is full of wild game — zebra and wildebeest and hartebeest. A jackal stops, a stone's-throw off, to watch your car go by. A few miles farther on, that trout-stream cuts a rocky cleft across the plain where a lioness and her cubs are lurking. And those wooded Aberdares are full of elephant and buffalo.

Alone with Africa. A stern, bare, testing life—a life for strong men who can fill their thought and time with the hard work of mastering virgin soil—no life at all for idlers. Africa, capricious as she is at times, respects and in the end rewards a worker. But she has no patience with the weakling or the fool, and anyone who dares to treat her merely as a romantic and secluded playground will learn, sooner or later, his terrible mistake.

The southward road from the highlands passes, as it nears Nairobi, through the Kikuyu Reserve. In some dis-

N

tricts this Reserve was interpenetrated by European settlement in its earlier days, so that here and there on one side
of the road the land is under native cultivation and on the
other side under European. The contrast is as marked as it
is inevitable. To the right, all the ground is cleared, well-
weeded—clean, close-grown crops ranged side by side—
long straight rows of coffee trees. To the left a few random
patches of maize with a banana tree or two lie scattered in
a waste of high grass and weeds. But at one point a progressive chief has looked across that road and learned.
Very little of his land is left to waste. The crops are relatively well ordered, the weeds few, the lines of bushes
straight. And the garden before his house or large-scale
hut is ablaze with flowers.

At Kabete, seven miles west of Nairobi, on rising ground
with a noble outlook over the Athi plain to the solitary
humped ridge of the Ngong Hills, stands the Government
Native Industrial Training Depot, a spacious little village
of bungalows, native dormitories, and workshops. Over
400 Africans are in training there, mostly sent from the
technical mission stations scattered about the colony. The
European staff consists of a principal, three technical
instructors, and nineteen artisan instructors. Walk from
group to group and shed to shed, and you will observe
each stage of apprenticeship to the building trade in
operation.

Out in the open a little class of new-comers, boys of
sixteen or so, are sitting with their slates before a black-
board acquiring (with remarkable speed) the requisite
elements of mathematics. Near by, some sixty pupil
carpenters are starting on the path which leads from
simple joinery to intricate cabinet-work, and they are
intensely interested in their job—so interested that they
give the intrusive visitors only a moment's glance. Pass on

to the 'shop' where cement blocks are being made for building; then to the glowing forge where the blacksmiths (true to their name for once) are beating out tools for the depots or welding metal trusses for the roof of the next big shed; then to the tailor's shop, where six young Africans in a row, pedalling away at Singer sewing-machines, are making all the shirts and 'shorts' required by their fellow-workers; and then to the dormitories, well aired and scrupulously clean and tidy. Visit, finally, one of the bungalows built for the European staff. Walls of neatly dressed cement blocks, a tiled roof, solid close-fitting doors of panelled wood, good tight window-frames, up-to-date brick hearths, plaster as smooth and firm as you could ever hope for in your house at home, paint well laid on, and all of it the work of Africans. That is no fantasy. It just is so.

By the end of this year the number of pupils will have risen to 600. It could be multiplied almost indefinitely if every application could be met. From every part of the country the demand of the Africans for this industrial education is insistent and increasing. And yesterday they were living a primitive life, unchanged for centuries, untouched by the outer world.

2. TANGANYIKA TERRITORY

Dar-es-Salaam is the centre of the Tanganyika Government but not of Tanganyika. It is a port of entry, belonging more to the sea than to the land; and, like Mombasa, it is an alien creation, half of the East, half of the West, not African. To reach the real centre, the real Africa, you must take train on the Central Railway, climb the rim of the highland belt, cross the Rift Valley, pass through leagues of dreary, dry, flat bush-country, until, over 500 miles from the sea and over 5000 feet above its level, you reach

Tabora, encircled by low stony hills and bowered in green mango trees. It is one of the nodal points in the old East African road system. The caravan routes from the three Great Lakes converge there; and in the palmy days of the Arab trade in slaves and ivory half a million carriers and captives, it is said, used to pass through Tabora every year. It is fitting that this ancient focus of African life should be linked with the memory of Africa's most single-minded servant. A mile or two outside the town may still be seen the half-ruined mud walls of the house where Livingstone lived in 1872.

One of the largest and most industrious of the Bantu tribes, the Wanyamwezi, dwells round about Tabora, which is therefore a centre of the new system of Native Administration, better described perhaps as the old system of tribal self-government, revivified, reformed, delimited, and supervised by the Mandatory Government. Under this system the domestic affairs of a tribe or a federation of kindred tribes are controlled by a Paramount Chief and a Council of Sub-Chiefs. Their administration is financed by a grant of one-quarter or more of the general hut and poll tax, together with the fees and fines from their own Native Courts. This revenue is paid into their Native Treasury and expended as they determine. Their annual budget is duly framed, discussed, and passed. To take for example the Kwimba Budget for 1928–9, from a revenue of 216,134 shillings, 74,340 are allocated to the salaries of the chiefs and headmen (smaller but safer incomes than the tribute and forced services they once obtained), 20,000 to the building of a school, 4600 to other educational charges, 12,000 to a campaign against the tsetse fly, 9000 to hospitals and dispensaries, 7680 to roads, 3000 to a demonstration seed farm, and so forth.

The writer was enabled to witness the judicial side of

this native self-government in operation. Close by Tabora
lives the Paramount Chief of the Wanyamwezi, Saidi bin
Fundikira, K.M.; and in the centre of his village stands
the Court-house—a spacious hall with a high-pitched
thick-thatched roof which slopes to within 10 feet of the
ground, supported on walls some 4 feet high. Between the
supports are open spaces letting in light and air. On this
occasion the body of the hall was pretty well filled by
the 'general public', while other tribesmen, lined up outside in the shade of the roof's edge, watched the proceed-
ings within over the low wall. At a table on a dais at the
end of the hall sat the seven judges. Chief Saidi himself
was not presiding, and sat apart. The president was one
of his sub-chiefs—a youngish man with a 'highbrow'
head and grave features which are perhaps to be found in
Africa more often than the casual traveller supposes. On
each side of him sat three very elderly elders. In front, on
the floor of the Court, stood plaintiff and defendant side
by side.

The case—one of those innumerable African disputes,
so puzzling to a European, about the financial side of
marriage—proceeded smoothly. There were no lawyers.
The litigants stated their claims themselves and were then
questioned by the Bench. Their witnesses were called and
likewise questioned. Then, after a brief discussion in
undertones, the six ancients delivered their opinions.
Finally the president gave judgement in the plaintiff's
favour. At once the whole audience, which all this time
had kept quite still and silent, clapped hands, including
the defendant. More or less a formality, no doubt; but
clearly the public believed that justice had been done. And
what is justice but the maintenance of rights upheld by
custom and the public will?

Near Tabora, also, is the Tanganyika Government

School for the sons of chiefs—for those, in fact, who will presently have to undertake the task of native administration. Its headmaster is an Englishman on the staff of the Education Department; and the school system, which is mainly his creation, is an adaptation of the English public school system. The boys are divided, in accordance with their origin, into tribes, roughly corresponding to 'houses', and each tribe elects a Mkuu and one or more Wakubwa, who roughly correspond to senior and junior prefects. These together form the school council, which is responsible for the maintenance of discipline outside the class-rooms.

Every offence against the school rules is tried by the council with the formalities of a Native Court. The charge, the defendant's case, the punishment are all briefly recorded in the council-book. The maximum punishments are three strokes of the cane, administered by the sergeant-major in the presence of an English master, and an hour a day of fatigue work for a week. Such rare cases as require severer treatment are dealt with by the headmaster, who only attends the council when he or it desires to discuss some question of school policy. Appeals from the council to the headmaster are permitted; but during the three years since the school began only one appeal has been made, and that one failed. Every judgement, moreover, must receive the headmaster's approval. He has only withheld it twice.

A rather formal, legalistic system of discipline? Yes; but a training in the formalities of judicial procedure and record is not the least useful element in the education of these boys. Some of them are already chiefs in their minority. All of them will one day be judges in their own Courts. One or two may be sitting before very long in that Court-house of Chief Saidi, a mile or so away. Nor is that the only 'practical' thing they learn. The welfare of the tribes they are to rule depends on agriculture and cattle farming. No less important, therefore, than the hours spent in the class-room—on speaking and writing English and (what is at least as valuable) on a better knowledge and use of their own Swahili, on the history and geography of their Territory and of the world in which it lies, on arithmetic, hygiene, nature study, singing—no less important are the hours spent on the school land, hoeing and ploughing and tending beasts. In more ways than one it is good that these young princelings should spend part of every day in picking ticks out of cattle.

New buildings are in course of construction—to form, when completed, a cloistered quadrangle. The fine long dining-hall is being temporarily used as a dormitory; and, since this new school is not in Buckingham or Dorset, the windows are blocked with hurdles to keep the lions out at night. At the time of the writer's visit the boys were away on their holidays. Some of them had taken friends from other tribes home with them. It is worth remembering that, not so very long ago, the chiefs of these tribes were almost certainly engaged in constant war with a view to capturing each other's sons and selling them to Arab slave-traders.

Akin to Tabora School and not far away from it is Kizigo School, which does for the sons of headmen what its neighbour does for the sons of chiefs. Its buildings are on a smaller scale—a circular open-sided Court-house with a conical thatched roof, flanked by plain square class-rooms and surrounded by trees and fields, and up the hill-side a cluster of 'beehive' huts, each containing at night a 'family' of six boys in charge of their elected 'father'. Discipline is kept and punishments recorded in the same way as at Tabora. Kizigo, in fact, is a smaller, simpler

Tabora. But there is this important difference: Kizigo is not the child of the Tanganyika Government. It was built and is maintained from the Treasury of Chief Saidi's Native Administration. It is controlled by his Council. Its headmaster is an African.

Luckily the boys at Kizigo were not on holiday, and the writer found them, about 100 strong, standing in two circles in the Court-house, big boys behind, small boys in front, very clean and spruce in white 'shorts' and shirts, and white teeth all a-grin. So standing, they sang their songs, in excellent time and tone and with quite obvious enjoyment. First 'Tanganyika', a patriotic song composed for them in Swahili, to the tune (and what could be more stirring?) of 'O my darling Clementine'. Next, the School Song, to the tune of 'Marching thro' Georgia'. Here is a translation of the first two verses:

> All we pupils are happy at our school.
> We live here together like one family.
> We will do our best to show that our
>   School is the best school of all.

> *Chorus—*
> The School! the School! Hurrah!
> The School! the School! Gladly we sing of it.
> We will try to prove by our efforts that our
>   School is the best school of all.

> Here we are taught the mysteries of wisdom.
> We are taught reverence for our King and
>   for Government.
> We are taught how we can help in building up
>   Our land that it may prosper.

It must be added that when, to finish off, they sang a Swahili version of 'God save the King', they were started in the wrong key, and some moments passed before the visitors realized that they ought to be on their feet.

Some months previously the Councillor in charge of the School had paid it a visit, on his own initiative, and unaccompanied by any white man. He was, as it happened, the same sub-chief who presided over that matrimonial case in the Native Court. And this, in translation, is the entry in the School Court-book recording his visit:

At a quarter to five came the School Councillor . . . and he asked the boys how they were and if they had any troubles. And the boys answered him, 'We are well and we have no troubles'. The School Councillor answered them, 'I am very glad to see you are all well and have no troubles at all. And I have something which I wish to say to you. And it is this. Listen, you boys! You were brought to this School by your parents. Do not think that you were brought here to learn reading and writing and arithmetic in order that you might do a clerk's work or a teacher's work. Far from it. You are the heirs of the land, and it is you who will take up the work of your parents. You have been brought here, moreover, that you may learn to be obedient, to stay at peace with men, to establish the land and behave well towards the Government. Further, you must show your ability and your obedience to the authority and the orders of your teachers—as when they tell you to cultivate the soil with a plough and oxen or with a hoe. This is the advice which I give you.' And he took his farewell and went his way.

So runs the record in the Court-book that lies on the table in that little round 'summer-house' in the heart of Africa. Ministers of Education, addressing Government schools in Europe, have probably, on occasion, made worse speeches.

3. The Spice Island of Zanzibar

Zanzibar belongs to the class of island colonies which have figured so often in the history of the British Empire—

'jumping-off places' for the penetration and exploitation of the adjacent mainland. But Zanzibar is not a British colony in fact or in form. Its colonists are not the few hundred Europeans who serve their time there in business or administration or mission-work, but the 40,000 Asiatics— the Arab landowners who conquered and occupied the island centuries ago and the Indian traders and bankers who followed on their heels. It is an Asiatic colony, an outpost of Asia overseas. Asia at Zanzibar impinges on Africa just as Europe impinges on Asia at Hong-Kong. And in form, likewise, Zanzibar is not a British colony, but an Arab Sultanate under British protection. Its sovereign is Seyyid Khalifa bin Harub. Its flag is its own, a plain scarlet ensign.

Zanzibar cannot be seen or comprehended by a new-comer from ground level. He is lost in a maze of deep narrow streets. His sense of direction is paralysed. If he catches, down some alley, a glimpse of blue water, he does not know whether it is the open sea or the harbour or the Creek which at high tide winds round the city and makes it almost an island. But let him climb the clock-tower of the Secretariat, and the whole of Zanzibar, its setting, its lineaments, its character are spread beneath him like a coloured map. Twenty miles to westward, if the air is dry, he will see the faint blue hills of Tanganyika. So near is Africa—and so far.

The life immediately below him is not African. The shipping in the harbour—a semicircle of brilliant blue hedged by a broken ring of coral-reefs and bright white sand-banks—belongs to other continents; a bunch of Arab dhows, two or three European steamships. And so with most of the city that spreads from the harbour-side. The greater part of it consists of flat-roofed white stone houses, with high thick walls, dark cool interiors, with windows opening on central courtyards and magnificent carved and metal-studded doors, all packed together and criss-crossed, like a jig-saw puzzle, by that maze of winding streets. Essentially in fact, an Arab town, cleaner in these days than most of its prototypes and healthier, but (since the Moslems of Zanzibar are mostly of the sterner sort) unadorned by the cluster of minarets which can sometimes save the dingiest of Oriental towns from unromantic ugliness.

At the seaward edge of this huddled, unplanned block of Asia, cutting it off from wind and water, is a belt of Europe, part of it old Arab houses modernized, part of it new-built, with bright red-tiled roofs. There is more order here and more space. Between the houses are plots and patches of green. The Union Jack, flying over one fine house and shady garden at the edge of the sea, betrays the home of the British Resident, First Minister and President of the Council. Not far beyond it the houses begin to peter out; then, among casuarina trees and mangoes, the tennis-courts and golf course; then the 'police lines'; and so at last the open country.

The city proper, then, is Asia with a European fringe. But it is hemmed in by Africa. Africans of a kind were there before ever the colonists came from oversea. Thousands more were stolen from the mainland to be the colonists' slaves. A mixed race now—called for convenience 'Swahili', the tongue they mostly speak—they still out-number the intruders by five to one. Their clusters of thatched mud-huts are dotted over the island and cling round the city itself like water displaced by a weight, lapping at its outskirts, creeping through them where they can. Close to the harbour front, where the Sultan's Palace and the Secretariat stand, a spit of sand juts out into the Creek. Except the usual village square in the middle, almost every foot of it above high-water mark is built on.

The huts are packed so close that sometimes the lanes between them are little more than a shoulder's-breadth wide. And beyond the Creek, among the encircling palms, along the water's edge, more huts and more are sprinkled, like the tents of a besieging army.

The northward exit from Zanzibar town has recently been improved and dignified by a new broad road which crosses and skirts the Creek and provides the townsfolk with a spacious and, whenever the sunset hour of exquisite light and colour coincides with high tide, a very lovely promenade. At the farther side of the Creek it plunges at once into a labyrinth of tropical vegetation—coconut palms, betel-nut palms, bananas, bread-fruit trees, mangoes, nutmegs, guavas, gums, and then, singly at first but soon in regiments, cloves and cloves and cloves. It was one of the greatest of Arab monarchs, Seyyid Said, who first brought the tree from Réunion in 1818. There are now between three and four millions of them growing on Zanzibar and its consort, Pemba. Those twin isles, in fact, have long usurped the historic fame of the Moluccas. They are the veritable 'Spice Islands' of to-day. Of every ten cloves served up in apple-pies or, less obviously, in chocolate creams, or utilized in strange derivatives of oil or scent —of every ten cloves in the world Zanzibar and Pemba produce nine.

Zanzibar is 54 miles in length by 24 at its broadest. Pemba is about half as big. And on both islands the belts of rich red soil which overlie the coral are thick with cloves. They are beautiful, well-proportioned, full-foliaged trees. Rank on rank, mile after mile, they cover the landscape like a dark-green sea undulating with the rise and fall of the ground. The construction of a road system in recent years—there are now nearly 120 miles of first-rate road in Zanzibar and nearly 60 miles in Pemba—has made

it easier than it once was for the visitor to traverse these
spice groves, and for their owners to market the fruit
thereof. There is no pleasanter way of spending those
sacred hours of the Tropics between tea-time and sunset
than to motor from Zanzibar along one of these roads—a
smooth white ribbon between dark walls of green.

After a few miles you should leave the car, and, shedding
some outer garments (for the 'cold weather' of July at
Zanzibar is nearly as hot as that of Bombay in December),
follow one of the narrow sandy paths that wind among the
trees. For a mile, perhaps, or more the cloves will encom-
pass you, and then you may strike a patch of poorer soil
and a jungle of palms and thorn-bushes and long coarse
grass; or you may emerge into a clearing and discover
there, half lost in creepers, the ruined walls of a *shamba*
where some Arab landowner, before the end of slavery
and the migration to the town, lived and lorded it with his
horses and his slaves. The path, if you choose the right
one, will lead finally to a little native village on the brink
of a long low ridge. The scent of spice is stronger here than
ever, for on the grass mats which cover the village square
innumerable cloves lie drying in the sun. But the air is
cooler; you have escaped from the languor of the groves:
and before you at last spreads the view you have earned in
dust and sweat. Westwards, across a plain of blended
greens, lies the sea, irradiated by the declining sun; and
southwards, in the distance, little white Zanzibar, wrapped
in a luminous haze, bewitched by the magic of space and
light, juts out, a pearl city, into the blue.

Sixty years ago Zanzibar was the curse of Africa. It was
the centre of the Arab slave trade. But it was at Zanzibar,
too, that the campaign against the Arab slave trade was
most effectively pursued and the essential steps taken
towards its final and complete extinction. To a student of

modern history, therefore, the two most interesting buildings in the island are, or ought to be, the house at Mbweni
and the cathedral at Zanzibar.

At Mbweni, four miles south of the city a small white
house stands on a promontory looking over a bay—an old
Arab house, square, solid, flat-roofed. Some fifty years ago
a great Scotsman made his home there whenever he could
escape from his work in Zanzibar. In the garden are still
growing many of the rare flowers and shrubs of East Africa
which were discovered by him and bear his name—some of
them so rare, it is said, that they can no longer be identified.
This keen botanist was also a doctor—a fellow-student, as
it happened, with Joseph Lister at Edinburgh—and his
life-work might well have been achieved in natural science
or in medicine but for the chance which took him as
Livingstone's lieutenant on the Zambezi Expedition of
1858–63. Those years determined John Kirk's career. He
had heard the call of Africa, which few who hear it can
ever again resist. Obeying it, he accepted in 1866 an official
appointment at Zanzibar; and there for twenty years he
laboured for the cause which Livingstone had preached—
the liberation of mid-Africa by British enterprise. The first
developments of British 'commerce and colonization' in
East Africa owed at least as much to Kirk as to any other
man of his day. But his greatest work was the part he
played in the abolition of the slave trade.

At Livingstone's side, in the region of the Lakes, he had
watched the far-flung tentacles of that foul monster pluck-
ing the life out of Africa. His office at Zanzibar was only a
few minutes' walk from the den to which it brought its
prey—the greatest slave-market of the age, where, huddled
in the dust and heat, those of the stolen youths and maidens
who had survived the rigours of the journey from their
distant homes awaited the prying eyes and probing fingers

of their purchasers. It must have been the crowning moment of Kirk's life when on a summer's day in 1873, mainly as the result of the trust and friendship which his personality had won from Sultan Burgash, the messengers came hot-foot from the Palace to clear the crowd from the slave-market and close its gates for ever.

On that same site the English cathedral now stands—its altar covering the place where once the slaves were flogged.

4. NORTHERN NIGERIA

The city of Kano is one of the focal points in Africa. Just over 700 miles inland by rail from Lagos and the Gulf of Guinea, it lies about midway across the northern fringe of Nigeria. Some 300 miles due west the Niger flows in from French Dahomey. Some 400 miles due east the Shari, approaching Lake Chad, marks the frontier of French Equatorial Africa. And this centre of Northern Nigeria is also the centre of Northern Africa. Draw a line a little north of west from Kano, and you reach the Atlantic near Bathurst, at 1700 miles. Follow the same northward slant to the east and you reach the Red Sea near Massawa, at 2000 miles. Go due north over the Sahara and you reach the Mediterranean near Tunis, at 1700 miles.

It was from these three quarters that, through long ages past, the streams of trade and culture and conquest converged on Nigeria—inundating the long, flat, fertile plains of the north, lapping round and climbing up the stony highlands between the Benue and the Niger, only checked at last by the belt of tropical forest, 200 miles or so in depth, barring the way to the sea. The conquerors came mainly from the north-east, pressing on stage by stage along the edge of the Sahara from the valley of the Nile. (The frontier of the Sudan is less than 500 miles from the frontier of Nigeria.) They overwhelmed the primitive aborigines, killing them, enslaving them, absorbing them into their social system and their blood, and so created a mingled race, mainly negroid, but with Berber and Arab elements, which now populates the greater part of 'Hausaland'. But all the earlier inhabitants were not thus submerged. Some of them took refuge in the rocky clefts of the highlands or in patches of dense 'bush'. Others fled southwards into the forest-belt, pushing their predecessors down towards the coast.

Commerce and civilization also came over the desert from the north. From Morocco to Timbuctoo and thence down the Niger, from Tunis across the mid-Sahara, from Tripoli or Benghazi or Assiut through Kanem or Wadai and round Lake Chad, ran the ancient caravan routes to Kano and its neighbours. And with trade in due course came Islam and its Arab culture, to Sokoto and Kano by the westward route from Morocco, to Bornu by the eastward route from Egypt and Arabia. Thus West Africa, like East, was penetrated and occupied by influences flowing out from Asia centuries before the first ships from Europe felt their way along the coast.

In the course of the sixteenth century this quasi-Oriental civilization reached its peak. Hausaland was at that time a dependency of the great Songhay Empire and shared something of its lustre. If Kano could not rival the Songhay capital, Timbuctoo, whose university matched its learning against that of Fez or Cairo, yet its name was widely known in the Moslem world, and Arab travellers and scholars came to visit it. But this golden age soon passed. At the close of the century Songhay was conquered by the Moors, and the old civilizing contact with the north was broken. For the next 250 years the whole Sudan from east to west was swept by anarchy and barbarism; and Hausaland, cut off from the outer world, starved of new blood and thought, lay stagnant and decaying. In race and culture it sank nearer to the negroid. In many respects, indeed, the primitive pagan life of the hills or the forest belt was cleaner and manlier than the degenerate Moslem life of Kano or Sokoto.

At the outset of the nineteenth century there was a transient revival. In 1802 Othman dan Fodio, scholar, statesman, and something of a saint, initiated the sort of militant puritanical reformation which Ibn Saud and his Wahabis have made familiar in the Arabia of our day. But it was not only a religious, it was also a political, almost a national, movement. For the chiefs whom Othman made the 'flag-bearers' of his holy war were members of his own Fulani race—that mysterious people who, centuries earlier, had wandered (it is thought) from Upper Egypt across to Senegal and thence percolated into Hausaland, a non-negroid people, slender, sharp-featured, with long, straight, black hair, and more highly gifted than the Hausas in the arts of organization and administration.

For a time the Fulani 'conquest' stimulated and purified Hausaland; but presently the Fulani of the towns—who, unlike their roaming cattle-driving kinsmen of the plains, had mingled their blood with darker strains—reverted to the licence and lethargy, the corruption and intrigue of earlier days, a disreputable oligarchy, living on the taxes they extorted from the Hausa peasantry and on the labour of the slaves they stole from 'pagan' districts. Slave-raiding, indeed, was the only occupation in which they maintained their old vigour and efficiency. When the hunting season opened they would mount their wiry little horses and sweep down on some wretched group of 'pagans' who had ventured too far from their fastnesses. It was a game that satisfied both the sporting and the acquisitive instincts.

For centuries past the rulers of Hausaland had thus obtained their living property, their labour-force, and the staple export of their country. Far back in the fifteenth century, when English yeomen were telling tales of Agincourt, the minstrels of Kano were honouring the warrior who had led its horsemen to easy victory and rapine among the southward tribes. 'Gatherer of the axes of the south', they sang; 'Gatherer of the youth of the south'.

From the sixteenth to the nineteenth century, the Europeans, who had sailed down to the Niger coastlands and were obtaining slaves there by the still easier method of buying them for muskets and strong drink, knew nothing of those Hausa States. Narrow as it was, the forest belt completely veiled them. And, when at last the veil was pierced, it was not from the Atlantic seaboard northwards that the first explorers made their way but by the old long route across the desert. Both Clapperton and Denham in 1822 and Barth in 1849 set out from Tripoli. European penetration from the south only began when Lagos became a British colony, and a Protectorate was established along the coast, and the Niger Company, armed with its charter, began to push its trade inland up the rivers. Even then British contact with the northern Emirates was casual and formal. The company's agents, seeking leave to trade on their southern borders, came and went. No stronger links were needed. Diplomatically speaking, Hausaland could be described as within the British 'sphere of influence'. And that sufficed till, fifty years ago, the French, expanding swiftly eastwards from their base on the Senegal, compelled us to confirm our claim by 'effective occupation'.

Then at last the forces of the modern world broke into that strange sanctuary where, walled in between desert and forest, a peculiar blend of African society, half of the

Negro South, half of the Moslem North, had preserved so long inviolate and so little changed except in its decay the life of the Middle Ages. It meant, of course, the end of those Fulani rulers' freedom—their freedom to misgovern and enslave—but for the mass of the people, for the stripped and famished peasantry of the plain, for the hunted 'pagans' in the hills, a new age of safety and order and fair play began when, on February 19, 1903, Lugard rode into Kano.

5. MOSLEM EMIRATES

Eastward from Kano the road runs straight across the North Nigerian plain, an endless plain, monotonously flat, closely cultivated with ground-nuts and cassava round every town and village, elsewhere an unbroken stretch of that familiar 'bushveld' which covers so much of mid-Africa from Lake Victoria to the Limpopo. One hundred and twenty miles from Kano lies Azare, seat of the Emir of Katagum. Like Kano the town is a maze of low rectangular one-storey pink mud huts—you can hardly call them houses—huddled close together, intersected by narrow winding alleyways. It would be difficult to find one's way about if some broader 'streets' had not been cut through the maze. The whole is encircled by a mud wall, once high enough, no doubt, to check a surprise attack, but now somewhat 'weathered' and unshapely.

At a roughly embattled gateway in this wall, just wide enough to take the car, a mounted trumpeter and four horsemen in brilliant scarlet robes are waiting to escort the Governor to the Emir's palace. Lining up, they canter abreast behind the car, flanked on either side (a pleasantly incongruous touch) by a similar scarlet 'outrider' pedalling hard head-down on a bicycle. The whole street is lined with people—men, women, and children—who sink to their knees and sometimes to their foreheads in the dust as the Governor passes. 'Zaki, Zaki!' they cry: 'Lion, Lion!' To which, at regular intervals, the outriders respond in high wailing unison, 'A-gaishe-ka': 'You are saluted'—presumably to spare the Governor the trouble of saying it himself.

Outside the palace wall the Emir makes obeisance to his 'overlord'. He bears himself well—a big, stalwart, coal-black African, dressed in flowing robes and swelling turban of coloured silk and satin, in his hand the silver-headed crown-capped staff of office. Beside him, bodies bent earthward, crouch the three members of his Council. At a little distance some twenty 'district heads' and 'village heads' have grouped themselves—the Emir's Civil Service.

The way to the audience-chamber lies through a series of dark twisting passages and little bare open courts. It is a gloomy room, some 20 feet square, ill-lighted by a few small high-set windows. Opposite the entrance stands, for ornament merely, a vast brass double-bedstead, complete with canopy, and against the wall a grandfather clock, striking the half-hours. There are one or two good rugs on the floor, but the only object of real value or beauty is a silver bowl.

Chairs are set for the Governor and his party, while the Emir sits or squats on a low dais, his robes billowing round him. The councillors are bidden enter, and crouch side by side, bodies bent, heads up, on the Emir's right. Then the discourse opens—the Governor speaking English, the Emir Hausa, the Resident interpreting—a discourse on the condition of the Emir's people, the effects of the depression, the low price of ground-nuts, the 'cuts' in salaries and in taxes, the prevalence of sleeping-sickness in some districts and the need for combating the tsetse fly, the operation of the Native Courts and the Emir's readiness to hear and redress all grievances, and so forth, till, at an hour's end, we emerge into brighter light and fresher air, and after ceremonious farewells drive off again through the kneeling crowds. 'Zaki, Zaki.' 'A-gaishe-ka.'

What, one wonders, do these black Moslems think of us white strangers who have broken so brusquely into their old, secluded, medieval life? Do they hate us and despise us for the 'kaffirs' that we are? There may be one or two sour fanatics who feel like that; but Africans, at any rate the Africans of the Tropics, are not bitter-minded; despite their age-long expiation of the curse of Ham, they seem somehow to have escaped the 'slave mentality'. Nor is Islam in Hausaland of the virile and passionate brand that may burst at any moment into flame. In blood and temper the Hausas are at least as near to the Niger creeks as to the sands of the Sahara. In the early years of the British occupation, it is true, there was an ugly little rising, led by an outlaw from over the French border; the call went out for war upon the 'infidels'; here and there a local fanatic assumed a mahdi's mantle. But the trouble was quickly scotched with the aid of the greater Emirs and especially the Emir of Sokoto, himself the 'Sarkin Musulmi', the acknowledged head of Islam in all the North except Bornu and the only natural leader of any true *jehad*. That was nearly thirty years ago; there has been little, if any, evidence of deep religious antagonism since; and some of those who know the North maintain that 'Mahdism' was never a real danger in Nigeria and only survives to-day in the files of the Secretariat.

But, apart from the difference of creed, do these Fulani, the conquerors of Hausaland a century back, rebel in their hearts against those who have conquered them? Now and again, no doubt, they feel the instinctive impatience of a subject race with alien rule; and maybe at times they remember with regret the days not so long past when they were free to fight and plunder their neighbours, to evade the law and buy injustice, to grind out the last pittance from their subject peasantry, and, above all else, to ride out any fine morning for a little brisk slave-hunting in the nearest 'pagan' preserve. But on the whole, surely, the balance is the other way. Old freedom is outweighed by new security. The British Resident and his subordinate officers may watch their ways so closely that any gross misgovernment is virtually impossible, may check so patiently the records of their courts that wealth or intrigue can rarely win a verdict, may supervise so carefully the assessment and collection of taxes that extortion is difficult and dangerous. But it is those same British who keep them on the seats of power—the Emir on his throne, the Ma'aji in his counting-house, the Hakim in his district, the Alkali on the bench. And, if their 'salaries' are no longer quite so personal or so elastic as they were, at least they are safe and regularly paid and not insubstantial. The Emir of Kano, for example, gets £6000 a year and allowances; a 'district-head' from £400 to £600; and in Kano the cost of living (for a peasant) is a penny a day. Nor, again, have the British robbed them of the outward symbols of their old estate. With their 'royal' pomp and panoply, their troops of armed retainers, the prostrate crowd at their palace gates, their trumpets and their drums, they still hold the stage: the Resident is hidden in the wings.

And, if the governing class thus acquiesce in British rule, there can be no question of the feelings of the governed. Not only on the poor Moslem villager, but also, and more so, on the pagan, the new order has bestowed a sense of safety in life, a security of property and person, that thirty years ago were unimaginable. Take the slave-hunting only: not a day dawned in the dry season when a pagan could be sure that he or his womenfolk or his children might not be raped away to slavery before the sun went down. And now even the dullest of them understand that the white men have completely stopped the big-scale slave-hunts and that the lesser slave-stealing and slave-trading by individuals are prohibited and punished by the law.

Not long ago, in a rural district of the North, two or three 'foreign' natives, having kidnapped or bought a few small children somewhere beyond the frontier, were leading them through the bush in the hope of a furtive and remunerative bargain in some wealthy town. They were observed by a couple of simple but sturdy peasants, who asked them whence they came. 'From a long way east', said the foreigners. 'And what are you doing with those little children?' 'They are our own children: we are taking them with us on our travels.' 'Nonsense', cried the peasants; 'nobody would take children of that age so far without their mothers.' And they haled them to the nearest native court, where in due course the culprits were convicted and sent to prison and the children freed. A pregnant commentary on thirty years of British rule.

6. Southwards of Lake Chad

It is two hours' drive from Azare to the border of the province of Bornu. In the days when Akbar reigned at Delhi and Drake was sailing round the world the dominion of Bornu stretched from Kano to Lake Chad and thence far north among the tribes of the Sahara. Nor in its decline was Bornu ever dominated or assimilated by its neighbours in Hausaland. Its people are still a slightly different people, with a little more of the Sudan in their blood, speaking Kanuri, not Hausa, linking their faith with Mecca by way of the Upper Nile, not through Morocco. The Shehu of Bornu yields no precedence to the Emir of Sokoto in the theocracy of Islam.

From the western border of the province the road runs straight as ever and across the same interminable plain, getting sandier and scrubbier now, on through the Shehu's capital at Yerwa (Maiduguri), across the mandated territories, till at 280 miles it reaches the French frontier proper at the river Shari. About eighty miles short of this and forty miles south of the shallow, shrinking margin of Lake Chad stands Dikwa, the most interesting of the Kanuri towns. Except for the brief period before the War, when, as the fortuitous outcome of the Anglo-Franco-German scramble in that secluded bit of Africa, it was torn from its natural and historical setting and included in the narrow northern tip of the German Cameroons, Dikwa was the eastward outpost of Bornu. And it was Dikwa that Rabeh the conqueror chose for his capital—fronting the land he had conquered, guarding the route by which he had come.

Rabeh was a foster-son of Zobeir Pasha, Gordon's famous or infamous friend and enemy, and like Zobeir he was a mighty hunter of slaves among the Nilotic tribes. When the Mahdi and the Khalifa made the Sudan too hot even for him he broke away westwards, and guided his followers, stage by stage, across the southern fringe of the Sahara. They numbered 500 horse and 1500 foot, equipped with rifles and breechloaders and two small cannon, a formidable little army; and when in 1893 Rabeh led them across the Shari to attack the far larger forces of Bornu, he was only once in danger—on the day the bold Kiari broke his line and took his camp—and then the better training of his men turned defeat into victory. Kiari dead, the Shehu a fugitive, all resistance at an end, Rabeh relaxed his rigorous discipline and let loose his savage veterans to murder and rape and rob and enslave the miserable people of Bornu.

The fort he built at Dikwa was the sign and seal of their subjugation—a solid square two-storeyed building, standing in a spacious compound where garrison and slaves were housed, surrounded by a stout 10-foot wall. There Rabeh lived for seven years, squeezing the country into starvation, draining away its manhood; and it might have been longer if, towards the end, he had not made his first and last great blunder. Resenting the intrusion of the white men who were now beginning to spy out the land along his borders and underestimating their power, he arrested a French scientific mission and hanged its leader, M. de Béhagle. That doomed him. For a time he fended off the punitive columns, but in 1900 he was killed in battle at Kusseri, and in 1901 his son and successor suffered the same fate at Gujba. The French were now, for a time, the masters of Bornu, and, installing as Shehu first Umar and then Bukar Garbai, they bade the latter, by way of reparation for the cost of their war with Rabeh, exact from his long-suffering people a fine of $80,000. Over $70,000 had actually been scraped together and paid over before the British intervened and established their claim to be the rightful 'protectors' of Bornu.

A generation has gone by. The emaciated country is beginning to recover. The days of Rabeh's tyranny and the brief French occupation are already half forgotten. Apart from Rabeh's Fort, there is only one material reminder—a statue of de Béhagle in the market-place at Dikwa. The simple inscription reads: *Pendu par Rabeh, il périt pour la liberté.* . . . The Union Jack flies over the Fort. The British District Officer sits in the high cool hall where Rabeh sat, beneath the inner window of the small square bedroom where Rabeh slept before he rode out to his last fight. He is the only white man in Dikwa, and for the four or five months of the rains communication with other white men is difficult and by motor quite impossible. At his back he has a handful of local native police. What does the ghost of Rabeh think of that?

From Dikwa our route bends southwards, and, after some forty miles, at last the monotony is broken. Away to the east, faintly blue at first, then deepening to the green of bush-clad slopes and the purple of morning shadows, stand the Mandara Mountains, rising to upwards of 4000 feet. Above the point where the road meets and skirts the foot-hills hundreds of natives are gathered to watch the cars go by. They stand in groups of three or four or a dozen on the big, smooth, round granite rocks that dot the slope, tall, lithe, naked or nearly so, silent, leaning on their long slender spears. Here and there a mountain stream runs babbling down between the rocks. The air is fresher, sweeter. The heat and languor of the sandy streets in Dikwa or Maiduguri seem suddenly far away. All that was Africa with an Asiatic tincture. This is Africa pure.

Saved by the hills and rocks from the raiding horsemen of the plain, these tribes have remained 'pagan', un-Moslemized, unenslaved, uncivilized. In a mean little village on the lower slopes—there are better, cleaner ones on the higher 'alps'—the huts are so small and their entrances so low that the occupant creeps out almost on all-fours like a dog from its kennel. Fiercely independent, scarcely less suspicious of new white 'trustees' than of old black tyrants, how can these primitives be known and befriended and helped to keep their footing when the tide of a new age rises slowly round them? The answer is hard to find in those hill-top villages where centuries have seen no change. But perhaps we may find it in the little 'pagan' school at the foot of the slope. It was opened about six years ago—and shunned. But now the suspicion and conservatism of the older generation are beginning to yield to patient persuasion; and when we visited the schoolhouse there were nearly thirty little 'day boys' sitting on the floor with their slates and struggling to write or to add up, or working with toes and fingers at miniature weaving-looms, or learning at a model forge how to weld the iron in which their hills abound. A slow business, no doubt; but already, surely, there is something hopeful in the contrast between the parent in his 'dog-kennel' and the child with his slate or loom.

South again, some sixty miles, to Mubi. The rest-house stands on the crest of a ridge, looking east across the river Yedseram and over wide green level country to the mountains, now rimming the horizon forty miles away, clothed in that lovely blue which, morning and evening, far-off hills in Africa always wear. The little flagstaff is flying the Union Jack, for the Governor is there. He is sitting now in front of the house. Facing him, on a mat, is the Lamido of Yola, who has come up from the south to pay his respects. He is a Fulani—we are no longer in Bornu—and one of purer stock than most, to judge by his delicate brownish complexion, his straight, fine nose, his slender hands. His eyes are fixed on the Governor, who is rounding off the hour's dialogue with a definition of good government, as the British understand it, in this backward African land. 'If in some far corner of the country a humble peasant suffers injustice from his village-head, and, though he be the poorest of the poor, can yet reach the ruler's ear and win redress, then that ruler is a good ruler. To give freedom to the poor and weak to live their own lives with their wives and children about them, to give them safety in their persons and their property, that is good government. . . .'

The sun is setting as the discourse ends. The flag flutters down. The file of blue-clad Nigerian police stand to attention. Their bugler sounds the Last Post. Over the plain those four long closing notes ring out—over the evening mist that is rising from the river and creeping low along the fields, away through space and silence to the blue hills, fast fading now into a starlit African night.

XI

IMPRESSIONS OF NIGERIA[1]

I

EUROPE took a long time to discover Nigeria. Its northern frontier is less than 2000 miles from the Mediterranean: Kano is no farther from Tunis than Edinburgh from Athens. Greek phalanx and Roman region penetrated deep into Asia: but in Africa, save where the Nile had cut a passage through it, the desert blocked their march; Rome got no farther south than Garama (Jerma) in the Fezzan, 400 miles from Tripoli. When Asia supplanted Europe along the Mediterranean coast, the southward road was still more firmly barred. The Arabs, less alien to the desert, made more use of the old caravan routes over the Sahara; right on to the eighteenth century a steady and lucrative trade in gold and slaves streamed up from the Western Sudan to Barbary; but, even when relations between Europe and the Moorish states were friendly, no European trader could join those caravans. From the fifteenth century onwards attempts were made to circumvent the barrier by sea, but without success. European penetration inland to the hidden gold-field was precluded first by the deadly climate of the forest belt and then by the growth of the slave trade, which, while it more than compensated sea-going Europe for the failure to appropriate the gold supply, made the exploration of the interior still more dangerous for white men owing to the opposition of the coastal chiefs who battened on the trade, and the

[1] April 1934.

213

hatred of the inland tribes who suffered from it. Those are the main reasons why the western section of mid-Africa was 'dark' so long. They explain the otherwise surprising fact that, whereas Alexander was on the Indus in 326 B.C., Marco Polo on the Yangtze in A.D. 1290, Vespucci on the Amazon in 1499, and Cartier on the St. Lawrence in 1535, it was not known in Europe even which way the Niger flowed till Mungo Park beheld it 'glittering to the morning sun and flowing to the eastward' near Segu in 1796, nor where it emerged into the sea till Richard Lander and his brother paddled down from Busa past the Benue to Brass in 1830.

Occupation, likewise, lagged behind discovery. After the abolition of the slave trade in 1807, hardy British traders maintained a precarious footing on the 'Oil Rivers', slowly building up a 'legitimate' trade in palm-oil instead of negroes; but it was only the prevention of slave-smuggling that attracted the attention of British Governments or of the public to the coast; that object alone determined the annexation of Lagos in 1860; and, in 1865, when slave-smuggling oversea was at last at an end, the House of Commons adopted the report of a Committee which declared:

That all further extension of territory or assumption of government or new treaties offering any protection to native tribes would be inexpedient and that the object of our policy should be to encourage in the natives the exercise of those qualities which may render it possible for us more and more to transfer to them the administration of all the governments with a view to our ultimate withdrawal from all, except, probably, Sierra Leone.

That such aspirations were not realized was mainly due to the international factor. To abandon British 'spheres of influence' to self-government was one thing; to abandon them to the rule of a rival European Power was another. British merchants were already confronted with French competition on the Niger; and it was only by buying out French companies and making a new series of 'protective' treaties with native chiefs that Britain was enabled to establish a prior claim to Southern Nigeria at the Berlin Conference of 1885. Again, in the next stage of the 'scramble', it was only Lugard's conquest and the annexation in 1901 that prevented French expansion over the edges of the North Nigerian plain.

Nigeria, then, is one of the latest arrivals in the British Empire. Lagos has been in it for 74 years, Rangoon 110, Singapore 115, Calcutta 248. Nigeria has been in it 33 years, Burma 48, Ceylon 138, Bengal 177, Jamaica 279. And, arriving so late, Nigeria is still relatively ill known. Little has been written about it, and, despite a brief vogue for Mary Kingsley, that little has not been much read. Personal visits to the country, except for those with duty or business there, have not been frequent. If Lagos lay on the direct sea-route to Cape Town, it would have been otherwise: but it is tucked too far under the great westward bulge of Africa, away from the traveller's 'beaten track', leading him nowhere. And by air the use of the straight route from England is obstructed by the vast intervening block of French territory. You can fly from London to Kenya by a regular weekly public service in five days. You cannot fly to Nigeria at all except by private arrangement. And yet this little-known and little-visited section of the Empire is by no means one of the least important. Its area is 372,674 square miles, the largest territory in the British Tropics. Its population is twenty millions, the next largest in the Empire (at a wide remove) to that of India, as large as that of all the Dominions together. The total value of its trade in 1930 was nearly £28 million, only exceeded in the

Colonial field by Malaya and Ceylon. Clearly Nigeria invites more interest than it has yet received from students of the Empire.

2

The following 'impressions'—they cannot claim to be more—are the fruit of a recent visit to Nigeria, comprising a stay of a week or so at Lagos and some 3000 miles of travel in the interior.

The variety of the country is one of the things that must first strike a stranger. The greatness of the river which has named it, the traditions of the old oil trade, the narratives of the pursuit of slave-smugglers in creeks and lagoons, might suggest that Nigeria is little else than a gigantic tangle of sluggish waterways and mangrove swamps, hemmed in by the 'primeval forest'. That is a passable description of the spreading delta system which covers most of the south-east. But it must not be supposed that this delta country is an unpopulated wilderness (very much the contrary; Owerri and Calabar provinces, for example, contain over 140 people to the square mile), nor that all Nigeria is like that! Westwards of Benin there are scarcely any rivers, the coastland has been widely cleared, and where the forest begins it is no black, impenetrable wall; some of it is not high-timbered forest at all, but thick 'bush' rather, broken by patches of cultivation and harbouring countless little villages. About 100 miles inland, moreover, beyond the latitude of the Benue-Niger junction, the whole character of the country changes. The Bauchi plateau, rising at its centre about Jos and the tin deposits to 4000 feet, spreads east and west to either frontier and north about 150 miles at an average height of over 1500 feet. It is dry there for half the year, and relatively cold in winter. The 'forest', needing perennial damp and warmth, is gone.

Parts of the plateau are rolling 'bush-veld'. Parts are studded with those smooth queer-shaped masses of granite so familiar elsewhere in Africa. The scenery is varied and attractive; some of the distant views magnificent. And then again the prospect changes. The plateau sinks to a vast level plain, only 1000 feet or less above sea-level, stretching infinitely northwards, getting sandier and barer, till it merges, away beyond the frontier, into the Sahara. Most of it is open parkland or thin 'bush'; but every town and village is encircled, sometimes for long distances, by stretches of close cultivation, especially of the universal ground-nut. The plain, indeed, is by no means barren. Its soil is rich, and it is watered by rivers which are filled to overflowing in the five months of the 'rains'. It is a sort of vast oasis between the forest and the desert, and on it were born and fattened the famous and wealthy Hausa States.

This physical variety has, of course, its human counterpart. In race the whole population, apart from European and Syrian immigrants, is negro or negroid. Invasion from the north, sometimes in waves, all the time in trickles, has brought into Hausaland a strain of alien blood—much of it Berber in origin, a little of it Arab, but only a strain. The earlier races of the plain and the plateau have prevailed. The Hausa is dominantly negroid. Even the Fulani —that peculiar fine-nosed, straight-haired, brown-faced people—have only kept pure in their roaming, standoffish, pastoral communities. The Fulani of the towns, including the great governing class, are now mostly black. And in the forest, of course, and all along the coast the people—allowing again for immigrants from other maritime territories up to Sierra Leone and for the descendants of freed slaves whose homes may have been anywhere— are the nearest approach to the aboriginal Nigerian. Even here, however, there is infinite variety, due, no doubt, to

P

unceasing movement and warfare and slave-raiding and a steady pressure of new-comers from north and east. If the Yoruba-speaking people of the west from Badagri to Benin are roughly akin, they are quite distinct from the Ibos and Ibibios and Efiks of the east; and in and around the delta country there are a multitude of smaller groups each with its own language and way of living.

Socially there are similar broad differences. The northern invaders introduced a civilization which, like that of Egypt and the Mediterranean littoral whence it came, has been for centuries past a Moslem civilization. There is a tradition, therefore, in Hausaland of organized large-scale administration, of the qualified 'Oriental' autocracy of an emir and his councillors, of civilized commercial and financial dealings, of Arab learning, of Islamic law. But in patches of 'bush' on the plain, and still more in the rocky fastnesses of the plateau, groups of pure Negroes evaded enslavement or assimilation, and still maintain an independent, primitive, 'animist' life. In Northern Nigeria there are no less than 3,750,000 of these 'pagans' (as they are ill called, whatever the origin of the name may be) in a population of 11,500,000. And except westwards, as in Ilorin, Islam and its culture have failed, like other things, to cross the line of the rivers and penetrate the forest. South of the forest, on the other hand, all along the coast and up the rivers, the people have felt the full shock of European contact. Lagos, with its European and African inhabitants, its banks and shops and public buildings, its crowded 'Marina', its quays and warehouses and offices, its spreading suburbs, is the leading British 'emporium' in Tropical Africa—the nearest, if distant, colleague of Calcutta or Bombay. The effect is the same, on a smaller scale, at other coastal or river-mouth towns like Port Harcourt or Calabar, or up the Niger as far as the steamboats go.

Onitsha, for example, has its water-front and shops and so forth, and its sophisticated Africans in European costume including sun-helmets, but mingled here with 'raw' natives from the neighbouring 'bush' in loin-cloths only, such as are rarely to be seen at Lagos. Not only in the towns, but throughout the coast strip and the delta country, Christianity is widespread: at a rough-and-ready estimate there are over 800,000 Christians in this area. Every townlet or substantial village has a church, and too often the absurdity of two; one wonders, indeed, if missionary propaganda has been as intensive anywhere else in the world outside Polynesia. And since above the elementary 'vernacular' stage the mission schools teach the 'three R's' and English, the more or less literate, more or less English-speaking, African is ubiquitous. So European culture and Christianity in the south stand over against quasi-Asiatic culture and Islam in the north, and between them, in the denser forest, on the rocky plateau, in the hills above the Benue, along the sides of the mountain ranges that flank the country on the east, are the 'pagans'—7,500,000 of them all told, with a culture and religion wholly African.

The political structure of the country is no less varied. Everywhere, of course, the Government of Nigeria, as the instrument of Parliament, is supreme, but it operates differently in different areas. For the 'Colony', consisting of Lagos and its neighbourhood, and the Southern Provinces of the 'Protectorate', the Governor is advised by the usual Executive and Legislative Councils, the former consisting solely of officials, the latter of twenty-six officials, thirteen nominated members (seven Europeans and six Africans), and four elected members (all Africans), three for Lagos and one for Calabar. The Governor legislates for the Northern Provinces by ordinance without a Council. Each province is administered by a Resident and district officers under his charge. Between them and the Government at Lagos are interposed a Lieutenant-Governor and Secretariat for the Southern Provinces at Enugu, and a Chief Commissioner (recently reduced from the status of lieutenant-governor) and Secretariat for the Northern Provinces at Kaduna — a duplication of administrative machinery which exists nowhere else in British Africa nor in any Indian province.

Established, advised, and controlled by this 'Crown Colony' Government are the Native Administrations, the initiation of which by Lugard thirty years ago entitles Nigeria to be regarded as the birthplace of 'indirect rule' in Tropical Africa. There are over 900 of them—175 in the north, 728 (including 'subordinate' units) in the south; and the purpose of them all is the same—to maintain and develop a form of local government which accords with the traditions and aptitudes of the people and to use it as a training for self-government. In each of them the administration is in African hands, guided and at need directed by British officials; in each there is a native court or courts, and, except in the units not yet fully organized in the south-east, in each there is a native treasury. They are all alike, too, in their subordination to the Nigerian Government: their authority is delegated under ordinance and commission of appointment; their law-making power is confined to bye-laws; they may not raise troops; they levy no taxes; their revenue consists mainly of a fraction, usually about 50 per cent, of the taxes laid by the Government, and their estimates for the spending of it, though initiative and responsibility are encouraged as far as possible, are subject to the Government's confirmation. But otherwise there is more diversity between them than there is between the Indian States. In the north, Kano Emirate has a population of over two millions, and its annual revenue

exceeds £200,000, while there are several minor Native
Administrations with populations of only 15,000 or so and
revenues of £1000. In the south, the Yoruba State of
Abeokuta has a population of over 430,000 and a revenue
of £50,000, while some of the newly formed administrations in the Ibo country are 'village groups' of 5000 or
6000 people with revenues proportionately small. Still
more striking are the differences in political structure. The
northern Emirates are Moslem autocracies qualified by
the Emir's need of the advice and support of the mainly
Fulani aristocracy or governing class, from which he
selects his Council. The Yoruba States in the south, being
mainly peopled by Christians or 'pagans', are at least as
different from the Emirates as a Hindu State in India from
a Moslem; but they are likewise governed by autocrats
and councils, though the latter are now becoming representative of more than one class and the former are obliged
to take account of the spread from the coast of education
and English ideas. In the south-east, on the other hand,
there are no large aggregations and no autocracy. The
tribes are broken up into multitudinous separate self-
regarding fragments whose social or political unity is often
limited to a 'clan' of a few thousand people or even to a
smaller 'village group'. Priests of a sort they have always
had, but only for priestly functions, and they know nothing
of kings. The Government's attempt, therefore, to set up
indirect rule on the northern model by selecting the most
suitable 'elder' and making him a 'warrant chief' was not
an unqualified success, and a patient enquiry has been in
progress now for some years past with a view to re-estab-
lishing those Native Administrations in a more real form
on the basis of an authority which the people recognize as
traditional and desire to obey. It appears that this authority
is generally a council, consisting primarily of the elders

of a village or an 'extended family' or a clan, combining executive and judicial functions, with a 'chairman' or spokesman at its head, but no chief. This system, seemingly, is not an oligarchy of old men, a gerontocracy: indeed it is markedly democratic or even egalitarian; meetings of council are attended by all and sundry, and young men of personality take an effective part in the discussions. On the extent to which conservative, 'animist' age can accord with educated, often Christian youth the success of this experiment will mainly depend. If in course of time it does succeed, it may help to make political and social progress easier in the south than in the north, where, except in the 'pagan preserves', the old African polity has been long eliminated by alien conquest and Islam.

So diversified is Nigeria, its land, its people, its civilization—more diversified than any other British territory in Africa. The Gold Coast is most like it, but not so complex. In Kenya the European element is a bigger and more complicating factor, but otherwise even Kenya and certainly Uganda or Tanganyika, despite their Arabs and Indians, seem almost homogeneous beside Nigeria.

3

One aspect of this diversity is dominant. The difference between north and south, the joint result of geography and history, overrides all others. How far does it break the unity of the Nigerian State and endanger its smooth progress in the future?

Not long ago there was a school of thought which seemed bent on widening the gulf. The north, it claimed, is part of the Sudan. Its association with the south is quite artificial and very recent, the result of British occupation. While the south is the home of negro barbarism, civilization has been planted in the north for a thousand years. True, it is Moslem civilization, but it has merits. The great and ancient city of Kano, with its traditions not only of commercial wealth but of high learning, is one of the wonders of Africa. The administrative system, in its articulation and regularity and in the efficiency of its personnel, is as immeasurably superior to the crude organization of a tribe or a clan as Islamic law to primitive native custom. And its monarchy, its ordered feudal society—are not these more suited to backward Africa than the illusion of democracy and the mimicry of parliamentary government for which the half-educated, half-Europeanized *intelligentsia* on the coast are hankering? Ought we not to aim at keeping this southern ferment at a distance, at strengthening the monarchical principle, at maintaining the Emirs' prestige and gradually enhancing their power, till they attain something like the status of the Indian Princes, leagued together in a separate, stable, independent Hausaland?

Such ideas have a natural attraction for some Englishmen. They correspond to the tendency in India to regard Islam as more congenial than Hinduism, to extol the Sikh at the expense of the Bengali, to tolerate the proud aloofness of an old-fashioned, ignorant country magnate more easily than the claim to equality asserted by a highly educated lawyer of the town. But that attitude in Nigeria was never dominant and is now fast disappearing. Naturally so; for it is rooted in fallacies. The north is not radically distinct. Call its people Sudanese if you will, but they are Negroes, none the less, with an Hamitic strain; theirs is the Niger, not the Nile. And what they have gained from farther north can be exaggerated. The visitor to Kano who expects to find another Fez or Cairo hidden in the heart of Africa will be as disappointed as Caillié was a century ago when he discovered Timbuctoo to be 'nothing but a mass of ill-looking houses built of earth'. The Emirates can no more compare with the Indian States than their squat mud buildings with the marble palaces and shrines of Rajputana, or their picturesque untidy mobs of horsemen with the smart 'imperial' cavalry of an Indian Prince. Their civilization is a survival from the past. The channels that once fed it from living springs of culture in the Mediterranean world have long been cut. Its only hope of reinvigoration now lies in European influences spreading from the south. Its administrative system, similarly, was corrupt and disordered when the British came. Its efficiency to-day is a tribute to the wisdom with which Lugard converted it to better uses and the patience with which his disciples in the Residencies have followed the course he set. Its future success depends, not on trying to protect its medievalism from new ideas—an impossible task in any case, for 'progress' emanates, so to speak, from every train from Lagos that steams into Kano—but on trying to adapt it gradually to modern needs. Nor, lastly, is a separate Hausaland conceivable. One can imagine it united with French West Africa, but not standing by itself. The railway alone binds North and South Nigeria together. Never again will the economic life of Hausaland, any more than its cultural life, be fed by the long caravan routes over the Sahara: till airships are as safe and economical as liners, it can only be fed from the sea. Nor in politics can anything be gained by separation. For all concerned, including the Emirs, it would surely be unfortunate to saddle Nigeria with the difficulties created in India by the peculiar status of the Princes. On all counts more unity, not less, is what Nigeria needs.

4

How does Nigeria live? What is the economic situation? The first impression is what one would expect. Like all tropical Africa, Nigeria is an agricultural country. There are large deposits of tin on the Bauchi plateau. Gold is found in several Northern Provinces, mostly alluvial. Coal is mined by the Government at Enugu, mainly for its railways. Iron, lead, lignite, mica and other minerals occur, but have scarcely yet been touched except by the natives in their locality. Trade in hides and skins is growing in the north. Every northern village has its handicrafts— spinning and weaving cotton, for example; there are a few old local industries catering for more than local needs, such as the brasswork at Calabar or Benin or the cloth-weaving and dyeing at Kano; and a soap factory at Apapa and a cigarette factory at Oshogbo have been established by British enterprise. But that is all: there is no sign as yet of the growth of large-scale industry as in India. The mass of economic activity is still on the land. The Nigerians are a nation of cultivators, working not on big estates or plantations but on their own small holdings.

Before the British occupation this cultivation, apart from the old palm-oil trade on the coast, was almost wholly for subsistence. The Nigerian grew his own little crop for food and his own cotton for clothing. If wars and slave-raids had permitted production in the interior for export, lack of transport facilities would have forbidden it. But when the British not only enforced peace but also built the long railway from the coast to Kano and motor roads to feed it, the economic life of Nigeria was swept with a rush into the stream of world trade. Ground-nuts and cotton were still grown for local consumption, but now in fast-increasing bulk for export also, and, side by side with a great expansion in the old palm-oil trade, there were new developments in palm-kernels and cocoa for export only. Between 1909 and 1929 the total value of Nigerian exports rose from about £4 million to nearly £18 million; and prices rose concurrently. By 1924–5 ground-nuts, for example, at Kano had reached £13 a ton, palm oil at Lagos £26, palm-kernels £15. Part of this new wealth was absorbed, of course, by merchants and shippers and other 'middle-men', but much of it reached the producers' pockets, and much of that came out again for the purchase of the manufactured goods provided by the outer world. So imports likewise increased. In 1908 their total value was £4,250,000, in 1928 £15,500,000.

Startling figures for so short a period of development; and no wonder they inspired dreams of an almost indefinite growth in the producing and consuming power of Nigeria. The potential competition of vegetable oils from elsewhere, notably Sumatra, seemed, indeed, the only cloud on a golden horizon when in 1930, two years or so later than Europe, Nigeria felt the impact of the world depression.

Its effects have been devastating. The value of exports dropped to £9,500,000 in 1932 and £9,025,000 in 1933, and the value of imports to £7,250,000 and £6,500,000. Prices have fallen headlong. Ground-nuts at Kano are now worth £2 a ton, palm oil at Lagos £6:10s. The output of tin was cut down to $33\frac{1}{3}$ per cent and then 40 per cent of what it had been in 1929, and it is still restricted to 50 per cent. The coal-field is partly closed. The number of wage-earners on mines is less than half what it was. But it is needless to multiply examples. The 'slump' is universal, and it has hit consumption, of course, as much as production. Most of those pockets are empty now, and 'Manchester goods' are harder to sell. If Nigerians of the poorer class could not buy cheap Russian or Japanese singlets and shoes and so forth, they could not buy such 'luxuries' at all.

Revenue has fallen automatically with the fall of trade. Half of it is derived from customs, and the direct taxation, which ranges roughly from 4s. to 8s. for each adult male, is increasingly difficult to collect and has been widely reduced. From 1925 to 1930, one year excepted, the revenue was well above £8,000,000. In 1931–2 it was £6,700,000, in 1932–3 £4,900,000, in 1933–4 £4,700,000. The yield of customs fell from £3,400,000 in 1928–9 to £2,400,000 in 1932–3. A profit on the railway of over £900,000 in 1928–9 became a loss last year of over £300,000, mainly owing to lack of freight. Drastic retrenchment has been enforced in every department, including a levy on officials' salaries; expenditure, which stood at £8,000,000 in 1931–2, was reduced to £4,900,000 in 1932–3, and £4,800,000 in 1933–4. But even that last figure, low as it was by comparison with the 'boom' years, meant a deficit of £147,000 on the year. Happily, there is a reserve fund of over £2,000,000; but, if there is no marked improvement in trade in the next few years, Nigeria, so recently regarded as a self-supporting colony *par excellence*, may have to beg for help from British taxpayers.

Poverty in Nigeria does not mean starvation. If world trade collapsed in chaos, the great mass of the Nigerian peasantry could go on living on their own produce as they did before the British occupation. But poverty does mean a lower yield of taxation, and consequently a diminution of those expensive social services—health, education, and the rest—on which the Nigerian's progress depends. In Nigeria, however, as elsewhere, nobody despairs. The depression will pass, they say. Prosperity of a sort will be recovered. But the most sanguine optimist realizes that the future can never quite equal the past. The golden dream has faded out. Unlimited wealth is not to be got from unlimited production of vegetable oils. There are limits to the world market, and there is not only the old competition in the Dutch East Indies and elsewhere, but whale oil has now been made sufficiently edible to compete, and is being largely imported into Britain under the recent trade agreement with Norway instead of Nigerian palm oil. There is room, no doubt, for improvement in the latter's quality. Produce inspection has already done much to standardize it, and farmers are now to be encouraged to better their palm cultivation by a rebate on the export duty on the output of approved plantations. Provision is to be made, moreover, from the reserve funds of native treasuries in the south to foster the co-operative system for which Mr. C. F. Strickland has just been conducting one of his crusades. In the north, similarly, reserve funds are being used to promote 'mixed farming' and to extend the cultivation of cotton. Such efforts as these may go far to save the Nigerian peasant from the worst effects of the fall in world prices; but the main need seems to be to broaden the basis of Nigerian economy by the development of new products, and it is a hopeful sign that a full enquiry is now being made into the commercial possibilities of the forests.

In the background of the economic scene there is one new feature no visitor to Nigeria can miss. The European firms, mostly British and mostly connected with Liverpool, have long combined the businesses of exporting and importing, of buying the Nigerians' produce and selling them manufactured goods. That is an old-standing custom; the novelty is the combination of nearly all these firms in one big concern. Apart from the one or two surviving

British units, a few foreign houses, and the African and Syrian merchants, the whole trade of the country seems to be in process of being monopolized by the United Africa Company. Will it attain the same kind of position in Nigeria as the United Fruit Company in Jamaica?

5

The economic development of Nigeria is one of the most striking results of the British occupation. Of its other results no full analysis, of course, can be attempted here, but two points may be stressed. The first is obvious enough —the familiar *pax Britannica*. But it is not so much the establishment of civilized government, of the mechanism of law and order that impresses one, as the creation in so short a time of the spirit or atmosphere of law and order. Except in the 'Colony' of Lagos and its neighbourhood, British rule is of very recent date. The Crown did not 'take over' from the Niger Company till 1900. Northern Nigeria was not effectively occupied till 1903. Most of the south-east was brought under control only some ten years later. Yet now peace is maintained unbroken from one end of the country to the other. Everyone was startled by the women's riots in Owerri and Calabar in 1929 because they were so unexpected, and they were due to peculiar circumstances which need not have arisen. And this tranquillity is not the product of intimidation. The Nigerians are not sullenly submitting to the power of rifles and machine-guns. There are no British 'regulars' in the country. The West African Frontier Force, of which only the commissioned officers and colour-sergeants are British, is about 3000 strong. The Nigerian Police Force is not much larger. Local order is mainly in the hands of constables locally enlisted by the native administrations.

Clearly, then, the quiescence of the people must be mainly due to their own recognition of the rule of law. Less than a generation ago a great part of the country away from the coast was constantly distracted by fighting and bloodshed between tribe and tribe or village and village. In the south-east, ' head-hunting ' and ' ritual murder ' were endemic. Slave-raiding on a big scale was the regular pastime of the governing class in the north. The sale or abduction of women and children for the slave trade was equally common in the south. But now these things only happen as crimes happen in other countries. A few cases of child-selling, for example, have been recently occasioned by the economic depression. In general it is understood that such practices, habitual though they were in the memory of all middle-aged Nigerians, are now forbidden and ought and can be punished by due forms of law. One illustration out of many may be cited. Not long ago, in the south-east, three girls of fourteen to sixteen years were collecting fire-wood in the 'bush' when they observed four strange men resting on the ground with two little boys, one of whom was tied up in a basket. They tiptoed away and reported what they had seen in their village. Four of the villagers went to investigate. Taken by surprise, the strangers tried first to bluster it out, and then, when they found it useless to deny that they were slave-trading, to buy the villagers' silence. But the villagers were not to be bribed: the culprits were taken before the District Officer, and were finally sentenced to heavy terms of imprisonment on the evidence of two of the girls and two simple peasant-farmers. Surely it is remarkable that understanding and acceptance of the rule of law should have become so widely and deeply rooted in so short a time.

The second point is the spread of education. In Southern Nigeria there was nothing that could be described as

formal education before the British came. The missions
were the first to introduce it; it was not till 1882, forty years
after the opening of the first mission school at Badagri,
that the Government established a Board of Education;
and it was not till 1903, when the Board was replaced
by a technical Education Department for the Southern
Provinces, that the Government took any substantial part
in education beyond supervising and meagrely assisting
missionary effort. In the north, in the old days, there were
no missions, but education of a sort was provided for
Moslems (though not, of course, for 'pagans') in the
Islamic schools, which taught boys, but not girls, the religious, social, and ethical doctrines of the Koran. The
number of these 'Koran schools' at the time of the British
occupation was roughly estimated at 20,000 and of pupils
at 250,000. There was no provision for further education
except that the few who had mastered Arabic at school
could acquire a training in law by attendance at the Alkalis'
courts. After the British occupation missions were encouraged to take the field in the 'pagan' areas, but not at first
in the Emirates for fear of wounding Moslem suscepti-
bilities and of sapping confidence in our promise of non-
interference in religion. The Government, however, was
able to take a hand in Moslem education by working
through the Native Administrations, and in 1910 an Education Department for the Northern Provinces was created.
In 1929 the two departments were amalgamated under a
single director with his headquarters at Lagos. Its expenditure for 1933 was estimated at nearly £250,000. In 1903
the Government spent only £2500 on education in all
Nigeria. So great has been the growth of its educational
activity in thirty years.

Of what has this activity consisted? In the Southern
Provinces, first, new institutions have been created,

especially for higher education. Secondly, larger grants have been made to the missionary bodies, who still provide the great majority of the schools. Thirdly, all non-Government schools, with the full co-operation of the missions, have been subjected to official supervision and control. Fourthly, the whole complex of institutions has been or is being co-ordinated in a carefully articulated but not too inelastic scheme of education. First come the elementary schools—2936 of them, with 173,499 pupils, of whom one-fifth are girls. Next, the middle schools, which aim at a six years' course for pupils between thirteen and nineteen: of these there are nineteen for boys and four for girls, with 986 and 88 pupils respectively. From these middle schools paths diverge to the centres or colleges for training primary or secondary teachers, of which there are seventeen with 722 male and 75 female pupils, or to apprenticeship in the Medical, Survey, Agricultural, and Engineering Departments of the Government, or to the higher college at Yaba, on the outskirts of Lagos, which provides not only a literary education, especially for the teaching profession, but also, in co-operation with Government departments, a technical education in medicine, engineering, agriculture, and so forth. The new buildings of this Yaba College have just been opened, and over 90 students are now at work there.

In the Northern Provinces an attempt has been made, with the close co-operation of the Emirs, the Native Administrations, and the religious and legal pundits, to broaden the teaching in the Koran schools, of which there are now 37,431 with 206,979 pupils, 1 per cent of them now being girls. Free courses are arranged from which Koran teachers may carry secular instruction back to their schools. But, over and above the Koran schools, the Native Administrations have built and maintained new elementary

schools of their own, of which there are now 112, including
those which have recently been started in some of the
'pagan' areas, while for the 'pagans' the missions have
provided 189 schools. The number of pupils at these two
kinds of elementary schools is 12,963, of whom 459 are
girls. Middle schools also have been established in the
north as in the south; there are thirteen of them with over
700 pupils. And, as in the south again, there are two training centres and a college for teachers (150 pupils), and a
higher college at Katsina (56 pupils) which aims at the
same sort of vocational education as Yaba. There is also
a special college at Toro for training teachers in 'pagan'
schools.

These figures, which could easily be doubled or trebled
if there were money or teachers enough to meet the greedy
and growing demand for education, say something in themselves of what has been done in thirty years. But the spirit
of the work is incommunicable. To catch it one must see
the schools and colleges at work—the middle school at
Maiduguri, for instance, far away in the north-east near
Lake Chad (in one class-room little Moslems of Bornu
intoning the Koran, in another learning the elements of
history from a 'first-class' Oxford graduate or reading
Kanuri with a newly trained compatriot from Katsina, in
others busy at agriculture, weaving, metalwork—a gym-
nastic class in the 'quad' outside); or the primary school
at Gwoza, at the foot of the Mandara Mountains, where a
handful of tiny 'pagans' are struggling with slates and
looms and anvils; or Yaba itself, the crown of the whole
structure, making a modest start, but not concealing the
magnitude of its ambitions, rivalling Achimota, bent on
becoming a Nigerian University. Do not such plans as
these—and particularly the enthusiasm of the men and
women teaching there—illustrate better than anything else

Q

the merits and the hopes of British rule or British partnership in Nigeria? There the African's patriotism seems at
its purest. There the Englishman's sense of 'trusteeship'
seems to burn with its whitest flame.

6

Whither is it all tending? What is the ultimate goal of
British rule in Nigeria? Such questions were probably
never asked before the war. They were seldom asked in
India. The immediate task of good administration was so
obvious and so absorbing. But in the last twenty years we
have been forced to think more about ultimates; and as
regards the destiny of tropical Africa our thinking has
taken definite shape. To those who take the Mandate
System seriously, as the British people certainly do, its
ultimate implication is clear, and it is no less clear that
our task in a territory which is not 'mandated' is morally
indistinguishable from our task in one that is. This is no
academic theorizing; it is our official policy. 'In Nigeria
proper, as in the Mandated Territory,' said Sir Donald
Cameron, the Governor, in his opening address to the
Legislative Council last year, 'our duty is gradually to
train the people so that—whatever may be the generations,
or even centuries, that it will take—they may ultimately
be able to "stand by themselves", in the words of Article 22
of the Covenant of the League of Nations.' The policy of
to-day, in fact, is the same in form as the policy of 1865.
But they are far apart in spirit. The keynotes of the 1865
Report were a lack of interest in West Africa, a desire to
evade responsibilities which seemed to promise no financial return, and a hope that the native peoples might
quickly, somehow or other, be found able to look after
themselves. It was something like a policy of 'scuttle'. But

no one to-day underestimates the amount to be done before British rule in West Africa genuinely achieves its object. No one desires to scamp that work or to hasten its end unwisely. No one would condemn Nigeria to Liberia's fate. The difficulty for our descendants, rather, will probably be in Nigeria, as it is for us in India, to determine when the time is ripe for 'Dominion Status', or whatever form or title self-government may take. But there, one suspects, as in India, circumstances rather than theories will strike the hour.

That it is easier to imagine African self-government in Nigeria than in East or South Africa is partly due to the difference of attitude or atmosphere in a country in which colonists of our own stock have not made and cannot make their homes. British settlers in Kenya speak and think of it as '*our* country'. The representatives of the British unofficial community in Northern Rhodesia asserted a few years ago that British rule there is 'primarily concerned with the furtherance of the interests of British subjects of British race'. And most South Africans tend to think of the Union in terms of its white inhabitants. Such ideas, such an attitude, in unofficial no less than in official circles are untenable in West Africa. Nigeria is manifestly for the Nigerians. Englishmen wish to retain a leading share in its economic development, but they do not think of it as *ours* or that *our* interests are paramount. The contrast, of course, arises from a difference of physical, not moral, temperature; and, lest we be too complacent about the idealism of the 'West African' school, it is worth perhaps recalling the story of the Nigerian who proposed to erect a colossal statue to the saviour of Nigeria. 'But who is it to be?' asked his European friend. 'One of the great emancipators? Wilberforce? Buxton?' 'No,' said the Nigerian; 'the Mosquito.'

Another reason why it is easier to take ultimate self-government in West Africa for granted is the higher stage of progress its inhabitants have reached. The peoples of the east are of the same great Negro race. Local infusions of other blood have not made them less capable of advance: some observers think the contrary. But the coastal community in the west, especially in the towns, has been much longer exposed to all the stimulating influences of European contact. Africans of high capacity and culture are by no means lacking in the east, but there are far more of them in the west. There are scores of educated Africans at Lagos and other towns, living in the same kind of houses, wearing the same sort of clothes, following much the same social and intellectual pursuits as Europeans. They read the current English books: one African secured, it was rumoured, the first copy in the country of Mr. Churchill's *Marlborough*: in another's consignment from England was Mr. Garvin's *Chamberlain*. Lagos alone produces five or six English newspapers, owned, edited, printed, and mainly written by Africans. There are Africans in the professions and in business—parsons, doctors, lawyers, schoolmasters, journalists, bankers, merchants, contractors. In Nigeria, and nowhere else save the Gold Coast and Sierra Leone, there are African members of the Legislative Council, and they are elected by African constituents. In the Secretariat, the Treasury, and the technical departments of the Civil Service there are fifty Africans holding 'superior posts' with salaries ranging from £315 to £840 a year. The whole of the clerical staff, except for one or two posts in the Secretariat, is African, and so is the subordinate staff in all the technical departments. Work, too, which used to be considered too difficult or too responsible for Africans is rapidly passing into their hands. It is stated, for example, that no more engine-drivers will be needed from oversea. More than one facile generalization about Africans would never have been made if its author had ever visited Nigeria; and however lacking as yet the Nigerians may be in political experience, however weak in the qualities which only experience strengthens, it seems absurd for anyone who has seen their vigorous and varied life to suppose that they will never be capable of providing themselves with some decent form of government.

But 'What form of government?' the critic will ask. 'Will not the Legislative Council in Nigeria, as in India, inevitably grow into a parliament; and can all variegated Nigeria be governed by a parliament mainly manned by the *intelligentsia* of the coast?' It would be foolish to prophesy what the political evolution of the country is going to be; but one or two comments may be hazarded. It certainly seems as if the urban population of the coast is already committed to the pursuit of parliamentary institutions. The Legislative Council at Lagos is likely to follow the same path as the Legislative Council at Calcutta. But the 'politicians' of the coast are not dreaming of imposing their sectional will on all Nigeria—on the northern Emirates, in particular: they are probably envisaging a parliament in which all sections of the country will be represented. It seems doubtful, however, if a unitary system is desirable or attainable. The orbit of the Legislative Council, instead of broadening, might well narrow to the Colony and the other urban centres of the south. In the south-east one can imagine the little Native Administrations gradually federating, as they have been doing in Tanganyika, until a South-East Federal Council represents them all. The scattered 'pagan' Administrations in the north might one day form a similar combination. And, meantime, the Emirates and the Yoruba States, becoming steadily more imbued with representative principles, might also draw together into a Northern and a Southern Federation. Then a pan-Nigerian Council could be composed of the representatives of these five federated groups. Intricate, no doubt, but not much more intricate than the contemplated government of India.

It is futile, perhaps, to dwell on the possibilities of a future which only time and events can determine. But it is difficult not to look forward in Nigeria. The last impression with which one sails away is the sense of youth and hope. Nigeria is no old, tired country, being stimulated into a vigour it does not naturally feel. There is no scent of decay in its air as in that of some eastern lands. In social life and culture, in economics, in politics, it is a country in the making.

XII

THE EXPLOITATION OF AFRICA[1]

EUROPE'S discovery of Africa — the real Africa of the tropical belt between the Sahara and the Zambezi—is a new thing. Only sixty years ago the centre of the continent was being penetrated for the first time by the great explorers. Only thirty years ago the 'partition' of this vast area among the leading Powers was in course of completion. Since then the country has been 'opened up' at a startling speed. By rail, by motor-car, by aeroplane Europeans have spied out the innermost recesses of what so lately was 'Darkest Africa'.

The full extent of the physical resources of mid-Africa is still unknown; but, though a tendency to exaggerate them still lingers on from the romantic days of Prester John and the Empire of Monomotapa, they are certainly substantial; and it is natural that Europe, especially in these days of economic stringency, should be thinking of profitable expansion in the continent next door where wealth lies waiting and where, otherwise than in Asia, the native population is as yet incapable of obtaining more than a fraction of it by its own unaided efforts. 'Economic Imperialists' in England are talking, though not so loudly as they did a year or two back, of developing her tropical 'estates'. M. Caillaux is reported to have said, some eighteen months ago, that a means of 'new prosperity' for Europe was to be found in the 'assiduous colonization' of Africa. Signor Mussolini has recently pointed out that

---

[1] *Christian Science Monitor:* weekly section, July 25, 1934.

Italy is the nearest of the Western Powers to Africa and confided to the Italians of to-day and to-morrow the special task of 'collaboration between Italy and the peoples of Africa'. Opinion in Germany is apparently divided, but a vocal section persistently demands the restoration of the mandated territories and the re-establishment of the old colonial empire.

That something will come of all this talk seems certain. What, then, does it imply in concrete terms? What exactly is it that Europe wants to get out of Africa, by what means can she get it, and how will the getting of it affect the African peoples?

It is sometimes said, more often with reference to Germany or Italy than other nations, that Africa can provide a home for 'surplus population'. One wonders at the outset why, if there is a difficulty in disposing of the surplus, the German and Italian Governments regard an increase in the birth-rate as so urgent a national duty. But, assuming the difficulty to be real, can Africa provide the required home? There are apparently not sufficient healthy highlands in mid-Africa for the permanent settlement of a very great number of European emigrants, nor is the healthiness of those that exist, compared with more temperate regions, yet determined beyond controversy. Settlement on a large scale, moreover, intensifies those difficulties as to the supply of land and labour which have already emerged in connexion with quite small settlements. And in the background of any big 'white colony' lurk the serious problems of economic competition between the races, and of their political and in the long run their social interrelations. One wonders again if Germans or Italians really contemplate the growth of new 'daughter nations' overseas under those conditions. Livingstone knew more of East and Central Africa than anyone else of his time and he favoured

European settlement on a small scale as an instrument of civilization. But 'the idea of a colony in Africa', he observed, 'as the term "colony" is usually understood, cannot be entertained'.

Associated with the want of a 'home' only in certain localities, and far more important, is the general economic need in which all commercial Europe shares. It is twofold. Europe wants first, or will want when the 'slump' is over, an increased supply of the raw materials to be found in Africa—its minerals and the varied products of its tropical soil: cotton, rubber, coffee, cocoa, ground nuts, palm oil, sisal, and the rest. It wants, secondly, an expanding market for its manufactures.

Of the raw materials minerals are in a class by themselves if only because no other product is so far beyond the present powers of the natives to obtain unaided. Unless the minerals are alluvial or so near the surface as to be very easily extracted, European enterprise is necessarily involved, and that raises problems as to the use of the land under which the minerals lie and of the native labour needed to 'work' them. Both these problems, if hastily or unwisely handled, may lead to grave injury to the natives. But this need not happen. It need not happen even in Kenya, where the first 'rush' at the Kakamega gold-field has acquired some notoriety. It ought not to happen on the North Rhodesian copper belt, where, it is said, the demand for native labour is to be reduced to a minimum by the installation of labour-saving machinery. It has not happened and it is not happening in the gold and diamond mines of Ashanti or the tin and coal mines of Nigeria.

No doubt, if gold were found in East Africa on as great a scale as in the Transvaal and a second Johannesburg sprang into being there, the whole situation would be changed. But the experts have not yet painted a prospect quite so gilded. And in the ordinary course, while every mining 'proposition' calls for the most careful attention and control by Government and, on proved necessity, even prohibition or postponement in the interests of the natives, there is apparently no real reason why they should suffer from mineral exploitation. On the contrary they *ought* to gain by it. The taxation of mineral output is the safest and richest means of revenue. And it is only more revenue that can give the tropical territories the full measure of public services they need. The maintenance of health, infant welfare, the extension of education, social improvements of all kinds, cost money. Indirect rule, which has been adopted in most of the British territories as a means of training their peoples in self-government, is less expensive than direct rule, but the stronger its financial basis, the more effective will be its work. Indeed the hope of human progress in Africa depends on Africa's capacity to pay for it; and, if minerals pay best, the more of them that can be exploited *without counteracting injury* the better.

It may be observed in passing that the taxation of minerals provides at least a partial solution of a difficult psychological problem. To the native's mind the removal of these precious metals from the soil on which he lives must seem akin to theft. He may not be able to dig them out himself, but he feels none the less that they belong to him or rather to his tribe. On no other point, probably, is it harder for him to believe that the theory of European 'trusteeship' is not a sham. Is the ideal method of meeting this difficulty impracticable? Are the risks of mineral exploitation too great for the Governments themselves to undertake it? If so, justice and good policy alike demand that private enterprise be taxed to the highest limit it will bear, so that the native may be convinced that all the surplus profit is retained in the country to finance his public services and that all the rest is payment for the capital, skill, and labour required to get the minerals out.

Minerals, however, though so valuable, are but one element in African economy. Industries of a kind there have always been. But, they have rarely got beyond the simple, though often graceful products of village handicraft for village use. Manufactures for export, like the dyed cloth and 'Morocco' leather of Kano, are only to be found in a few advanced and 'urbanized' localities. The economic life of Africa is agricultural and pastoral. So it has been since time began. If Europe had never discovered Africa, the Africans would still be tilling the soil for foodstuffs and herding cattle for milk and hides or just as a form of living property. What the coming of Europe has meant is a stimulus to these millions of African country folk to do more than scrape the ground for their own subsistence. For centuries past they had exported alluvial gold dust, ivory, a few local manufactures, and, in terrible volume, slaves, but not agricultural produce. In 1929—to take some of the British territories before the 'depression' hit them— Nigeria exported palm oil and kernels, ground nuts, cocoa, and cotton lint worth over £13 million; the Gold Coast, similar products worth over £10 million; Kenya and Uganda, mainly cotton and coffee worth over £7 million. In 1901 the total exports of the same four territories together were worth under £4 million. The vast difference is due to British occupation.

How has it made the difference? First, by building the roads and railways and providing the ships which made it possible for North Nigerian ground nuts, Gold Coast cocoa, East African coffee to be sold in Europe and America. Second, by attracting and safeguarding the European merchants and bankers needed to manage the oversea trade and finance it. Third, by providing expert official aid and advice as to improved cultivation, seed, anti-pest measures, marketing methods, and so forth. Fourth, by the participation of British settlers or planters in the work of production.

The effect on the African peoples concerned can be gauged from the fact that of almost all that mounting volume of exports they have been the producers. The fourth of those factors is relatively small. There are no European plantations in Nigeria or the Gold Coast. There are only about 17,000 Europeans in Kenya, and about 10,000 more in Uganda and Tanganyika, and probably less than a fifth of the 27,000 are permanent farmers or plantation managers. And, while their share in the increase of production has been substantial, the great bulk of it has been the work of the natives themselves, mostly peasantry tilling their own or the communal land; and it is to the natives, producers and middlemen, that the great bulk of the profit above the cost of export has gone. Even in that minor field of European production, moreover, at least a fraction of the yield has been paid to the native in wages for his labour.

All in all, then, the profit to the Africans themselves has been very great. Vast multitudes of country people, who used to be content with 'subsistence cultivation', have discovered what it is to have money to spend. Some of it has gone in taxes by which, as has been observed, the means of transport and other public services are provided. The rest of it, not being for the most part instinctive hoarders, they have spent. On what? Partly on more and better food and other local amenities. Mainly on manufactured articles imported from Europe. And thereby they are meeting the second great need which Europe seeks to satisfy in Africa —the need of markets. The following table of imports for 1901 and twenty-eight years later speaks for itself:

	1901	1929
Nigeria	£2,242,000	£13,193,000
Gold Coast . . .	1,795,000	10,082,000
Kenya and Uganda . .	539,000	9,740,000

As soon as world trade recovers, the African markets seem capable of an expansion only limited by a corresponding increase of profitable production and thereby of local purchasing power. But the production must be profitable, and there lie dangers. First there is the danger of over-concentration on a particular crop. That has happened in West Africa where the fortunes made in the cocoa boom led to so much new planting that there is now more cocoa than the world needs or even perhaps will need when the 'slump' is over. But it ought to be possible to deal with that problem by stimulating demand for the product in question, especially the local demand, and by developing other marketable crops. A second danger is the possibility that some of the main African products may be cultivated elsewhere in better quality or at lower cost. It is said, for instance, that the vegetable oils of the Dutch East Indies may thus presently drive those of West Africa out of the market. And this has inspired the argument that in order to improve quality and decrease cost the system of native ownership and cultivation should be replaced by a system of large-scale plantations under European management. But apart from the question whether the native, who in either case does the work, will do it better for wages than to grow his own crop, such a policy would raise the fundamental question of African rights in African soil. In British West Africa, indeed, it would mean such a dislocation of the whole social order that the Government has repeatedly and unequivocally declared itself against it. And in East Africa, while a limited number of European plantations may serve a useful purpose in training natives by employment and example to improve their own cultivation, its indefinite extension seems undesirable if only because it tends to weaken the sense of self-reliance and of the need for voluntary co-operative effort on which the ultimate well-being of African society depends. The better way in the end to meet competition, however slow it may seem, is surely to encourage by all possible means the native cultivator to improve his own methods and to co-operate with others, and to continue and expand, as far as budgets permit, the patient work that is being done by the agricultural and forestry departments.

With agricultural production, then, as with minerals, it seems as if the economic development of Africa can proceed, as if Europe can obtain what she wants from Africa, not merely without injury to the Africans but to their advantage, *provided that the process is wisely and firmly controlled*. In Britain—the writer cannot speak for other countries—the will to control it exists. British public opinion will never revert to the mentality of the old slave-owners. It will not be persuaded again to regard the black race as divinely ordained to serve the white. And that attitude will be all the stronger because in its make-up the British humanitarian tradition will be combined, not for the first time, with British business sagacity. The lesson of the earlier exploitation of the Congo has not been missed. It is a mistake to kill hens if you want eggs.

XIII

THE FUTURE OF COLONIAL
TRUSTEESHIP [1]

I

THE term 'trusteeship' is commonly and often rather
loosely used to denote the character of British rule over
backward peoples. The idea of a political trust goes back
to the days of Burke and the great emancipators, but, like
so much else in British history, it long remained a principle or tradition not formulated in any document nor
expressed in any specific pledge. It was not till 1885 that
the British Government, in conjunction with the other
signatories of the Berlin Act, definitely undertook in one
particular field—the British territories within the Congo
basin in Africa—to watch over the preservation of the
native tribes, and to care for the improvement of the conditions of their moral and material well-being. More
recent and of wider scope are the formulas and pledges
connected with the Covenant of the League of Nations.
Article 23 includes an undertaking 'to secure just treatment of the native inhabitants' of territories under its
signatories' control. Article 22 declares that to the territories taken from the former German and Turkish Empires,

which are inhabited by peoples not yet able to stand by themselves under the strenuous conditions of the modern world,
there should be applied the principle that the well-being and
development of such peoples form a sacred trust of civilization.

[1] *Round Table*, No. 96, September 1934.

And in accepting the mandate for Tanganyika, for example, the British Government pledged itself 'to promote to the utmost the material and moral well-being and the social progress of its inhabitants'; and *inter alia* 'to respect the rights and safeguard the interests of the native population' with regard to land, and to 'ensure to all nationals of States members of the League of Nations, on the same footing as to (its) own nationals . . . complete economic, commercial and industrial equality'. The same or similar undertakings are involved in the other mandates.

The subscription of these formulas and pledges meant no departure from the British tradition. The mandate system, indeed, was regarded as the embodiment of that tradition. It was said by high officials, with experience of both fields, that the administration of a Mandated Territory was no different from that of a Crown Colony. And on at least two occasions the identity in principle has been officially admitted. In the White Paper of 1923 on the position of Indians in Kenya, His Majesty's Government recorded their opinion (re-affirmed in the 1927 White Paper), that

the annexation of the East Africa Protectorate . . . in no way derogates from this fundamental conception of the duty of the Government to the native races. As in the Uganda Protectorate, so in the Kenya Colony, the principle of trusteeship for the natives, no less than in the Mandated Territory of Tanganyika, is unassailable.

And in his address to the Legislative Council in 1933 the Governor of Nigeria declared that

in Nigeria proper, as in the Mandated Territory, our duty is gradually to train the people so that—whatever may be the generations or even centuries that it will take—they may ultimately be able to 'stand by themselves', in the words of Article 22 of the Covenant.

Nor, of course, can the extension of the principle be confined to Africa. If the principles of trusteeship are right in Kenya and Nigeria, they are right in Malaya or Fiji.

It is sometimes asserted that the theory of trusteeship is a masterpiece of hypocrisy, a cloak to cover the naked selfishness of 'economic imperialism'. It is true, of course, that our occupation of tropical territories was never altruistic. We wanted new supplies of raw materials and new markets for our manufactures; and occupation was the only way to prevent these raw materials and markets from coming under the control of rival foreign Powers. But higher motives were honestly linked with the economic and political. The British humanitarian tradition is an historical fact. We did give a lead to the world a century ago in abolishing the Slave Trade and Slavery; and more than once since then the extension of British rule has largely been determined by a genuine desire to protect the peoples concerned from those and kindred evils. Nor have we ever admitted that the economic development of the Tropics is necessarily injurious to the welfare of the natives, that (to quote the famous jibe) 'philanthropy and five per cent' are incompatible. Wilberforce urged that the expansion of 'legitimate' trade was one of the surest methods of killing the slave trade. Livingstone linked commerce with Christianity as a means of fulfilling our duty to 'civilize' Africa. And it is becoming more and more obvious in these days that the execution of a 'trust' for the welfare of the natives, involving as it does the provision of costly public services for their physical and social advancement, depends for its efficiency on an adequate local revenue, which in turn depends on economic development.

The nature of our economic system before the War enabled us to assert a second claim. Most other colonial

Powers, including the United States, maintained a privileged position for themselves in the commerce of their colonies. We, being free-traders, disclaimed all preference on principle. Foreigners were as free as British subjects to trade in British colonies. The products of foreign colonies competed openly with those of British colonies in the British market. British interests, it is true, enjoyed some indirect advantages from the fact of British rule, but the value of these can be exaggerated, and the 'open door' was genuinely open. And this could be pleaded as a sort of justification or excuse for the relatively large size of our colonial empire. 'We develop it', said Mr. Joseph Chamberlain, 'as trustees of civilization for the commerce of the world'—a text which Lord Lugard cited, in his classical study of African administration, to illustrate his well-known doctrine of the 'dual mandate', half for the natives, half for the world.

It may be observed that, while in two of the three classes of Mandated Territories the 'open door' has similarly been maintained, if not for the whole world, at least for the members of the League, and, by subsequent arrangement, for the United States, no reference is made in the Covenant to any such secondary trust. And indeed, though the welfare of the natives is no more our sole object or interest in maintaining the colonies than it was in acquiring them, nevertheless it seems undesirable, if not dangerous, to give to the term 'trust' or 'mandate' such a double application. For one thing, it is doubtful whether British public opinion was ever really interested in promoting world trade apart from the British share in it: we maintained the 'open door' because we thought it paid us, economically and politically. For another, the second use of the term tends to blur and weaken the effect of the first. It ignores the possibility of conflict between the economic development of the Tropics and the protection of the natives; whereas, of course, the danger of such a conflict is inherent in the colonial problem, and applies to the principle of trusteeship its severest test.

2

There can be little doubt that the British people desire to maintain the principle of trusteeship. The public interest in the centenary of the abolition of slavery shows that we are still proud of our humanitarian tradition; and to those who look ahead it seems clear that, even in relatively backward countries, the increasing stimulant of European contact and the steady growth of education will make it progressively harder to govern or to trade with peoples who believe that their interests are deliberately subordinated to those of the ruling Power. As regards principles and methods of government, our policy still accords, on the whole, with these ideas. Constitutional reforms in Ceylon and the West Indies, the development of indirect administration in Tropical Africa, the scheme of decentralization in Malaya, and the closer attention given to education—all this and much more is inspired by an honest desire to help the peoples concerned, sooner or later according to the varying standards of their past achievement and present capacity, to stand on their own feet. The only difference, indeed, from pre-War policy is a clearer realization that, however long it may take to reach it, some kind of self-government is everywhere the ultimate goal.

But in the economic field there have been changes since the War. The revolution in our economic system at home was bound to affect our economic ideas about the Empire as a whole. Just as in the nineteenth century, after the downfall of protection, we attempted to impose free trade on our 'white' colonies—and were only prevented by the powers of self-government they had already attained—so now the natural tendency is to bring our 'black' and 'brown' colonies within the new system of imperial preference. M. André Siegfried, one of the British Empire's friendliest critics, prophesied a few years ago that under the pressure of world economic forces we would try to refashion our tropical Empire into a closed economic area of the eighteenth century mercantilist type; [1] and that indeed is what some of our own imperial enthusiasts demand from time to time, in the belief that our economic problems can be solved by an exclusive 'exploitation of our tropical estate'. Nothing so drastic, of course, has yet occurred, but one or two things have been done that point in that direction.

(i) Already at the close of the War the 'open door' was no longer quite open. Differential duties were temporarily laid on the export of palm-kernels from West Africa in order to foster the manufacture of vegetable oil in this country at Germany's expense. Small preferences were also arranged between Great Britain and the West Indies and one or two other colonies. But it was not till the Ottawa Conference that the preferential principle was extended to cover almost every part of the Empire in which it was not ruled out, as it is for instance in the Congo basin, by the treaty rights of foreign Powers. The Colonial Secretary himself went to Ottawa to represent the colonies, and, speaking in the House of Commons on July 12 last, he claimed that the agreements he had secured there had not only benefited British and Dominion exporters to the colonies, but had also helped the native producers to fight the economic depression by widening

[1] *England's Crisis*. (Jonathan Cape. 1931.)

and safeguarding their markets in Great Britain and the Dominions.

This article is not concerned with economic controversy nor with the effect on international relations of a closing or partial closing of the 'open door'. It must suffice for the moment to stress the fact that it is no longer open. There has been relatively little discussion of this aspect of the Ottawa policy; public opinion seems scarcely to have realised that, whatever its merits, it was a radical departure from pre-War principles, and that it differentiates the economic status of those colonies to which it has been applied from that of a mandated territory. We can no longer claim to be trustees for the commerce of the world. It should not be forgotten, moreover, that, while the Ottawa agreements between Great Britain and the Dominions were concluded between democratic Governments representing their peoples, those affecting the colonies were concluded by the Secretary of State on their behalf, and that, although he doubtless consulted their Governments, he was in a position in most cases to put his decisions into effect, whatever local opinion might be. Only seven of the colonies are sufficiently advanced to possess legislative bodies that are not controlled by an official majority; and in one of those, Ceylon, where the new constitution has not yet secured political harmony, the State Council repudiated an important part of the preferential agreement.

(ii) These points require still greater emphasis with regard to the recent imposition of anti-Japanese duties and quotas. On May 7 last the President of the Board of Trade announced in the House of Commons that

the Governments of the colonies and protectorates for which such action would be appropriate would be asked to introduce import quotas which, except in the case of West Africa, would apply to all foreign imports of cotton and rayon goods. . . . In the most important of the West African colonies . . . there were treaty obligations which precluded differentiation in favour of our own goods. It was for this reason that on May 16 of last year notice had been given to release the West African colonies from their obligations under the Anglo-Japanese treaty, and action there would be limited to Japanese goods.

On the face of it those measures are intended to serve no other purpose than the protection of British exports from Japanese competition: they are a move in the world-wide conflict between this country and Japan. It can be argued, of course, that the interests of the colonies—political, strategic, financial, commercial—are so closely linked with our own that any sacrifices they may make are made in a common cause. But has it been adequately recognized that it *is* a sacrifice for the poorer natives of the Tropics to be deprived of the chance of buying cheap Japanese goods? The Nairobi correspondent of *The Times* reported that East African opinion did not regret that the imposition of the duties in East Africa was barred by the Congo treaties.

It is felt (he wrote) that the limited native purchasing power has been used, money circulated, and trade kept alive by Japanese goods at a critical time, which would have been less probably the case with more expensive British articles. An example of such indirect benefit comes from Tanganyika, where medical officers declare that the purchase of cheap Japanese rubber shoes has done more to prevent hookworm disease than all the efforts of the health department.[1]

It is much the same in West Africa. Hard-hit as they have been by the fall in the price of ground-nuts and palm products, the poorer natives in Nigeria are still able to buy cheap Japanese shoes or singlets, but not the more expensive British product. It is the same story in Ceylon.

[1] *The Times*, May 11, 1934.

A high tariff on Japanese cotton piece goods (to quote again from a correspondent of *The Times*) would not, it is believed, in any way increase the sale of the British commodity; it would merely deprive the consumer of something which he demands and is now just able to afford.

In Malaya anxiety as to the effect of the duties on the *entrepôt* trade is stiffened by a traditional attachment to free trade, which in the course of the last century raised Singapore from an obscure village to one of the world's great ports.

It is not surprising, therefore, that the imposition of the duties has met with some local opposition. In Nigeria and the Gold Coast, it is true, the requisite measures were accepted by the unofficial members of the Legislative Councils, but it was pointed out that, if the cost of living was to be raised in Nigeria to protect British trade, Great Britain should do more than she has done for Nigerian products. At Singapore, on the other hand, the unofficial members of Council unanimously opposed the Bill, which could therefore be carried only by the votes of the official *bloc*. In Ceylon, after some hesitation, which was apparently due to a desire to bargain with the British Government for the better protection of Ceylonese products in the British market, the Board of Ministers decided to withhold support from the duties, and to 'leave it to the Secretary of State to treat the question as one of Imperial significance, if he desired, and to take such steps as he thought fit'.[1] An Order-in-Council has since been made, vesting in the Governor of Ceylon power to regulate textile imports by quota.

It would be impossible (said the Secretary of State) that Ceylon should be excluded from a broad imperial policy of

[1] *The Times*, July 21, 1934.

this kind, which is regarded as essential in the economic interests of the Empire as a whole.

It may be that this local opposition is inspired by a false or narrow conception of the ultimate interests of the colonies concerned; but in brushing it aside how much consideration has the British Government given to those interests? Mr. Runciman's announcement of the Government's decision was of a brief official character: he merely stated that, pending a settlement by co-operation with the Japanese, action must be taken to prevent their 'continuously expanding their exports in our markets to the detriment of Lancashire'. The Government were thus 'obliged to resume their liberty to take such action as they deemed necessary to safeguard our commercial interests'. As regards the colonial markets, the action mentioned would be taken 'with a view to reinstating this country in the position in those markets which she held before the present abnormal period'. A reasoned explanation of the Government's policy was not to be expected on this occasion; but since it was only in the colonial sections of 'our markets' that immediate action was to be taken, it is strange that Mr. Runciman could not find room for a single sentence to show that anything but 'the detriment of Lancashire' and '*our* commercial interests' had been considered.

(iii) A third example of new tendencies may be taken from a different field. The air service provided by Imperial Airways between London and South Africa by way of the Sudan, Uganda, Kenya, Tanganyika, and the Rhodesias is aided by a subsidy which amounts this year to £246,000. Of this total Great Britain provides £100,000, South Africa £94,000, and Southern Rhodesia £10,000. The residue of £42,000 is made up by Kenya (£15,000), Uganda and Tanganyika (£10,000 each), Sudan (£5000), and Northern

Rhodesia (£2000). Those five territories are not, like the first three, self-governing. They are all under 'trust'. One of them is 'mandated'. Their total revenues have averaged in recent years about £10 to £12 million. No doubt they share in benefits that the service confers on all the territories it traverses. No doubt, too, there are political and strategic questions to be taken into account. But the disproportion between a payment by Tanganyika, for example, of over one two-hundredth of its revenue and a payment by Great Britain of less than one seven-thousandth is marked. Sir Edward Grigg went so far as to say in the debate on the Air estimates on March 19 that 'the proportion in which the subsidy is divided is an exploitation of the African taxpayer for the benefit of the taxpayer here'. No one supposes, if that be so, that it was deliberately intended; but it seems doubtful if the relative utility and cost of the service to the African native and the Englishman at home were reckoned up with a due sense of our responsibility as 'trustees', and it is satisfactory that Sir Philip Sassoon promised that this aspect of the question would be fully considered.

3

The point to be repeated and emphasized about these three examples of our recent policy in the colonial field is that the policy is new. It assumes a different relationship between Great Britain and the colonies than that of the pre-War trusteeship, or at least a different conception of trusteeship. The old theory, as defined at the outset of this article, was that the interest of the ward was the Government's overriding concern. Private commercial enterprise was certainly encouraged, but, broadly speaking, in the belief that it did not injure and should not be permitted to injure the peoples under 'trust'. We were content with the incidental or indirect advantages that accrued to us from British rule. We did not ask the peoples ruled to pay for more than the local cost thereof, and, when they could not meet even that, we made good the deficiency ourselves. The new policy is on other lines. It can hardly be said, perhaps, to be based as yet on any very definite theory. Things seem to have been done to meet particular needs or to fit in with other policies, without considering their logical implications. But at least the outline of a new colonial doctrine seems to be taking shape, a doctrine that tends to regard colonial territories less as a class in themselves and more as an integral part of the Empire, and to identify their interests more closely with those of the Empire as a whole. It suggests that their new path of progress lies in imperial co-operation. Where treaties permit, it substitutes reciprocal 'Ottawa' preferences for the 'open door', and with the same proviso it calls for aid in Great Britain's economic conflict with Japan. It takes for granted a subvention to an imperial air service. Going one step farther, it might perhaps assert that the colonies, enjoying the general benefits, the freedom and security, inherent in their connexion with the Empire, should share also in its general burdens over and above the local cost of their administration. The conception of the relationship between ourselves and the colonies, in fact, would seem to be no longer that of trusteeship, but rather that of partnership.

In principle, no one can quarrel with that. Partnership in the colonies, as in India, is the natural outcome of trusteeship. It has been said, indeed, that the separate consideration given to the colonies at Ottawa implied a rise in their status, and that the discussion of the new preferences in their legislatures was a step in the direction of fiscal autonomy. There would be more force in that if the

majority of most colonial legislatures were not bound to
vote in the last resort as the Colonial Secretary in London
wished, and if the only important colony that possesses a
real measure of fiscal autonomy, Ceylon, had not disagreed
with the British Government's proposals. There is danger,
indeed, in regarding peoples as partners who, in fact, are
still only wards. It may lead to imposing on wards what
partners would refuse. George III's ministers believed
themselves justified in asking the American colonies to
contribute to imperial defence. The attempt to impose free
trade on Canada in the eighteen-fifties was inspired by a
quite genuine belief that it was good for her. To be a just
judge in one's own cause demands a superhuman virtue,
and, if indeed such a doctrine as that outlined above is to
be adopted, let us take care to define it clearly and truth-
fully. To talk of 'co-operation' unless we are sure it is
voluntary goes far to justify what is said abroad of our
national hypocrisy.

We are face to face in fact with an imperial issue of
quite first-rate importance. Let us recognize it as such
betimes, and not allow it to be decided by a series of
hand-to-mouth decisions, without thinking out the principles involved. Above all, it must not be decided without
the fullest public discussion; for the final responsibility
lies with the British people. The 'trusteeship' for the welfare of the millions of coloured peoples is not vested in
their colonial Governments. In most of the colonies the
Governor can secure his end in the legislative as well as the
executive field by ordering, if need be, the official majority
in the legislature to vote as he directs them. But the
Governor is under the instructions of the Secretary of
State, who is himself the agent of Parliament, and, more
particularly, of the House of Commons, which represents
and is responsible to the British people.

Theirs, then, is the ultimate responsibility. Their opinion must decide the issue. It must not be settled by a policy of drift or in 'a fit of absence of mind' without consulting them. And so far no such consultation has taken place. Neither in Parliament nor outside it has there been any real public discussion of the new colonial policy. Full attention was given to the part played by the Dominions in the Ottawa agreements, but scarcely any to that of the colonies. The anti-Japanese duties were announced without even a bare reference to their interests. Nor can it be pleaded that public opinion in this matter can be taken for granted. It is impossible to say what it is. Is it, for instance, convinced that the application of 'imperial preference' in the colonies is economically or morally justified? Has it considered and decided to face the reactions of such a policy on the attitude of other nations towards the British Empire, especially that of the United States?

Nor is it British public opinion only that must in these days be consulted. Every effort should be made to inform the educated section of any community concerned as to the purpose of our policies and, as far as possible, to obtain its views. It need not be assumed that they will differ from our own. In 1919, while the African members of the Gold Coast Legislative Council voted against the palm-kernel export duty, those of the Nigerian Council voted for it because Sir Frederick Lugard had straightforwardly appealed to them to recognize what they owed to British rule. What is almost certain, on the other hand, to provoke dissent and antagonism is to impose a measure, especially an economic measure, on a colony without troubling to explain and justify it as clearly and fully as possible. The suspicion that the political ideals of our 'trusteeship' do not conform with our economic purposes is unhappily as inevitable in the colonies as it used to be in India; but it is not yet so widespread, and everything possible must be done to combat it. Not only in Ceylon and the West Indies, but in more politically backward communities in Africa and elsewhere, the educated native is closely watching what we do and how we do it. And at all costs we must try —and it is not by any means impossible—to convince him of our sincerity and to keep his good-will. For, however we interpret our 'trust', every student of colonial problems knows that its successful execution depends, and will increasingly depend as time passes, on the sympathy and co-operation of the native peoples.

XIV

THE MEMORY OF WILBERFORCE[1]

You are engaged all this week in remembering William Wilberforce, and you have done me the honour of asking me to take part in this commemoration and to speak to you about the life and work of your greatest fellow-citizen. But I suspect you are already, or soon will be, fairly familiar with that great story. You have been provided with a feast of lectures and sermons and newspaper articles and plays about Wilberforce. You have learnt about him by looking at documents and pictures and slave relics and waxworks at the Centenary Exhibition. One or two of you may even have read my book. So I propose to spend my time not in telling over again that famous tale, but in discussing its significance and in asking why and to what purpose we should remember it to-day.

I cannot help wondering, at the outset, what Wilberforce himself would have thought. Suppose that by some miracle of relativity this afternoon could be made to coincide in time with an afternoon rather more than a century ago; and that one of us had been delegated to visit Mr. Wilberforce and ask him his opinion of this commemoration. Imagine our representative walking up and down that sunny path in the Highwood garden beside the man whose name all England honoured—old and frail and bent, but unconquerably young in spirit, and seizing with unfailing gusto an opportunity of talking.

[1] Guildhall, Hull, July 25, 1933: *Hibbert Journal*, October 1933.

There might be a little difficulty, to begin with, in persuading Wilberforce to believe in your commemoration. He would be startled, I think—for his humble opinion of himself was quite unaffected—by the idea of the nation paying honour to him a hundred years after his death. But, if he could be got to face the fact and take it seriously, I can guess what his first comment would be. 'I do hope', he would say, 'you are not making too much of *me*. I could have done nothing without the others.' That, of course, is true; and it is right, it is unquestionably what Wilberforce would have wished, that, when we are honouring him, we should not forget those others who worked before him and with him and after him for the triumph of their common cause—Granville Sharp, the pioneer, who, almost single-handed, deleted slavery from England: William Dillwyn and the little nucleus of Quakers round which the first Abolitionist forces were mobilized: James Ramsay, vicar of Teston, giving all his leisure and in the end his life to denouncing the evil he had seen and hated in St. Kitt's: Thomas Clarkson, indefatigable investigator, journeyman, propagandist, who did more than anyone else to furnish the ammunition for the great battle on the Slave Trade: Henry Thornton and Charles Grant, men of high standing in the field of finance and government, yet giving the best of themselves to philanthropy, and always at Wilberforce's elbow with encouragement and practical advice: Zachary Macaulay, so quiet and unobtrusive, little known to the contemporary world, almost lost in the shadow of his more famous friends, yet the man of action whose governorship saved Sierra Leone and the man of mind whose incredible industry and invincible memory made him the intellectual mainstay, the encyclopaedist, of the Abolition movement: James Stephen and the two younger Stephens, and the younger Grants and Babington

and Gisborne and the Venns and the other members of
the 'Clapham Sect': and last but not least, Thomas Fowell
Buxton, a Joshua to Wilberforce's Moses, chosen by the
veteran he revered to lead the army of Emancipation into
the Promised Land, chief organizer of its victory in Parliament a hundred years ago. . . . Yes: we must give all
those names the honour due to them. But we can never
feel about them all we feel about Wilberforce. He was so
easily, so visibly, for his own day as for ours, the greatest
of them.

But we must return to Highwood, and listen to our
representative putting to Wilberforce his first question:
'What do you think, sir, is the primary significance of your
work, the lesson of the abolition of the slave system?'
Surely you can hear the instant answer: 'It was God's
work. It signifies the triumph of His will over human
selfishness. It teaches that no obstacle of interest or prejudice is irremovable by faith and prayer.'

That may be old-fashioned language to some of us; but,
however we phrase it, we must agree that Wilberforce's
achievement was a striking example—perhaps the most
striking one can think of in modern history—of the power
of pure idealism in the practical world. Consider the sheer
greatness of what was done. In 1783, though slaves had
ceased to exist on the soil of the British Isles for ten years
past, slavery and the slave trade were still regarded by
almost everyone as a necessary and permanent element in
the life of the overseas Empire: and this realistic or fatalistic assumption was solidly buttressed not only by the
unbroken tradition of mercantilist imperialism, by the
settled convictions of officials and experts, of statesmen
and diplomatists and admirals for generations past, but
also by one of the most powerful 'vested interests' ever
embedded in our society and politics—plantation pro-

prietors, mortgagees, bankers, sugar merchants, bond-holders, ship-owners, insurance agents, all who shared in the prosperity of Liverpool and Bristol, all the multitude of men and women whose livelihood depended in some degree, directly or indirectly, on the ownership of slaves or the trade which supplied them. Indeed the hold of the British slave system on men's minds and pockets seemed so unshakable that Burke, no faint-hearted humanitarian, described the abolition of the trade alone as 'a very chimerical object'. Yet, in the course of only fifty years, not only the trade but the whole or almost the whole of the British slave system was torn up by the roots and destroyed. The more one looks at that revolution in thought and conduct, the more astonishing it seems. The demolition of the whole social and economic basis of colonial life in the Tropics was the least of its results. It transformed the relations between white men and black, between Europe and Africa; and on that account it must be regarded by all far-sighted historians as one of the transcendent events in the history of mankind. But, if the magnitude of the change is so impressive, no less impressive is the means by which it was brought about. For it was the outcome not merely of a change of mind, but of that far rarer thing, a change of heart. It was a moral revolution.

Some years before the War a German historian tried laboriously to prove that the abolition of the British slave trade was a characteristic mixture of hypocrisy and greed. Influenced, so he would have it, by a section of opinion, commercial and colonial, which stood to gain by the abolition of the trade, the British Government just 'put it across'. Motives, it is true, are seldom unmixed, and certainly there were some little groups who thought their interests were served at each stage of the Abolition movement

S

—slave-owners on some of the older West Indian colonies in 1807, East Indian sugar merchants in 1833. But to anybody who has seriously studied the details of the Abolitionist crusade and knows what really happened not only in Downing Street and in Parliament, but throughout the country, it seems almost ludicrous to imagine that the destruction of the British slave system was imposed on an ignorant and docile electorate by a dictatorial ministry at the bidding of 'sinister interests'. The British slave system was destroyed for the simple reason that it involved a degree of cruelty and injustice which the conscience of the average man and woman in this country could no longer tolerate: they knew little and cared less about those few individuals who stood to gain: they knew that the country as a whole must lose; and they were ready to pay 'the price of virtue', as Fox called it, by the loss of all the profits of the slave trade in 1807 and by the extraction from taxpayers' pockets of twenty million pounds for compensation to the slave-owners in 1833. There has never been a less 'sectional' or a more 'popular' movement in England than the Anti-Slavery movement, and never one in which the moral motive was so pure.

But that raises a further question. The slave system had existed for a century and a half. Why was it that the conscience of the British people, so sluggish all those years, was stirred just when it was, and stirred so sharply? The main reason, unquestionably, was the Evangelical Revival which spread through England in the second half of the eighteenth century like fire in dry grass and kindled to new life the sense of Christian duty. There were other influences working in the same direction—ideas of the 'noble savage', of 'natural rights', of the 'brotherhood of man', ideas of the Age of Revolution, American and French —but the mainspring of the whole humanitarian movement in England, of the great resurgence of missionary effort overseas, of the new interest in and sympathy with the backward races in Asia or in Africa, of the new doctrine of imperial 'trusteeship', was the Evangelical spirit; and it was as the exponent and interpreter, nay, the embodiment, of that spirit that Wilberforce persuaded Parliament to write those 'virtuous pages' of English history on which the downfall of the slave system is described.

It was not an easy task. The landowners and country gentlemen who composed the great majority of both Houses were mostly churchmen of the old school, not Evangelicals. Practitioners by birth and training of English common sense, apt to regard 'enthusiasm' as deplorably bad taste, cautious, conservative, hard-headed, sentimental at heart but robustly contemptuous of sentiment, champions of the rights of property—and slaves were property as much as stocks or manor-houses or 'rotten boroughs'— how was it that such an audience listened to Wilberforce's sermons—listened and were interested, attracted, excited, conscience-stricken, converted! It was not only the man's eloquence, his beautiful voice, the ease and charm of his manner, the effective presentation of evidence resulting from months of toil: that would account for the attention of the House of Commons, but not for its conversion. Nor was it only the good taste and good sense with which he argued his case. It is easy enough to denounce old-established abuses without advancing by a day the time of their removal. But Wilberforce had none of the professional zealot's failings. He was restrained, he was not too emotional, he was never morbid; he made it clear that the narration of horrors was an unsavoury and distasteful business; above all, he remembered that the men who were implicated in the slave system, the slave-traders and the slave-owners, were human beings; he tried to understand their case and to concede what in justice or equity they could claim; he never impeached them wholesale as a class. But the real secret of Wilberforce's strength and power was something greater than good taste and good sense, something far more impressive and convincing—his utter disinterestedness. No one will believe an agitator who has anything to gain from his agitation. The most eloquent sermon is unconvincing if the preacher's sincerity is suspect. And the chief reason why those hard-headed members of Parliament could not help believing Wilberforce and could scarcely help being converted by him was the sheer impossibility of questioning his motives. Obviously it was not money, nor political ambition, nor party interest, nor mere personal vanity that prompted him to attack the slave system. It could only be what he said it was—his conscience and his faith. And something in those members of Parliament, and in the whole body of the people they represented, responded to the call. The conscience of all England was awakened. That, in a word, is how the slave system was abolished. Not because it was good policy or good business to abolish it—it was neither, it was the opposite—but simply because of its iniquity.

That, surely, is a lesson for our post-War cynics. Idealism, it appears, is not after all a romantic illusion, a perquisite of ineffectual angels, a solace for the soft-hearted and soft-headed, a sort of compound of cotton-wool and chloroform. It may be that individual life is often a pursuit of selfish ends. It may be that politics is often no more than a mask for the strife of rival interests. But the lives and works of Wilberforce and the 'Saints' are certain proof that not merely individuals but the common will, the State itself, *can* rise on occasion to the height of pure unselfishness. Let us take heart then. I know that civilized people are quite extraordinarily shy of admitting (except, perhaps, in church) that they want to be good. But let us be shameless, just for once, at any rate here in Hull and in this Commemoration Week, and confess that we do want to be good, in politics as in other things, in our national and international and imperial life, and affirm, remembering our ancestors and Wilberforce, that we can be good if we are given a good lead, and that the leadership we want—the whole world is crying out for it—is moral leadership.

There is another question I should like our delegate to put to Wilberforce: 'What practical purpose should this commemoration serve? Memories should be inspirations. To what end should these inspire us?' Again I cannot doubt his answer. 'Our work', he would surely say, 'was only a beginning. The greatest tribute you can pay us is to finish it. Much has been done since our day; but is slavery still practised among men, and have you made atonement yet to Africa?'

Slavery, of course, is still alive—in Abyssinia, in Arabia, in China and other backward lands—and it is natural and right that memories of 1833 should prompt us to do all we can to promote its abolition. Our country has kept its place, ever since Wilberforce put it there, in the van of that old crusade. The British Anti-Slavery Society is the most vigilant and active and influential organization of its kind in the world. More power to its elbow and more money in its chest! And it is British initiative that has kept the question of slavery to the front at Geneva and done most to secure the institution of the new Permanent Committee of the League of Nations whose business it will be to see to it that the question of slavery never drops again into the background. That we should pledge our-selves not to relax our efforts for universal Emancipation may seem, perhaps, the most obvious tribute we can pay to the memory of the Great Emancipators. But it is not the only task of which those memories should remind us, nor in a sense the most directly ours, the closest to our hand. Those five million slaves that still exist are practically all in foreign lands; we can only try by patient and considerate diplomacy to persuade the rulers of those lands to do what seems to us, but not yet to most of them, their duty. Nor even in this can we work single-handed; it is an international business; broadly speaking, we can only act with and through the League. But, if we think of the race we actually enslaved rather than of slavery in general, if we look at Tropical Africa, the old slave-trader's preserve, rather than Arabia or China, the case is different. Over a vast area of Tropical Africa we are ourselves the rulers. There we can do, of ourselves and by ourselves, precisely what we wish. In so far as atonement is possible at all, it is in our power to make it.

I put the word 'atonement' in Wilberforce's mouth because he used it himself—and so did Pitt; and if it seems a rather sentimental or melodramatic word, consider these two facts. First, that the population of mid-Africa is very much smaller than that of other comparable regions of the world. Second, that the European Slave Trade stole away from Africa from first to last at least twenty million Africans and killed at least as many in the process—and those figures might stand as well as any others for the incalculable volume of the Arab Slave Trade. No serious modern investigator can question that the second fact is connected with the first. Remember, too, that the operation of the slave trade made the barbarism of Africa yet more barbarous, intensified and perpetuated intertribal warfare, closed the country to the more natural and civilizing agencies of trade and science, made the 'dark continent' darker. And since *that* was what was done and since for most of a century Englishmen did more of it than any other people, was 'atonement' too high-pitched a word for Wilberforce—or us—to use?

It implied, of course, something more than the abolition of the slave system. It implied a 'positive policy'; and Wilberforce had some definite ideas as to what it should be. In his eyes the best reparation we could make to the Africans was the gift of Christianity; but mission-work was only to be part, if the best and most promising part, of an attempt to raise the Africans from savagery to civilization. He wanted, also, in place of the old slave trade to build up and expand a 'legitimate' trade; he believed that normal commercial intercourse between Englishmen and Africans would be beneficial to both. Nor, as the Sierra Leone adventure shows, did he shrink from colonization. 'Christianity, commerce, colonization'—those were Wilberforce's, as later they were Livingstone's, three instruments of atonement.

Well, those instruments have been used since Wilberforce's day to far greater effect than he ever dreamed. Christianity? The whole of Africa is dotted with mission stations, and four-fifths of the education of its natives is in missionary hands. Commerce? The whole of Africa has been opened up and brought within the web of the world's trade. Colonization? The whole of Africa (except Abyssinia and Liberia) has been cut up into colonies or protectorates or mandated territories under the rule, direct or indirect, of various European Powers, and Europeans have settled as colonists wherever the climate has permitted it.

'But,' you may ask, 'is all that "atonement"? Have those three instruments all been used as Wilberforce would have wished? The missions, no doubt, were planted with no other purpose than to help the Africans; but what of the

commerce and colonization? Is it not said that the motive
for the European partition of Africa, for that hasty and
notorious "scramble", was simply to obtain raw materials
for European industries and markets for European goods?
Is there no sting in the witticism that "Europe first robbed
Africa of the Africans and then robbed the Africans of
Africa"? What about greed and hypocrisy now?'

It would take a lecture, a course of lectures, to deal
properly with those questions, and I can only say one or
two things here and now. And first, while of course I
admit that economic motives played a very big part in the
extension of British rule in Africa, I also assert—and I defy
authoritative contradiction—that materialism was often
blended with idealism, that there were other motives at
work besides the economic, and that one of the most potent
of them was the old humanitarian tradition, the wish to
give the Africans the blessings of peace and good government and specially to free them, as only thus they could
be freed, from the age-long curse of the slave trade. In
the shaping of the public opinion which determined the
course of British imperialism in Africa the name of Livingstone has been as powerful as that of Rhodes. Secondly,
I claim—and again it is indefeasible—that while at certain
times and in certain places there have been exceptions to
the rule, some of them grave exceptions, not to be ignored
or palliated, nevertheless, in general, the government of
British Tropical Africa has been conducted in the spirit
of that 'trusteeship' which was first enunciated in Wilberforce's day as the true principle of our relationship with
backward peoples. For long years past now, a host of
officials, high and low, in all departments—executive,
judicial, educational, medical, agricultural—have laboured
hard, and often at cost of health and life itself, with as pure
a zeal for the welfare of the Africans as that of any mission-

ary. And it is right to add that, if many private individuals
have sought only their private gain in Africa, reckless of
what injury they did, others have pursued their lawful
avocations—in the business-house, in the up-country store,
on the farm—without forgetting the special responsibility
that lies on white men living and dealing with ignorant,
credulous, relatively defenceless black men. It would be
true, in short, to say that, when the statesmen gathered at
Paris fourteen years ago defined in Article XXII of the
Covenant of the League the rules that were to govern the
administration of 'mandated' areas, they were reaffirming
the rules that *on the whole* had actually governed for years
past the administration of the British tropics. *On the whole*,
we had applied, and we do apply, to our government of
peoples 'not yet able to stand by themselves under the
strenuous conditions of the modern world . . . the principle
that the well-being and development of such peoples form
a sacred trust of civilization'.

So far, so good; but we must not be too complacent.
Those economic motives are still in the picture, in the fore-
ground of it. Europe demands no less insistently to-day
than at the period of the 'partition' that the resources of
Africa as a producer and a customer should be developed
to the full for the benefit of all the world. In itself that
seems to me a legitimate demand. Africa as well as Europe
is part of the world, and on the face of it should be the
first to benefit from her own development. That was
Wilberforce's own belief, and Livingstone's. But it is not
therefore certain to come true. Africa *should* benefit, but
it is not certain that she *will*. Her future, it is often said,
is one great question mark—so swift and so disturbing to
the whole framework of African society has been the intrusion of economic forces from without. And it is evident
enough that, if the pace is hastened beyond reason, if

short cuts to wealth are attempted without sufficient regard for the welfare of the Africans who in the last resort produce it, if excessive demands on land or labour make it impossible for African society to traverse this age of transition without complete collapse, then indeed the last state of Africa will be worse than the first; then, so far from atonement for past injury, we may prove to have done as much harm in the twentieth as in the eighteenth century, and with far less excuse.

That may happen. The idea of 'getting rich quick' in Africa may prove too tempting to Europe in her need; and there are politicians and journalists, both in this country and elsewhere, who tell us that one of the surest means of recovery in Europe is a more assiduous colonization and exploitation of Africa. But much will depend in the future as in the past on England's example, and personally I cannot believe that she will give the wrong one. Mistakes, no doubt, will be made in British Africa as elsewhere. Reactionary and selfish things may be done behind the scenes. But, whenever the main issues which will really determine the fate of the continent are brought, as from time to time they must be brought, into the limelight at the front of the stage, then I am sure that the right decisions will be taken. And, if you ask me why I am so confident, I refer you to this commemoration. In the last resort the British people will do justice to Africa because they are heirs and guardians of a great tradition. If they are asked to choose plainly between right and wrong in Africa, they will obey their consciences as their ancestors obeyed theirs. If Europe needs a lead in its dealings with Africa, they will give it again as they gave it in 1807 and 1833. To-morrow, no less than to-day, England will remember Wilberforce.

Postscript on the Meaning of Dominion Status [1]

(1) DOMINION Status as it is to-day is the outcome of a long period of growth by which the major groups of self-governing Colonies (as they were once called) have obtained a position of equal nationhood with Great Britain. It has been a gradual process, varying in pace and method as between one Dominion and another; and at each stage it has been controlled not by preconceived theories but by circumstances. It was the War which brought it to its climax; for the equal nationhood of the Dominions was recognized in principle when their Prime Ministers sat with the British War Cabinet to constitute the Imperial War Cabinet in 1917 and when they were separately represented at the Paris Conference and separately signed and ratified the Treaty of Versailles, under which they became separate members of the League of Nations.

(2) This fact of equality in national status was affirmed by the Imperial Conference of 1926. The well-known sentence adopted by the representatives of all the nations of the British Commonwealth defined the Dominions and Great Britain as autonomous communities within the British Empire, equal in status, in no way subordinate one to another in any aspect of their domestic or external affairs, though united by a common allegiance to the Crown and freely associated as members of the British Commonwealth of Nations.

As Sir Robert Borden and General Smuts pointed out at the time, this definition made no change in the actual position. It was only an agreed interpretation of existing facts.

(3) In a later section of the Report of the Imperial Conference of 1926 it was said that 'existing administrative, legislative, and judicial forms are admittedly not wholly in accord with the position as described in Section II'—a reference to the definition quoted above. The Conference, accordingly, recommended certain changes in administrative practice in order to make the form correspond with the fact of equal nationhood, and on the legislative side it recommended the appointment of a committee of legal experts to examine and report on the means of bringing about the same result.

This committee, which was styled a 'Conference on the Operation of Dominion Legislation and Merchant Shipping Legislation', met in 1929, and recommended, *inter alia*, the passing of a 'declaratory enactment' by the Parliament of the United Kingdom, the terms of which it defined.

The Imperial Conference met again in 1930. In his opening speech the British Prime Minister said: 'It is now our task to consider, upon

---

[1] Extract from a letter published in *The Times*, February 20, 1935.

the basis of our experience, how to give practical effect to the declarations of 1926'. The Conference approved the Report of the 1929 Conference, and embodied it in its own Report with certain additions. Accordingly, the 'declaratory enactment', known as the Statute of Westminster, was passed in 1931. It is entitled 'an Act to give effect to certain resolutions passed by Imperial Conferences held in the years 1926 and 1930', and its purpose is similarly defined in the preamble.

It is thus evident that there is not, as is sometimes asserted, any difference of principle between the Declaration of 1926 and the Statute of Westminster. On the contrary, there is an essential unity. Historically and logically, the one proceeds from the other: they mark successive stages, not necessarily the last, in the single process of establishing 'equal nationhood'. The Statute does not concede something which the Declaration withheld. It only changes legal forms to square with what the Declaration asserted to be political facts.

(4) It should further be observed that the actual application of Dominion Status is not uniform. All the Dominions have not yet chosen to exercise all the powers inherent in it. Among several examples may be cited the fact that Australia and New Zealand have neither adopted those sections of the Statute of Westminster which do not apply to them unless adopted, nor appointed their own diplomatic representatives at any foreign capitals.

(5) Lastly, it may be useful to correct a mistake which is commonly made both in this country and in India. Dominion Status in principle has nothing to do with the form or type of internal constitution in a Dominion. It is only concerned with the external position. It is a matter, so to speak, of the 'international' relations between the nations of the Commonwealth. It fixes that relationship as one of equality. It may be hard to imagine the Commonwealth as anything but an association of States under parliamentary government; but Dominion Status does not require a Dominion's internal constitution to be parliamentary. A Dominion might enjoy Dominion Status under any domestic *régime*, provided (1) that it maintained allegiance to the Crown; (2) that it contained no element of subordination to any other member of the Commonwealth; and (3) that it accepted free association with the other members.

Anyone who wishes to consult the relevant documents will find them conveniently collected, with an authoritative introduction by Professor Berriedale Keith, in a little volume published by the Oxford University Press under the title *Speeches and Documents on the British Dominions, 1918–31*.

Printed in Great Britain by R. & R. CLARK, LIMITED, *Edinburgh.*

NEW MACMILLAN BOOKS

THE ESSENTIALS OF PARLIAMENTARY DEMOCRACY

By R. BASSETT

WITH HORACE PLUNKETT IN IRELAND

By R. A. ANDERSON

THE ENDLESS ADVENTURE

By F. S. OLIVER

Vol. III.   10s. *net.*

Previously published :

Vol. I. THE RISE OF ROBERT WALPOLE TO THE HEAD OF AFFAIRS : 1710–1727.   15s. *net.*

Vol. II. WALPOLE AND THE FIRST PARLIAMENT OF GEORGE THE SECOND : 1727–1735.   15s. *net.*

LORD BROUGHAM

By G. T. GARRATT

With portraits and reproductions of contemporary cartoons and prints.

SIR WALTER RALEGH
The Last of the Elizabethans

By EDWARD THOMPSON

MACMILLAN AND CO., LTD., LONDON

NEW MACMILLAN BOOKS

PRINCIPLES OF ECONOMIC PLANNING
By G. D. H. COLE. *6s. net.*

THE PLEASURES OF PLANNING
By IAN MacDONALD HOROBIN, M.P.
4s. 6d. net.

CIVILISATION AND THE GROWTH OF LAW
By WILLIAM A. ROBSON, PH.D., B.SC. (ECON.)

STUDIES IN MODERN HISTORY
DISRAELI, GLADSTONE AND THE EASTERN QUESTION
A Study in Diplomacy and Party Politics
By PROF. R. W. SETON-WATSON, D.LITT., PH.D., F.B.A.
With Illustrations and Map. 21s. net.

THE STRUGGLE FOR SUPREMACY IN GERMANY, 1859–1866
By PROFESSOR HEINRICH FRIEDJUNG
Translated by A. J. P. TAYLOR *and* W. L. McELWEE
15s. net.

MACMILLAN AND CO., LTD., LONDON